T0207707

GROWING WHOLE

A Lifelong Spiritual Journey

GLORIA CRAWFORD HENDERSON

WESTBOW
PRESS®
A DIVISION OF THOMAS NELSON
& ZONDERVAN

WestBow Press books may be ordered through booksellers or by contacting:

WestBow Press
A Division of Thomas Nelson & Zondervan
1663 Liberty Drive
Bloomington, IN 47403
www.westbowpress.com
844-714-3454

Interior Image Credit: G. Crawford Henderson

ISBN: 978-1-6642-5148-9 (sc)
ISBN: 978-1-6642-5149-6 (hc)
ISBN: 978-1-6642-5147-2 (e)

Library of Congress Control Number: 2021924019

Print information available on the last page.

WestBow Press rev. date: 12/31/2021

DEDICATION

I dedicate this book to my family. May the infinite bond of fellowship, friendship, love, and respect remain unbroken and transition with us into eternity.

A special memorial tribute to my father, Robert Crawford, Sr., for his encouragement, love, and support. He was an outstanding role model, confidant, and friend. His dedication to his family was unwavering and the lessons he taught me have shaped my worldview in myriad ways. He is ever-present in my soul.

A special thank-you to my husband, Marvin, for the untold hours he spent editing and offering invaluable insight.

Names of the individuals in my stories are fictitious. Details and settings were altered to protect privacy.

CONTENTS

Part II   Growing Whole

Part III   The Dichotomy of Emotions

Part IV   Life Gets Better

PREFACE

God created a beautiful universe and filled it with physical and spiritual phenomena that are far too mystical and wondrous for the human brain to comprehend. Then He created living beings to inhabit this vast province. Finally, the crown jewel of His creative genius was humankind, to whom He assigned the role of caretaker.

Through a relationship breach of mammoth proportions, the perfect, heavenly fellowship between God and His protégé was severed, and everything changed. Since the breach, humans have longed to reconnect with their original source, and they have devised interesting strategies to assist in that effort. Though misguided to say the least, the biblical story of the Tower of Babel is a bold human attempt to reach God. This story offers several lessons, but the most profound one is that we cannot reach God through external human initiatives. He devised a masterful redemption plan, but we do not control it. Through God's grace, we are privileged to reconnect with Him. The path home is possible only because of the divine gift of salvation, not human ingenuity.

This book is the story of one woman's spiritual awakening. I was born into a Christian household, so I have always known about God, and in my early years, I thought that was sufficient. I participated in the rituals common to my faith, and I engaged in activities of daily living much as others did. I identified my life goals, and I implemented strategies to achieve them. I was taught that education and hard work were the tickets to happiness, so that was the direction I traveled. My primary roles of wife and mother brought unimaginable happiness to my life.

At some point during my middle years though, it became clear that something important was missing. What started out as a faint feeling of emptiness grew into a keen awareness that the calling on my life included more than working long hours in one stressful job after another. There was a loneliness deep inside that I could not explain. By secular standards, I should have been happy and content. I was ashamed to admit my feelings of uneasiness to anyone because in accordance with worldly norms, I was living a dream life. So I kept quiet and went about my days as expected all the while hoping the disturbance in my spirit would subside. But it did not.

I felt more and more uncomfortable with the lifestyle I had settled into. I prayed for divine guidance, and after much self-examination and soul searching, I got the clarity I needed. I came to realize that knowing *about* God and *knowing* God were not the same. It was no longer enough for me to have a relationship with Him based on rituals; I needed a more intimate friendship with Him. With that recognition, I set out on a lifelong spiritual journey of growing whole.

At that point, I was a spiritually broken Christian, but on some level, I understood what I needed to do. Much like establishing a friendship with a fellow human, becoming friends with God would require my attention, commitment, time, and trust. I understood I would get to know Him better if He became an integral part of my life rather than a convenient accessory, someone I would connect with when I needed His help.

As we spent more one-on-one time together, our relationship became personal. I learned to rely on and trust Him to guide my life. I felt His presence and heard His voice, and as I grew closer, my feelings of brokenness subsided. The joy that surpasses human understanding was becoming a reality, not just something I claimed because other Christians professed it. The pain of loneliness waned, and I was being transformed from a state of spiritual brokenness to oneness with God and wholeness with myself and others.

Along the pathway to wholeness I have enjoyed many accomplishments, but I have also had my share of missteps. There were moments of pure joy, but I would find heartache just around the corner. I have laughed and cried, and I have loved and lost. I have progressed, and I have regressed, but through it all, I have grown closer to God.

Growing whole is a lifelong endeavor, and every experience contributes to the outcome—some more than others. For me, being a product of the segregated, rural south and being the child of strict, hardworking, blue-collar parents figure prominently in the person I am today. Each of these circumstances offered pertinent messages that are permanent parts of my psyche.

Segregation taught me that I had to work harder and smarter than others. In some ways, my strict, hardworking parents taught me the same lesson. I am a loner by nature. Getting to know the right people and attending social gatherings to rub shoulders with the who's who did not appeal to me. I much preferred being in a quiet corner reading a good book. So I decided long ago that my contribution to society would be through the medium of hard work just as my early experiences had taught me.

During my search for inner peace, though, I learned something far more profound. Opening my heart and inviting others in was an important by-product of the decision to pursue wholeness. I let go of my need to control circumstances and people and trusted that God's perfect plan would unfold as it should. Learning to walk in the spiritual space of gratitude and humility continues to transform me and nudge me closer to the Christ-centered lifestyle I desire.

It has taken me decades to understand the spiritual value of some of life's most important lessons. In my younger years I was busy doing things and did not take the time to appreciate the therapeutic value of simply being. Because I kept silent about my insecurities and perceived shortcomings for fear of being misjudged and misunderstood, I told no one of my feeling that something important was missing in my life. If I had been more open and forthright, perhaps I would be further along on my journey toward wholeness. Possibly I should have abandoned my tough-girl façade earlier. But then, maybe the knowledge, understanding, and wisdom I needed was revealed to me exactly when it was supposed to be.

As a life coach, I see how the agony of spiritual brokenness expresses itself in everyday situations. How we feel inside is revealed in myriad ways. Our intentions, thoughts, words, and deeds are contaminated by brokenness. Rather than choosing to see the best in people, we actively search for the worst. Rather than seeking blameless resolution when a problem arises, we choose to criticize, falsely judge, and mistrust. Rather than giving others the benefit of the doubt, we opt instead to gossip about them and attack their character. Rather than extending feelings of love and compassion when someone is hurting, we find some degree of pleasure in their pain. Perhaps we do this to feel better about our own misery, but it is hurtful, and it only adds to our brokenness.

In my youth, I mistakenly equated wisdom with the aging process. I have since learned that one has little to do with the other. Unless we proactively address our spiritual brokenness, it becomes increasingly problematic as we age. Years of guilt and regret continue piling on our shoulders, weighing us down, and robbing us of vitality. Without God, we cannot undo the damage. Wholeness begins with a willingness to take ownership of our messes and remove the façade we created to hide our emptiness. My journey has been one of slowly eliminating the false pretenses and figuring out who I am and what really matters at my authentic core. When we know ourselves and God, life has meaning and sacred purpose thrives.

Finding the courage to share my story is a privilege of epic proportions. The essential purpose of this book is twofold—to inform and to inspire. First, I believe that others will benefit from my transparency. Second, authoring this book was motivational and therapeutic. We all find God in our own ways and in our own time; that makes our journeys uniquely ours. How or when we get there is far less important than getting there. Without His fellowship and friendship, finding meaning and pursuing sacred purpose through Him will not make sense. We might even ridicule those who believe in His promises and revelations. We all serve someone or something. In the final analysis, it is a personal decision; the choice of who or what we serve is ours.

I am awed by the many examples of God's intervention on my behalf. In hindsight, I can see Him steering me back in the right direction when I veered off course. I can hear His soft, still voice encouraging me when I desperately needed comforting. I can see God protecting me from danger and preserving my dignity. I can feel His gentle touch as He nudges me closer to realizing my goals. I can see Him patiently molding me into His character and image. I am filled with gratitude and humility when I consider how His love and friendship have given my life meaning. He has offered me so many second chances even though I did not deserve them.

The spiritual significance of the blessing of aging is profound. With divinely inspired foresight, insight, and hindsight, I look forward to continuing my journey toward growing whole. We cannot change the past, and we do not know what the future holds. However, the beauty of now is that we are here for the fulfillment of sacred purpose, and that is all that matters.

I hope the revelations in this book will serve as a call to action for others. Finding God is the only true pathway to healing. As we are transformed from spiritual brokenness to wholeness, life has meaning and sacred purpose abounds.

This is not a book about religious rituals; it is a candid discussion of how life gets better when we choose compassion over judgment, fellowship over isolation, love over fear, and spiritual awakening over religious rituals. When we give ourselves permission to be slowly molded from the inside out into the character and image of God, we are growing whole.

Introduction

Life is complicated. In spite of all the tools we have at our disposal to help us interpret its meaning and purpose, we still have far more questions than answers about it.

We sense the need to belong to something bigger than ourselves, but beyond this feeling of insufficiency lies a sea of confusion, so we continue to search. We innately know something important is missing, but fear and uncertainty creep in. So we settle. Whoever and whatever show up in our lives, we accept and muddle through. To make the unbearable a little more bearable, we try to convince ourselves that this is all we deserve. But a faint whisper deep inside is telling us something different—that we are in fact worthy. So we struggle. This internal-external misalignment causes significant damage and further undermines our self-images. In the meantime, the harmful effects of the damage permeate every aspect of our being, and we devolve into someone we are disappointed in and can hardly recognize. So we overcompensate. Because we realize the authentic, private self is broken by sin and separation, we mistakenly create a pretend public persona that we think is more presentable to the world. This is a mistake because we waste time and energy promoting a false image that does not reflect God's perfect work. With all our flaws, the authentic versions of ourselves are exactly what God intended. The people He created and the false personae we create do not align, and there is discord. So we search.

Some choose to rely on their physical prowess to find the answers they seek. Armed with natural gifts and talents plus the five-sensory abilities to hear, see, smell, taste, and touch, they try to find meaning and purpose in the secular realm. Others readily acknowledge their human limitations; they accept their inability to find the joy and peace they desperately need, so they ask for help.

The profound questions about life that humankind has grappled with for eons can be addressed only in the context of faith. Everyone has purpose, which is elevated to a sacred status when God ordains it. For our existence to have meaning and sacred purpose, we must establish a Christ-centered lifestyle. This requires a willingness to accept that God created everyone and everything. As a result, reality, relevance, and truth are defined by Him. Nothing matters unless He says it does. For Him, love of God, self, and others matters most. The requirement to love is the cornerstone of our Christian faith; nothing else is more important. This love is realized, received, and reciprocated through fellowship and relationships.

Structurally, God's spiritual essence is revealed to us in the Bible as the Trinity of Father, Son, and Holy Spirit. The universe He created is similarly structured; it is three-dimensional space, matter, and time. Humankind, whom He created in His image, is tripartite—body, soul, and spirit. This three-dimensional relationship pattern is repeated several times in the Bible. It is also amazingly consistent throughout the universe and in humankind. From a spiritual perspective, the number three represents completeness, harmony, interconnectedness, and interdependence. These same characteristics help form the basic building blocks of loving relationships.

We learn to love as God loves us through fellowship with humankind and nature. We can readily identify emotions related to familial and romantic love and love of a beautifully adorned flower garden. But learning to love as God loves does not come easily; it is a lifelong process that takes concerted effort. *Growing Whole* is a blueprint for those who choose to expand their capacity to love beyond worldly expressions.

Becoming one with God, ourselves, and others and glorifying Him in the process are excellent examples of sacred purpose. They are the most important callings for every human being. As we grow in knowledge, understanding, and wisdom, we innately position ourselves to implement these callings. Because of our unique gifts, talents, and personalities, sacred purpose manifests itself in different ways, but the overarching mission is the same. This never-ending process is steeped in love, and as life unfolds, this truth will continue to reveal itself in myriad ways. Our holy mission is clear. Learning how to complete this mission in a world that prefers the secular over the sacred is our life's work.

The meaning of life is far too complicated to fully comprehend solely from a physical, five-sensory perspective. As critical as these senses are, they cannot offer us the complete picture. We are multisensory beings with physical and spiritual qualities for good reason. Most of life exists beyond our finite, physical nature. The bodies that present us to the world take shape in the womb. They have dates of birth and dates of death. They are useful to us during our lives, but at the point of death, we will part ways.

The spiritual essence of humankind is indisputable. From this multisensory perspective, life begins long before conception. Many decisions about the course of our journey have already been made. *Who will our parents and our life partners be? What will our challenges and opportunities look like? Where will the major plots of our personal life stories take place? How will our existence impact others? Why does our particular journey matter?* The answers to these questions are not entirely in our capacity to decide. Much of this work lies solely within the purview of God. Predeterminations have been made to support His divine will. Our task is to fully utilize the circumstances and events of our lives to bring us closer in resemblance to the character and image of God.

The agony and the joy of life lie deep in the contours of our search for answers. Life begins much like a jigsaw puzzle. As experiences unfold, we connect more and more pieces and a picture emerges that offers important clues about why we came here in the first place. At the beginning of the process, most puzzle enthusiasts lay out all the sections face up. They then start with the less complicated parts, usually the edges. By sorting the remaining pieces into groups of similar shapes or colors, they make it easier to orient them in the right direction. The closer they get to the end, the more challenging their task becomes. At this stage, many puzzlers including me give up and walk away in frustration. However, those who press on find that at some point, it gets easier as you put more and more of the pieces in place.

Every event and experience in my life have merged synergistically to make this book a practical reality. *Growing Whole* represents God's loving patience with me. Over time, He gently redirected my attention from egotistical pursuits and toward spiritual enlightenment. I am so grateful for the gift of time. Longevity has blessed me with appreciation and insight that expand with age. In my daily dialogue with God, I now have the time and space to linger in His presence and fully enjoy the benefit of His divine essence.

I have written and rewritten *Growing Whole* several times. It continued to evolve as I better understood the voice of God and faced my insecurities and uncertainties about the receptivity of my message. *Who am I to consider I have sufficient wisdom to share with others?* was a question I had. With this book, I finally have the courage to embrace what I believe is my twofold, sacred purpose—to record the valuable lessons I have learned about spirituality and growing whole and to spend the remainder of my time in the earthly realm describing what this looks like from my vantage point. The lens through which I view the world becomes clearer with age. New levels of consciousness appear almost daily. Many of the superficial, worldly trappings I clung to in my youth no longer take center stage. As my transformation continues to unfold, life gets better!

With much gratitude and heartfelt thanks, I humbly offer my thoughts to you for your consideration. I pray the ideas presented in *Growing Whole* are received with the same level of positivity they are offered. I tried diligently to present the messages in a reader-friendly format. I include in boxes at the end of chapters important points to ponder. Please use this book as a practical guide and revisit it often. Even if you disagree with a particular message, your thoughtful contemplation of its merits and demerits will move you closer to an understanding of the meaning of life and its sacred purpose as it applies to you.

If you are willing to consider the biblical explanation of life and its essential nature, you may find that *Growing Whole* is an interesting read. If however you are sure that a big bang brought you here, you may choose an alternative way to spend the next few hours. If you decide to linger, I encourage you to consider the views set forth in this book with an open heart and mind. The present and future promises it reveals can alter the trajectory of your life. Because you are here, some level of awakening may be stirring within. Enjoy the read!

PART I

PERSPECTIVES ON THE
MEANING OF LIFE

1

LIFE'S DIVINELY INSPIRED INTERRUPTIONS

> Hold your own plans loosely and stay ready to submit to His. Consider them to be more important, more desirable than anything you could dream up on your own. He has come down to you with intentionality and purpose because He loves you and knows that you are never more secure than when you're in His will. (Priscilla Shirer[1])

Herodotus, the father of ancient history, recorded in the mid-400s BC that oak trees contained the gift of prophecy in their boughs. In some cultures, oaks are considered cosmic storehouses of wisdom and towering strength. Throughout literature, oaks are respected as stately, wise, and humble; they are equated with revered elders who survived and thrived despite challenges.

I love everything about oak trees; they are the essence of strength, durability, natural beauty, and diversity—traits I admire. They present themselves in several varieties all of which I appreciate, but my absolute favorite is the live oak. Her longevity and visible evidence of continued growth and productivity are impressive. Her deep roots support her graceful branches.

She can live for hundreds of years. She is forever green, and she exudes

---

[1] https://goodreads/priscilla_shirer_15514706.

character. Her sweet, edible acorns feed animals and birds, and her roots are sufficiently deep to offer a solid foundation for the sprawling branches she births and nurtures for centuries. Her length of years harbors many secrets, and she generously offers us glimpses of her historical role as a natural, environmental wonder.

My unbreakable spiritual bond with her began when I was a child, and she has consistently captured my imagination and respect for decades. My father loved oak trees and he taught me to do the same by regularly sharing his adoration of them with me. I clung to his words and at some point I internalized the emotion and high regard inherent in his heartfelt gratitude as he thanked God for their beauty and strength.

The Call

It was a rare moment for me. I was sitting in my office at work experiencing the bliss of uninterrupted solace. I was lost in thought enjoying the stately oaks peeking over the building on the south end of the office complex. The lush greenery was a welcome sight; it flanked acres of parking spaces. I remembered when this area was one of the most picturesque in the city and filled with breathtaking examples of nature's bounty and variety. At that point, however, it was mostly concrete and asphalt.

The phone rang. It sounded far off because I was lost in the nirvana of the moment. My assistant buzzed me and said, "Your doctor is on Line Two."

I picked up the phone and immediately sensed that her usually upbeat tempo was subdued. She said, "I have some bad news. You have a brain tumor."

I could still hear her speaking, but after she dropped that bombshell I lost the capacity to understand what she was saying. She was calm. I was hysterical. I couldn't breathe. The walls were closing in. A storm cloud appeared on the horizon, and the beautiful blue sky I had been enjoying just seconds earlier was covered over. I felt faint. I resisted the urge to throw up. I was off balance and about to fall out of my chair when I realized I had to pull myself together at least long enough to get home. Then I could fall apart. I am not sure how we ended the conversation, but I grabbed my personal belongings and started running. That was almost twenty years ago. I never went back to that building.

The news of the brain tumor ended my career as a top-level government manager, which was not a bad feat for a Black female who had grown up in the segregated south where remnants of second-class status were prevalent.

I always had a strong work ethic. I learned that from my parents. For the majority of my life, I was driven to succeed, to prove I had a brain, and to earn others' respect. To some extent, the segregation and racism I had experienced contributed to my strong drive to prove my self-worth. The impact on me was twofold. First, I erected a thick wall around my heart to protect it from demeaning expressions of disdain and disrespect. In my attempt to protect my heart though, I created another problem for myself. It took years of concentrated effort and spiritual growth before I would allow others to penetrate that wall.

Second, I developed the egotistical need to prove I did not fit the stereotype of being dimwitted and mentally slow perpetuated by those with racist attitudes. Making it to the level of division director fed my ego, but the cost to my health was great. For three years, I had managed two large statewide programs simultaneously. No other clear-thinking professional would have allowed management to put him or her in such an untenable position, but I was desperate to prove my ability and value.

For years, I suffered from intense headaches. Sometimes, they were so strong that I thought my skull would burst. I took a variety of over-the-counter drugs to soothe the pain, but at some point, my efforts to self-medicate stopped working. I was forced to visit my doctor to ask for help, and she wisely insisted that I get a magnetic resonance image (MRI). The results of that test changed my life that morning.

For the next year and a half, I was in and out of doctors' offices, hospitals, and clinics. Prior to this experience I hardly ever relied on the medical treatment model. I was an avid proponent of self-care and prevention, but that time, I had allowed the ravages of stress to have their way, and treatment appeared to be the only reasonable option.

With an extensive background in health care administration and health practitioner regulation, I knew I would not appreciate being caught up in what I had long before dubbed medical madness. Even so, I was not prepared for the roller-coaster ride that unfolded. I was exposed to enough MRIs, second opinions, and brain scans to last several lifetimes. I was referred to numerous physicians none of whom communicated with the others. I spent far more time recreating my medical history each time I visited a different practitioner than actually interacting with the doctor. During one visit, the physician was face to face with me for a whopping two minutes. I timed it. The follow-up reports would sometimes indicate the tumor had grown. Other reports would indicate it had shrunk. No matter what the X-rays suggested, every specialist I worked with recommended the same thing ... surgery.

One day as I was waiting for another MRI, I had an epiphany. As I watched a parade of senior citizens traipse in and out of the doctor's office in almost robotic precision, I saw my future being hijacked by the tumor. I envisioned endless treks from one health care facility to another, and I made a pivotal quality-of-life decision. I was acutely aware of the dangers of surgery considering the location of the tumor. I did not like the prognoses, which ranged from complete recovery to death to— even worse—permanent disability. I refused to accept the vision of a life controlled by a tumor. I decided to approach this challenge the same way I had approached serious challenges innumerable times before—from a spiritual perspective.

At that point, I was several years into the conscious pursuit of answers to my deep questions about life's meaning. The strict religious teachings of my childhood had been heavy on form, process, and rote memory of Bible verses. However, my ability to see how the words applied to my life in everyday terms was limited. I expected this major challenge to offer me invaluable life lessons, and it did not disappoint me in that respect. In learning how to navigate the complexities of this life-altering situation, I gained skills and increased my stamina in many ways. After that fateful morning, I never discussed the tumor with my doctors again.

Pay Attention to the Wisdom of Your Body

I am now keenly aware of the clear message my brain was sending me during that experience. It was no longer willing to compete in the stressful environment I had unwittingly created, and it was simply rebelling. I now recognize that I was being oriented to the reality of aging. In my younger days, I could stretch my mind and body in several directions as I tried to manage my roles as a wife, mother, lifelong student, career woman, and community volunteer. By age fifty, I was beginning to receive subtle messages to slow down and take better care of myself. The message from the tumor got my undivided attention. At some point, the tumor and I must have agreed to peacefully coexist, and I hardly ever think about it unless asked.

People are shocked when I say that I consider the news of the tumor a blessing. I was in an extremely stressful job with only a smidgen of a support system at work. I was trying desperately to make a positive difference in people's lives, but without a systemic reordering of priorities in the organization, any progress I could make would have been incremental at best. Although I felt my health deteriorating, I struggled to hold onto the great salary and the title. I told myself that I was giving voice to those who could not speak on their own behalf. I knew deep inside though that my ego was also heavily invested.

My reasons for hanging on varied and were far more substantial than the ego-boosting adrenaline that accompanied my Good Samaritan mindset. I had chosen to be a public servant. I earned a bachelor's degree in political science and a master's degree in public administration because I saw myself building and sustaining an honorable career in government. Becoming a top-level manager was a dream come true. The next tier up was department head, and that was within my grasp. Even during my stress-related health scares, I really wanted to linger there for a while longer, but destiny and fate said no. *What now? What do I do knowing that this significant part of my life must end rather abruptly?* I wondered. I enjoyed working. It was an important part of my self-image. For the first time in my life, I faced the death of a big dream. This was a moment of reckoning, and the season for learning the spiritual value of true humility was upon me.

The Therapeutic Value of Dreaming

I have always been a dreamer. Growing up in a rural part of the city, I spent many summer days passing away the time fantasizing about my fabulous future. I was fixated on the thought of living in California with an unobstructed view of the Pacific Ocean. In my dream, I saw and heard the waves crushing against the monstrous boulders on the shore. I envisioned sitting on my balcony for hours basking in the sun and contemplating, meditating, praying, and reading. I gave no thought to how I would finance this fabulous lifestyle, however. My eleven-year-old brain supposed that fabulous lifestyles were free.

That fantasy never materialized, but it served its intended purpose; it taught me to dream big. That was an important skill to develop. Sometimes during my childhood, I found it hard to envision life beyond the invisible, yet clearly delineated barriers erected all around my race to keep us in our place. So we had to become adept at peeking through the cracks in the walls to get a glimpse of life unfettered by the reality of second-class status. Sometimes, big dreams were all we had.

If you ever find yourself too burdened to move forward, start dreaming, meditating, and praying. My best ideas surface often when my mind wanders into the territory of dreaming. While in this creative space, the energy of anticipation reduces stress and activates your subconscious problem-solving skills. When you dream, a particular moment in time can be instantly transformed from unbearable to enjoyable. At will, you can create a stream of consciousness that whisks you away from undesirable situations to your safe haven. When the magnitude of a personal circumstance overwhelms you, desperately needed respite appears in the form of a wandering mind.

Know When to Pause and Reset

For the preceding thirty years, I had worked hard to prove myself worthy in a world that was controlled by people who were culturally and racially different from me, and I had become proficient at navigating this glaring imbalance. I was finally comfortable with the ongoing scrutiny that came with being one of a few minorities in a sea of majorities.

But then suddenly, a potentially life-threatening illness had shifted the trajectory of my life in ways my dreams had never envisioned. I had to ask myself some probing questions: *Does my earlier than expected exit mean failure in some way? What will I do with myself now that twelve-hour workdays are no longer a reality? How will I satisfy the strong desire to be productive? What will my new normal look like?* These and other questions haunted me until I gave myself the gift of humble acceptance. When I did,

I discovered I was exactly where I was supposed to be. Once I pressed pause and sat quietly long enough to hear the voice of God, I received the divine guidance I needed. So I pressed reset and moved forward.

Taking time to sit still in the newly informed reality of my life gave me much-needed clarity about the ill effects of imbalance. When we sacrifice one dimension of our lives to satisfy another, we create a ripple effect that can have devastating consequences. Our well-being relies on balance and harmony; when this basic spiritual principle is ignored, we suffer.

I decided to set out on a course of miraculous discovery rather than continuing to exist in a woe-is-me mindset. I am a planner by nature. My childhood dreams were bolstered by my need to set goals and create mental blueprints of how I could materialize them. At least three different scenarios were usually under consideration. This was a comfortable life strategy for me, and I was most at peace when I was envisioning, planning, and doing. In this moment though, what mattered most was silence and stillness. I needed to linger for a while in a space of simply being. I knew that I would be okay, that I just needed time to get my bearings and do some serious self-examination and soul searching.

With prayer, meditation, and quiet reflection as my companions, I could breathe deeply. The rhythm of elongated inhaling, exhaling, and pausing offered me the previously unrealized benefit of complete surrender. Something magical was happening. There I was resting in full awareness that this circumstance had been predestined with my spiritual growth in mind. Somehow, I knew that life on the other side of this challenge would be much improved as a result of the interruption. I have never looked back. Leaving that stressful job was one of the best decisions I ever made. My attention and energy shifted to where it should have been all along—to meaning and sacred purpose.

Excellent Examples from a Loving Father

In addition to being a lover of oak trees, I am a deep thinker and a loner. It is in my DNA. My father was smart, resourceful, strategic, extremely generous, and compassionate. He was also a deep, introspective thinker, someone who loved his time alone, and an all-around great man. We lived on a twenty-one-acre family farm. With six children, it was usually noisy in the house, so whenever Dad needed to go deep inside himself, he would announce that he was about to "walk the fence line." We came to understand that a trip along the outer boundaries of the property meant he needed quiet time to think.

Years prior, he had single-handedly fenced the entire acreage. I imagine at some point as he was digging a hole, inserting a post, pouring concrete, or attaching wire, he must have made a spiritual connection to the property he had worked so hard to obtain, maintain, and retain. Dad never allowed himself any luxuries; the land was his haven, his healing place, his spiritual retreat. A few hours later after his alone time, he would reappear ready to continue the endless chores associated with providing for his large family, working multiple jobs, and managing the farm.

He had an unbelievably tough life. Each time I listened to stories about his childhood, my heart broke all over again. He rarely allowed himself to open the wounds of his past, but my mother and aunt painted a detailed picture of his younger years for me. I often tried to put myself in his place and understand the fear and insecurity that must have been his constant companions but to no avail.

His mom died when he was only nine. Soon after, his father showed signs of spiraling down. He began to drown his sorrows in alcohol to escape the reality of having to raise three children alone. Being the oldest, my father was forced to deal with horrors that grown-ups let alone children should not have to endure. He encountered insurmountable challenges as he struggled to care for and protect his siblings from the ravages of dysfunction and despair. Despite his troubled background, he was the most optimistic person I have ever met.

As I observed him and his responses to events in his life, I often found myself asking the why, what, and who questions. *Why was his life riddled with such pain? Why was he so joyful considering his sad history? What was the unique combination of biology and environment that made him so determined to be a great father? Who was his role model?* I did not need to ask what made him happy. It was always clear to me that his large family made his tough life worthwhile.

Over the years, Dad provided me with invaluable character-building lessons. We were far more than father and daughter; we were friends. He was one of the few people who really understood me. We would sit for hours enjoying fascinating conversations about any topic. From current events and entertainment to history, the latest news, and religion, he always seemed to know more about the issues than I did. Whatever the topic, he regularly had valuable words of wisdom that I cherished. He had a robust laugh that seemed even more pronounced because he almost always pulled off his signature baseball cap and scratched his head as he burst into roaring laughter. This image remains with me even today. I miss him terribly. He will forever be my primary source of earthly inspiration. I learned so much from him. His generosity, gratitude, positive attitude, resilience, and laughter were contagious.

Meaning and Purpose

I have always paid close attention to the older people in my life. My mom often referred to me as what she called an old soul. As a child I would eavesdrop on adult discussions and particularly women's conversations. We all can learn so much by observing the female gender. We women value relationships. We are curious, and we ask penetrating questions. With ease, we cut through the fluff and get to the details; we are adept at separating the authentic from the superficial. We open our souls, and we listen empathically. We inspire, and we are far less likely than men are to require ego boosters. We do not hide our feelings behind veiled bravado, and we are usually willing to be vulnerable. There are many blessings unique to the female gender. Our ability to offer much-needed therapy to each other is one of our most endearing qualities.

Many of the conversations I was not supposed to hear embedded themselves in my psyche and greatly influenced my formative years. I clearly remember a discussion about growing old and the inherent fears of living too long. As you might imagine, it was impossible for my young heart and mind to comprehend the complexity of that dialogue. It was at once thought provoking yet disturbingly eerie. *Is there such a thing as living too long?* With maturity, I came to realize the answer to this question is a resounding "Yes ... maybe." If we are not properly prepared for longevity and its innate challenges, our last days can feel much more like a curse than a blessing.

During my teenage years, my grandmother was a caretaker for a woman in her mid-nineties. Whenever Granny was ill and unable to work, I was assigned to fill in for her when I was not in school. I can still hear Mrs. Enright crying out to God. She slept most of the time, but her waking hours were spent praying to die. She was bedridden, and it was a significant challenge to keep bedsores off her body. I felt so helpless during her pleas for relief from the pain and from the reality of the situation. She was still breathing, but she was not really living. I struggled to find meaning in those uncomfortable moments. *What's the purpose of her existence beyond independence and dignity? Why am I destined to witness the agony of her last years?* There was a spiritual lesson there, but it would take time and focused effort on my part to grasp it.

The subtle signs of aging present us with mixed messages that are sometimes hard to decipher. One of its most profoundly positive by-products though is awareness and enlightenment. Along with the aches and pains, those blessed with longevity witness revolutionary changes that unfold slowly and catapult us to a newly discovered level of growth. We are closer to God than ever, and our center of consciousness has shifted to what truly matters—our sacred purpose. Longevity is by divine design, and the reasons are far more complex than simply getting older and continuing to occupy space. In the words of Carl Jung,

> A human being would certainly not grow to be 70 or 80 years old if this longevity had no meaning for the species to which he belongs. The afternoon of human life must also have a significance of its own and cannot be merely a pitiful appendage to life's morning.[2]

Regardless of our ages or stages, when our lives have meaning and purpose, we have an unobstructed vision of who we are and why we are here. Our urge to become the best version of ourselves compels us to expand and grow. This basic need is not related to our ages; throughout life, we are inexplicably drawn to completeness and wholeness. This gives life its gusto.

From an early age we are taught to think about the question *"What do you want to be when you grow up?"* From a secular perspective, this question

---

[2] https://brainyquote/carl_jung_717969.

offers us the opportunity to envision a dream life that includes elements of whatever is important to us. Our response might relate to money, position, power, or prestige. As we mature, we continue to refine our goals, and over time, they morph into what we believe is our destiny.

From a spiritual perspective though, meaning and purpose have nothing to do with secular goals. In this dimension of our being, the reasons for our existence are far greater than accomplishing personal aspirations. The pertinent questions are *Why am I here?* and *What is the true meaning of life?* Our belief systems, core values, higher callings, morals, and principles are the gold standard, and they provide the spiritual backdrop for meaning and sacred purpose.

The story of Viktor Frankl is one of my favorite sources of inspiration. Dr. Frankl developed logotherapy, a form of psychotherapy, after surviving life in four Nazi concentration camps in the 1940s. The essence of Frankl's theory is threefold. First, while we cannot avoid suffering and trauma, life has meaning even under the most horrific conditions. Second, the pursuit of meaning is the strongest of all human passions. Third, everything can be taken from us except the last of the human freedoms, the freedom to choose our attitude. Frankl, his wife, his parents, and other family members were first deported to a Nazi death camp in 1942. He was the only member of his family to survive.

After release, Frankl published *Man's Search for Meaning*, which recorded the atrocities he and others endured in the camps. By the time of his death in 1997, his book had been published in twenty-four languages and was an international best seller. The details of how he made the conscious decision to remain positive are riveting. In his foreword to the 2006 edition of the book, Rabbi Harold Kushner said,

> Viktor Frankl's Man's Search for Meaning is one of the great books of our time. The book is less about his travails, what he suffered and lost, than it is about the sources of his strength to survive. He describes poignantly those prisoners who gave up on life, who had lost all hope for a future, and were inevitably the first to die. They died less from lack of food or medicine than from lack of hope, lack of something to live for. By contrast, Frankl kept hope

alive with a two-tiered vision. First, by summoning up thoughts of his wife and the prospect of seeing her again. Secondly by dreaming of lecturing after the war about the psychological lessons learned from the Auschwitz experience. Suffering in and of itself is meaningless; we give our suffering meaning by the way in which we respond to it.[3]

By envisioning life beyond the horrors of living in concentration camps, Frankl found meaning and purpose. Despite the terrible conditions, his will to live offered desperately needed hope, and it made the difference between life and death.

Lessons Learned

Life's lessons often present themselves to us in ways we cannot appreciate because we lack the insight, knowledge, understanding, and wisdom to fully comprehend and embrace meaning and sacred purpose. I used to think that when I became a grown-up, I would have the answers to my provocative questions and that the good life of my dreams would materialize in curious and exciting ways.

I now know that while there is something very liberating and promising about getting older, longevity does not come with a guarantee of easy living. Rather, the more time we are blessed to spend in the earthly realm the longer we are required to use our gifts and talents to pursue meaningful ways to contribute to God's kingdom building metanarrative.

Having learned this valuable lesson, I can finally rest in the knowledge that our lives and our individual stories matter. They are integral to God's grand story and we are here to participate in the fulfillment of His prophecy.

Making known to us the mystery of his will, according to his purpose, which he set forth in Christ as a plan for the fullness of time, to unite all things in him, things in heaven and things on earth. (Ephesians 1:9-10 ESV)

---

[3] Viktor Frankl, *Man's Search for Meaning* (Beacon Press, 2006).

This passage speaks to God's divine will, His purpose, His timetable that is in accordance with His will, the fulfillment of prophecy, and ultimately the unification of heaven and earth. It gives context to our lives and it helps us to make sense of how we fit into the kingdom story. Without a clear sense of purpose we have no basis upon which to build our lives. But when we understand why we are here we have the opportunity to make conscious decisions about whether our chosen lifestyle will contribute to or detract from Gods metanarrative, which is the overarching story that gives context, meaning, and purpose for all of life.

Regardless of the choices we make, the kingdom story will unfold as God intends. Ultimately, goodness, kindness, and love will prevail. In the meantime, in order for our existence in the earthly realm to have meaning, the circumstances and events of our lives must be experienced through the lens of sacred purpose. No matter how challenging and confusing life gets, we can rest assured that everything is as it should be. Nothing occurs outside the authority and permission of God. For reasons beyond our capacity to comprehend and under circumstances we sometimes find unbearable, the human spirit will continue its quest for divinity. I am reminded of one of my favorite scriptures.

And we know that for those who love God all things work together for good, for those who are called according to his purpose. (Romans 8:28 ESV)

Chapter 1: Important Points

- When life presents you with a major setback, spend time in prayer and meditation so you can better understand the intended spiritual message.
- Pay close attention to the wisdom of your body. It speaks to you in myriad ways.
- Life often presents opportunities through challenges. No matter the situation, always look closely for the lessons you need to learn.
- Things often happen for reasons you cannot control. When this is your experience, pray for the peace that comes with acceptance.
- Dream freely and laugh loudly and often.
- Wisdom comes from sacred and secular sources. Use your gift of spiritual discernment to reconcile inconsistencies between the two. Rely on God to guide you.
- Respect and enjoy the company of the elders in your family and your circle of friends. You can learn so much from those who have already experienced the challenges you face. Find ways to express love and appreciation for their sacrifices in support of your dreams.
- Guard your heart, but do not allow life's circumstances to shut off its valves.
- To grow spiritually, you must do so within the context of love, fellowship, and relationship.
- Life's lessons are divinely designed to move us closer to meaningfulness and sacred purpose. Often, we lack the insight, knowledge, understanding, and wisdom to fully comprehend and embrace what God is trying to teach us.

2

LIVE WELL TO AGE WELL

Spending time with God through prayer and His Word
is a prerequisite for having a great life and fulfilling your
purpose. (Joyce Meyer[4])

Every stage of history has unique challenges and opportunities. God's
timing is always perfect, and it is no coincidence that we are here at this
moment in history. Our gifts and talents have been perfectly appropriated
to help us find the answers to our deep questions about the meaning of life
and to contribute to the universal manifestation of sacred purpose.

To Serve This Present Age

We are currently amid a revolutionary transformation that appears
to have been thrust upon us without sufficient warning. Logically, we
know this is not the case, but our emotional uneasiness manifests itself in
paranoid ways. As a result, we are scrambling for the insight, knowledge,
understanding, and wisdom required to respond efficiently and effectively.

We are witnessing firsthand an extraordinary transformation of the
collective mindset regarding elderhood. Historically and particularly in
Western cultures, longevity was viewed as little more than the immediate
precursor to death. Discussions of chronic pain, disease, frailty, and

---

[4] https://bainyquote/joyce_meyer_565164.

infirmity are commonly associated with aging. However, reality is forcing us to reframe the conversation. Advances in medical technology, a focus on corporate and individual health, and quality of life decisions to reduce stress, eat right, and become more active have resulted in substantial gains in life expectancy. The number of centenarians continues to increase at a rapid rate worldwide. People are making significant contributions toward improving the human condition well into their eighties and nineties. In the United States, we just elected a president who was seventy-eight years old when he took the oath of office!

The longevity phenomenon is ushering in a whole new developmental stage in the human life cycle. Gone is the three-stage model of education, career, and retirement. Multiple careers and associated retirements are becoming the new normal. People are remaining engaged in the vibrant energy that accompanies active involvement well into their seventies and eighties.

There is nothing accidental or inconsequential about your being here at this moment and witnessing unprecedented changes related to aging. Life as we know it is undergoing a fundamental restructuring. The essential message is that we are here for reasons beyond occupying space. Elders have a role to play and a story to tell about the age of longevity we are ushering in. We are divinely designed for this exciting moment in history.

Many of our familiar guideposts are embroiled in a tumultuous drama that seems to be spiraling downward and threatening America's safety and security. As a nation, we have never lived up to the promises espoused in the founding documents establishing a government of the people, by the people, and for the people. The democratic ideals set forth in the Declaration of Independence and the Constitution remain unrealized. For example, the principles of domestic tranquility, equality, justice, and the right to life, liberty, and the pursuit of happiness are foreign to many hardworking citizens. They toil in the "vineyard" day after day trying to feed, clothe, and shelter their families, but the American dream eludes them. Glaring examples of inhumane treatment, vulnerable children and elders being routinely victimized, and the extreme, egotistical pursuit of money and power at the expense of others permeate our society.

Stakeholders are impatient with incremental efforts to make things right. Ills such as ongoing battles between the haves and the have nots, entitlement, greed, jealousy, hatred, unearned privilege, racism, and unwarranted fear are as prominent in American culture today as they were centuries ago.

Under the guise of freedom of religion and personal independence, early settlers left their homeland, traveled to the new world, then set in motion some of the most sadistic examples of how human beings can treat others. The indigenous native population was nearly eradicated, and people from a faraway land and culture were relegated to the impersonal status of property that could be bought and sold at will.

Even today, rather than modeling attitudes and behaviors that highlight the best versions of ourselves, we often march in lockstep with the commercialized principles of a consumer-based society whose policies and practices suppress the vulnerable and offer loopholes to those who abuse them. Addiction, chemical pollution, depression, poverty, and terrorism are commonplace in our society, and far too few of us are outraged about it.

America bears witness to numerous human rights failures. Just as has been the case historically, the potential for peace seems to be inextricably tied to the character and personality of our leaders. If they are kind and benevolent, we can breathe easier and expect government to attempt to live up to its promises in humane ways. If on the other hand our leaders display narcissistic and maniacal tendencies, people will suffer and die needlessly. In the meantime, those of us who survive feel helpless. In the twenty-first century, this simply should not be our reality.

To make matters worse, our spiritual leaders often coopt sacred purpose in favor of superficial, selfish pursuits and secular rewards. Church congregations are manipulated into ignoring blatant, untoward practices that confuse the membership and blur the lines of right and wrong. As a result, efforts to further the kingdom metanarrative are thwarted. People are turning away from religious institutions in droves; they sense the hypocrisy and want no part of it. A Pew Research Center survey conducted in 2018 and 2019 offers interesting insights into America's changing religious landscape.

> In the United States, the decline of Christianity continues at a rapid pace. 65% of American adults describe themselves as Christians when asked about their religion, down 12

percentage points over the past decade. Meanwhile, the religiously unaffiliated share of the population, consisting of people who describe their religious identity as atheist, agnostic, or "nothing in particular," now stands at 26%, up from 12% in 2009.[5]

These trends are broad based and apply across demographic categories. Survey participants offered the following comments as reasons they were not affiliated with any religion: "too many Christians doing un-Christian things," "organized religious groups are more divisive than uniting," "religion is not a religion anymore, it is a business," "it is all about money," and "the clergy sex abuse scandals."

In a different but related survey conducted in 2019 and 2020, the Pew Research Center found that Black Americans were more religious than the general population was. Further, the survey indicated, "Religion has long figured prominently in the lives of Black Americans. When segregation was the law of the land, Black churches served as important places for racial solidarity and civic activity." The research also confirmed that "Black Americans still relied heavily on prayer to help them make major decisions, and they view opposing racism as essential to their religious faith."[6]

The data presented in both reports indicate that younger survey respondents were less connected to religious practices than older Americans were. These findings present challenges and opportunities to people of faith. To serve this present age thoughtful consideration must be afforded to the long-term implications of waning interest in religion.

As we struggle for the redemption of our souls, we simultaneously struggle for the redemption of America's soul. Current events are crying out for enlightened elders. Armed with decades of experience and insight, we now have the knowledge, understanding, and wisdom to make positive contributions to our country's efforts to grow whole. We can run for public office or actively support candidates who share our political views. We can educate ourselves on the details of issues under consideration by government officials and hold our leaders accountable. We can engage in

[5] Pew Research Center (https://www.pewforum.org/?attachment_id=32199).
[6] Pew Research Center (https://pewforum.org/2021/02/16/faith-among-black-americans/pf_02-16-21_black-religion-00-0/).

civil discourse, organize food banks, or cosponsor events that offer children safe environments in which they can laugh, learn, and play.

We can volunteer to babysit for single mothers so they can have a few hours each week to themselves. We can mentor or tutor children who are reading below grade level, serve in soup kitchens, or volunteer as foster grandparents. We can join church ministries that focus on community outreach. We can chronicle our families' histories to preserve their legacies and educate our heirs.

We can visit senior citizen centers, write our life stories to encourage and motivate others, or check on neighbors who live alone. We can rescue abused animals or volunteer at summer youth camps. We can offer apprenticeship opportunities to young people so they can learn valuable skills. We can staff phone banks to help gather valuable information from public opinion polls, and we can fundraise. We can sponsor excursions to our native homelands so participants can begin to sense their connection to world history. We can volunteer at nature conservation corps. We can offer to use our expertise to teach a class at our churches. We can walk the dogs of those who are bedridden, or clean their houses, or sit with them and listen to their stories. We can conduct or sponsor research to help find cures for Alzheimer's or sickle cell anemia.

There are so many creative and stimulating outlets for our gifts and talents. From an everyday perspective, this level of faith in action is the lifeblood of sacred purpose. There is so much work to be done, and if it is not done by us, who will do it?

In the context of living well to age well, when life has purpose, it has meaning. When we have a reason to get out of bed in the morning, we arise with a sense of urgency. When we commit ourselves to causes that matter, we elevate our souls beyond the level of ego-centeredness, and we connect with God. When we leave the sanctuary pews and put our faith into action, sacred purpose thrives.

Why Am I Here?

In many respects, this is a how-to book about transitioning from the middle years to elderhood, but it goes deeper than that. It is a call to action for each of us regardless of our ages or stages to grasp the urgency of sacred purpose and develop personalized strategies to help ensure its successful implementation. We must make a positive difference; this is precisely why we are here.

With the publication of *The Purpose Driven Life* (2002), Pastor Rick Warren impressed upon us the need to ask ourselves, *What on earth am I here for?* He answered that question this way.

> It all starts with God. The purpose of your life is far greater than your own personal fulfillment, your peace of mind, or even your happiness. It is far greater than your family, your career, or even your wildest dreams and ambitions. If you want to know why you were placed on this planet, you must begin with God. You were born by his purpose and for his purpose.[7]

I applaud those who have consciously chosen to achieve sacred purpose. First things first though. To serve this present age, we must be spiritually fit for service. First, our internal house must be in order. Colossians 3:12–14 (ESV) reminds us,

> Put on then, as God's chosen ones, holy and beloved, compassionate hearts, kindness, humility, meekness, and patience, bearing with one another and, if one has a complaint against another, forgiving each other; as the Lord has forgiven you, so you also must forgive. And above all these put on love, which binds everything together in perfect harmony.

If we are not committed, grounded, and unshakable in our resolve, we will tire and give up when trouble comes. In Jeremiah 17:8 (NIV), we find these inspiring words.

> He will be like a tree planted by the water that sends out its roots by the stream. It does not fear when heat comes;

---

[7] Rick Warren, *The Purpose Driven Life* (Zondervan, 2002).

its leaves are always green. It has no worries in a year of drought and never fails to bear fruit.

Each of us must seek clarity from God about His vision for our lives. We must also be open and available to what He reveals to us, and all our efforts to implement the vision must humbly glorify Him.

The Victim and the Spiritual Giant

This is a story about the dichotomy of a victim and a spiritual giant. Given the same series of circumstances, they approach their challenges dissimilarly. As a result, their outcomes are drastically different. Both the victim and the spiritual giant were born to alcoholic parents; the prevalent details of their stories included abuse, chronic neglect, and extreme poverty. Beyond the obvious by-products of being born into households with dire circumstances such as these, consider the ill effects of existing year after year in an environment devoid of vision, safety, and security and the blessed energy that accompanies achievement and positive stimulation. There were no responsible role models in either home, food was scarce, and preventive health care was nonexistent.

The victim grew into an angry young woman who bullied her neighbors and classmates. At age fifteen, she fell in love with a man twice her age, quit school, moved into his barren apartment, and had three children in four years. In the fifth year of their relationship, she and her boyfriend agreed to part ways. Over time, she decided she could not care for the children, so they became wards of the state and were moved from foster home to foster home until they aged out at eighteen. She eventually reconsidered and decided she wanted to reestablish a relationship with her children. She spent years searching for them, but once she found them, they wanted nothing to do with her. Alone and severely depressed, she eventually committed suicide.

The spiritual giant decided early in life that she would rise above the dire circumstances of her childhood. She envisioned a bright future in which she could help people who grew up in deprived environments like hers. She studied hard, was awarded a full scholarship to college, and graduated with honors. Because of her long-standing desire to help people in need, she became a psychologist and worked her way through the ranks into an executive-level position. She made significant contributions toward improving processes by streamlining procedures and reducing the amount of time it took for children who became wards of the state to be adopted. Over time, many of her protocols were duplicated in other government agencies in her state and other areas of the country. She continues to enjoy a rewarding career that serves children.

The victim grew weary and lost hope. As a result, she disengaged from life and withdrew emotionally, physically, and psychologically. Given the choice to soar or succumb, she chose to succumb. Her extreme anger and negativity stripped her of any possibility of joy and peace, and she made a series of shortsighted decisions that eventually led to her unfortunate demise. The spiritual giant, when confronted with the same negative situation, remained hopeful. She chose to engage life on positive terms and was motivated to use her pain to make life better for others. Through prayer and introspection, the spiritual giant accepted that while the circumstances of her life were almost unbearable at times, she pressed forward. Despite her struggles, she found meaning and sacred purpose. We can choose to be victims or spiritual giants.

We can find other outstanding examples of spiritual giants. Their lives tell stories of triumph over tragedy, turning obstacles into stepping-stones, and overcoming formidable odds. Thankfully, when we weep, God mercifully sends us committed visionaries to help ease our pain, to inspire us, and to remind us of His divine order and sacred purpose even amid our chaos.

Servant leaders such as Archbishop Desmond Tutu, Gandhi, Dr. Martin Luther King Jr., Moses, Nelson Mandela, Nehemiah, and Mother Teresa brought much-needed messages of hope and peace. Despite their own struggles, they spoke out against injustice at great personal risk. Each approached sacred purpose differently. In accordance with their unique personalities and stations in life, they took stands against injustice. They are outstanding examples of what spiritual giants can accomplish. They stirred the pots of social activism. They led movements. They softened the hearts and minds of millions. They saw needs and unselfishly responded. They risked their lives to offer the world their unique gifts and talents. They served the common good. Their personal sacrifices and testimonies highlight what love for humankind and a strong sense of fairness look like. In their own ways, they filled leadership voids of their days and left rich legacies that will motivate readers for eons.

The central theme of Chapter Two is this: If you expect to age well, you must first learn to live well. You will see this theme repeated throughout the book. This essential message is critical to our capacity to find meaning and live out our sacred purpose. Living well is far more expansive than our own comfort and well-being. It even extends beyond concern for the comfort and well-being of our family and friends. Living well requires us to do our part to help improve the human condition.

We are here for a short while, and our mission is to further the cause of fairness and justice by learning to love beyond selfish pursuits. We must love our way out of the messes we have created. Love is far more than an emotion; it is who we must become and how we must intend, think, speak, and act. Love is the energy that fuels our desire to move beyond the trivial, worldly pursuits that undergird our egos. Love removes any remnants of fear-driven urges and makes room in our hearts and minds to propel us closer to wholeness.

For each of us, the opportunities to glorify God are endless. The lifelong process of growing whole requires sacrifice and service, and when we allow our lives to be guided by this level of commitment, life has meaning and we will be living in the space of sacred purpose.

Wisdom of the Aged

Most of the elders of my youth were rural neighbors. Occasionally, after church and Sunday dinner, time was set aside for visitation with friends and relatives who lived in the city or other distant communities. Sometimes, they would make the lengthy drive to visit us, and sometimes, we would reciprocate. During these gatherings, the grown-ups engaged in thoughtful conversations while the youngsters frolicked on well-manicured lawns, many of which were adorned with colorful flower beds. I always enjoyed the variety of plants that were strategically located across the sprawling country lawns, and flowerbeds still invoke feelings of enchantment.

Excitement was in the air whenever we expected company. We rarely interacted with people beyond our community boundaries, so those were special occasions. My siblings and I were always happy to hear our parents announce their plans to visit friends and relatives since, beyond church and school, that was the extent of our social lives.

I have fond memories of our large family piling into the car and driving along winding country roads and trails. Miles of hickory trees, towering oaks, and sweet gums gracefully arced toward each other and met in the middle of beautiful, canopied roads that appeared magical. Despite the busyness and noise of my siblings, I managed to fully immerse myself in the wonder of this spiritual experience. Even today, a canopy road drive is blissful.

I also paid close attention to my parents' conversations during these long, Sunday afternoon drives. Because there was so much noise in the back seat, they probably thought no one was listening to them, but I was. I felt secure as I heard them discuss current events, plans for the upcoming week, issues relating to us children, and other interesting topics. I learned a lot about grown-up challenges during these trips, but I also learned the value of friendship in a marriage. My parents could talk about any and everything, and they were always cordial and respectful toward each other. I never witnessed a single argument or cross word between them though I am sure there were some. I never told either one of them this, but I really appreciate the picture of marital friendship they painted for me during our lengthy Sunday afternoon drives.

In those days, telephones were available in our neighborhood, but only the more affluent could afford them. Even then, they were party lines, lines that more than one home shared. Imagine picking up your phone to place a call and hearing others' voices on the line. When that happened, we would simply wait for those callers to hang up and then make a call. The phone company published rules of etiquette for using party lines, but not everyone followed them. I remember a few community disputes resulting from someone eavesdropping on others' conversations. Despite the occasional mishap, though, the elders made sure the spirit of cooperation prevailed. In the process, they taught us valuable lessons about respecting the privacy of our neighbors.

Collectively, the elders of my youth impacted my worldview in myriad ways, and I am grateful for the outward display of overall wellness that projected strength despite their struggles. I am also eternally indebted to them for the fond memories, the thought-provoking conversations, the behaviors they modeled, and their shining examples of dignity and self-worth. Their lives mattered, and their lifestyles provided me with glaring examples of compassion, fellowship, and love. When neighbors were hungry or sick, they banded together to care for and feed them. Such acts of kindness demonstrated the level of love that makes God smile.

Years ago, a female elder in my church unknowingly served as a spiritual mentor for me. I was drawn to her because of her calm persona and her big smile that lit up the room. Her face revealed years of hard work and lack of care. Her hair was usually brittle and unkempt. She looked older than her years, and she was not particularly concerned about the unhealthy food choices she consistently made.

From a spiritual perspective though, she had an angelic allure I admired. My life was especially hectic, and being around her was a welcome relief. I took advantage of every opportunity to work with her on church projects, and I got to know her quite well. Her Christian faith was deep despite a tumultuous life with more than her share of challenges and disappointments. She had six children from four men. She also raised three children who were not biologically connected to her. She worked two jobs six days a week to make ends meet, but she always reserved Sundays for church, relaxation, and rest. Hers was not a life you would desire to emulate, but her loving demeanor, soft heart, tenacity, and unbreakable spirit spoke volumes about her strength of character. She left an indelible imprint on my life, and the wisdom she unwittingly passed on to me is much appreciated. I am forever grateful for the privilege of spending quality time with her.

The Faith-in-Action Challenge

For some time now, God has gently but clearly nudged me toward the realization that life for those who have a compelling reason to exist is far more enjoyable than it is for those who do not. Each of us is created and uniquely molded with greatness in mind. No matter our circumstances, our stories do not end until our last breath. However, realization of our potential is situational. We are often presented with opportunities to soar. After seeking spiritual guidance, realizing our personal goals and our sacred purpose requires us to act. Our mantra should be, "By faith, we act, and by action, we glorify God." Faith in action raises the level of our energy, and creativity and inspiration flourish. In this space, we contribute to the common good. Nobody can tell our stories better than we can. The central theme of our autobiographies should be that we served humankind well. So it is incumbent upon each of us to use every breath to engage in activities that make the world a better place. In doing so, we move closer to the state of oneness with God and wholeness with self and others.

Educational attainment, productive careers, and successful child rearing are important milestones that should be celebrated, but there is still so much other work to be done. The gift of longevity comes with certain responsibilities that connect us to the meaning and sacredness of life. Longevity offers a freedom that was not available to us during our young and middle years. Many of the demands on our time and attention are no longer present. For whatever reason, God chose us to serve this present age. As we find creative ways to accomplish our mission, we blaze virgin trails and reframe the conversation about aging. Longer lifespans and extended golden years position us to redefine elderhood.

Our challenge is to find creative and fulfilling ways to realize lifelong vitality through service. We should thoughtfully consider our roles in raising the level of awareness about aging and the possibilities it offers. We are poised to serve as role models to guide dialogue and influence attitudes about the escalating population of elders. Public policy conversations are underway, and decisions about a vast array of issues that affect us are occurring. We should insist on being at the table so that our views and voices are heard.

If you decide growing whole is a viable choice for you, get serious about it. Waiting for the hearts and minds of others to change, allowing external events to control your destiny, or taking the road of least resistance are excuses for mediocracy. Going along with what is unfair and unjust, tolerating less than our best, and settling for a mundane existence while biding our time and awaiting the grim reaper is not an acceptable life strategy. We must become comfortable with being uncomfortable. We must be willing to ask ourselves the hard questions and face the harsh truth. We must acquire the skills of self-agitation, stir internal ashes, and ignite the flames that support expansion and growth. We must disturb our habits and patterns in revolutionary ways and insist on nothing less than our best. We must acquire the courage to "overturn the tables of the moneychangers and the seats of those who sold pigeons" (Matthew 21:12 ESV) if necessary.

When you subconsciously agree to function below par, over time, you settle into an inferior mindset and give others permission to do the same. You see yourself as less than, so you expect others to see you that way. To know of your divine inheritance but allow the world and its superficial trappings to separate you from it amounts to living life in a default position. In effect, you are on the sidelines watching your story being narrated by someone who has no clue about your authenticity. Life is not a spectator sport. It requires active participation and a deep understanding of and appreciation for who you are and what you stand for.

Our stories unfold in interesting and remarkable ways. We have the power to ensure our lives have meaning beyond selfish endeavors. Our legacies must include the active pursuit of sacred purpose. We must live in accordance with standards that celebrate and honor our humanness. The gift of life is so precious. God selected us to be here. Each of us is a unique creation with a divinely designed journey that will prepare us for sacred purpose. There are so many natural and man-made wonders for us to enjoy and opportunities to be of service. There are people who love us, and there are dreams to pursue. By confronting unwarranted fears and reconciling differences between our inner and outer selves, we alter destructive patterns, raise the level of energy expended on our behalf, and live in spiritual abundance that brings joy to our souls.

Chapter 2 Important Points

- To age well, you must live well. Living well expands you beyond your own comfort zones. It includes assisting others in their quest for comfort and well-being.
- The longevity phenomenon is changing life as you know it. Educate yourself about its implications for your life.
- The gift of time is a blessing that comes with responsibilities.
- There are myriad ways to implement sacred purpose. Find your calling and put your faith into action.
- Life's circumstances challenge you but do not define you.
- The life stories of spiritual giants can be inspirational. Like us, they overcame struggles and risked their comfort and safety to serve. Are you a victim or a spiritual giant? The choice is yours.
- America still needs to live up to its promise of equality and justice for all. Consider how you can help set the agenda for policy discussions.
- You are here to serve regardless of age, stage, or life circumstances.
- Elders have a wealth of knowledge, understanding, and wisdom to share. Spending time with them is mutually beneficial.
- You never know who is watching you. Growing whole requires you to glorify God in all your endeavors.
- Nothing happens outside the authority and permission of God.
- The challenge before you is to find creative and fulfilling ways to realize lifelong vitality through service.

PART II

GROWING WHOLE

3

FROM BROKENNESS TO ONENESS AND WHOLENESS

> But our brokenness is also the source of our common humanity, the basis for our shared search for comfort, meaning, and healing. Our shared vulnerability and imperfection nurtures and sustains our capacity for compassion.(Bryan Stevenson[8])

The doctrine of the Trinity is foundational to the Christian faith. This means there is one God who eternally exists as three persons—the Father as Creator, the Son as Savior, and the Holy Spirit as Comforter. Structurally, we see this three-dimensional relationship pattern repeat itself throughout His creations.

With His supreme power, He created a vast universe that consists of space, matter, and time. Space is the mathematical equation of depth, height, and length. Matter represents the physical features of the universe, which include energy, motion, and observable substances. Time is experienced as past, present, and future.

Humankind is tripartite as well—body, soul, and spirit. Even in our human imperfections and spiritual brokenness, we reflect God's image. Our finite minds cannot fully comprehend the reality of an omnipotent, omnipresent, and omniscient God. So we accept by faith that He created

---

[8] https://goodreads/bryan_stevenson_4396806.

us and that His divine spiritual energy is actively at work in us. Nothing is wasted. God uses all the resources in space, matter, and time to accomplish His perfect, transformative will.

Knowing that God has every detail of life covered should give us the comfort and confidence we need to relax in the awareness that things are exactly as they should be. Even when our circumstances bring heartache and pain, there is always a God-ordained positive aspect. Trying to explain the nature of God, His universe, and His greatest creation, humankind, is impossible. We are curious beings who are in constant search mode. Seeking answers to our questions is as natural as breathing. However, once we accept that God really is in control and there is divine order, meaning, and sacred purpose even amid chaos, we free ourselves from the egotistical tendency to think we need to have all the answers. Scripture tells us that we cannot reconcile our broken relationship with God through human ingenuity. There is only one pathway, which is through faith in the Trinity.

At our core, we understand that we are part of something bigger than ourselves. We comprehend that life has meaning and sacred purpose beyond us. We believe that our stories are parts of a metanarrative that continues to unfold. We even accept the challenge to add value to the big picture, the universe-wide story.

We live, love, and coexist under the direction of a supreme God. He created a universe that is complex and mystical. We inhabit a small corner of this vast domain for divinely designed reasons. There are so many things about God's story that we do not and will not understand at least in this life, yet we are driven to search for answers. The energy we expend while searching fuels spiritual expansion and growth and continues to reveal the promises of God in new and exciting ways.

There are precious few certainties in life, but the gift of time grants us sufficient knowledge, understanding, and wisdom to support our desire to continue the cycle of expansion and growth. As we reach higher levels of Christ-centered consciousness, we alter the lens through which we see the universe in ways that move us closer to the essential reason for our existence, meaning, and sacred purpose.

Being Molded into the Character and Image of God

Every life has an important story to tell. While the main events, settings, and intended messages differ, each of our stories matters greatly to the collective human condition. Some are biographies that read like X-rated novels, others serve as inspirational memoirs, and many are tell-all confessions meant to clear slates and make amends. As the plots unfold, our stories are sometimes filled with exciting, unexpected adventures that keep readers on the edge of their seats while others are more sedate and predictable. Regardless of their level of suspense, our individual life stories are a part of God's kingdom metanarrative that began with the creation of humankind. In our daily lives, our central themes develop in a multitude of ways. Many details of our stories are private and uniquely ours, but the meaning and purpose of existence for each of us is the same. Our single, universal mission is to use our gifts and talents in ways that glorify God and support His kingdom.

There is great variety in the personalities who participate in the human earthly experience. From the sassy to the serious and from the scientific to the artsy, from the worldly to the naive, and from the sophisticated to the less cultured, our personae offer important clues about how our stories will unfold as we breathe life into the legacies we create. While much of our journey is divinely predetermined, each of us has the free will to be active participants in the development of our individual narratives. Equipped with the essential tools we need to explore the meaning of life; we make decisions and engage in various activities that help or hinder us. From a spiritual perspective, nothing is neutral; everything matters. The energy force of our being is either expanding in the direction of oneness with God and wholeness with self and others or is withering in that respect.

Growing whole is a lifelong process of being molded into the character and image of God. For centuries, the phrase *image of God* has been a subject of discussion in religious circles. Genesis 1:26–27 and 9:6 tell us that God made man in His own image. We see in 2 Corinthians 4:4 (ESV) a reference to Jesus being the "image of God." Even today churches throughout Western cultures prominently display pictures of Jesus as a bearded white man with long, wavy, light brown or blond hair and often with blue eyes. I remember a similar image on the wall behind the pulpit of my childhood church, and it confused me. In church, I was taught that

Jesus was born in Bethlehem, a small town a few miles south of Jerusalem. In school, I was taught that people who lived in that part of the world were brown or tan. I remember expressing my confusion in the form of a query to my Sunday school teacher one morning. Rather than answer the question, she quickly admonished me for being impudent. Thankfully, I discovered John 4:24, and my curiosity was satisfied—God is spirit.

In view of this revelation, what does image of God mean? For the answer to this question, we must consult the original source. The Bible describes God in several ways, but the following five characteristics are commonly referenced. God is many things including the following.

1. The Creator of the universe and everything in it including humankind
2. Unconditional love
3. The Trinity of Father, Son, and Holy Spirit
4. Omnipotent, omnipresent, and omniscient
5. Eternal and infinite

God is sufficiently mysterious that our limited human capacity cannot comprehend His fullness. While we will never know everything about Him, the Bible tells us exactly what we need to know to become more like Him. When we establish our intention to be molded into His character and image, the positive energy of transformation is activated. As we diligently pursue meaning and sacred purpose, the light we shine further illuminates His myriad qualities.

Growing whole rather than simply growing old is a practical discussion about healing our broken spirits. We do this primarily by reconciling our severed relationship with God. We must take specific actions to realize the joy and inner peace we yearn for. The closer we get to wholeness the more meaningful life becomes. The more compassionate, forgiving, and loving we are, the more holiness we exude. *Growing Whole* offers a detailed roadmap for anyone who intends to become more Christlike.

The Divinity of Oneness with God

We are imperfect spiritual beings who are living, loving, and serving others in an imperfect physical world while actively engaging in activities that transform our brokenness into wholeness. In our tripartite human form, we possess a body, soul, and spirit.

Our body represents the physical essence of who we are. It provides visible evidence of our presence in the earthly realm, occupies space, and possesses distinct features that distinguish us from others. In this aspect of our being we function on the level of world-centeredness and our desires, impulses, and instincts are determined by external, secular stimuli. We rely primarily on our five physical senses to navigate life.

Our soul represents the non-physical essence of who we are and includes the heart, mind, gifts and talents, personality, self-awareness, will, and everything else about us that is non-physical.

In this aspect of our being we function on the level of ego-centeredness and our emotions, intellect, and thoughts are determined by selfish stimuli and what works best for us. This is where God accomplishes His redemptive work in us through salvation (being delivered from sin) and sanctification (being purified of sin). This is also where the work of growing whole (balancing and integrating the twelve functional dimensions of humankind in ways that support spiritual growth) is manifested.

Our spirit represents the duality of our humanness and holiness. All humans have spirits. One of the many accomplishments of the salvation experience is the immediate transformation of the spirit to holy status. In partnership with the Holy Spirit, we cocreate a new normal for our lives. As we gain knowledge, understanding, and wisdom, we are no longer controlled by the world or the ego. In this aspect of our being we function on the level of Christ-centeredness. We are learning to live in accordance with biblical teachings. Our convictions, which are the principles that guide our lives, undergo purging, purification, and transformative processes that alter our worldview in revolutionary ways. Our code of conduct is elevated, and our sense of fairness and justice heightens. Attitudes and behaviors we used to tolerate are no longer acceptable. We are being transformed into the character and image of God.

Our partnership with the Holy Spirit serves us in three important ways.

1. By expanding our capacity to love
2. By improving our relationships with God, self, and others
3. By increasing divinely inspired revelation

There are many explanations for the existence of God and His creations. Whether you accept the results of science-based research, theories of evolution, religious doctrine, or your own opinion, the choice is yours. For me though, Christian theology offers the perfect explanation for life. The three-dimensional universe and tripartite humankind were created by God, and His spiritual energy permeates all that is.

The mysteries of God, the universe, and humankind are far too complex and expansive to be understood during our brief period as mortals. No matter how curious or smart we are, some things are reserved for after our transition to the immortal realm. In the meantime though, what we know is this—we are here to accomplish specific goals. First among them is to internalize and implement sacred purpose. All humans share the oneness of this common life mission. We are all here to reconcile broken relationships with God, with ourselves, and with others. We are not here to antagonize, compete with, disrespect, or fear each other. We are here to transition from worldly, ego-centered physical beings to our Christ-centered spiritual essence. In between these two spaces, the physical and the spiritual, is the human soul. This is where every immaterial thing that makes us who we are resides.

Unresolved pain from past disappointments and wounds needs to be appropriately attended to and put in its proper place. So when we decide to grow whole rather than simply grow old, we are in effect making the life-altering decision to raise our level of consciousness from worldly and ego-centered to Christ-centered. This individual mandate has universal implications, and sacred purpose is deeply embedded in its transformation imperative.

The Tripartite Nature of Humankind

> Now may the God of peace himself sanctify you completely; and may your whole spirit and soul and body be kept blameless at the coming of our Lord Jesus Christ. (1 Thessalonians 5:23 ESV)

Humans are tripartite. We are spiritual beings who occupy physical bodies, and we possess souls, the essence of who we are. When we die, the physical body eventually fades away, but the spirit and the soul are eternal.

"The dust returns to the ground it came from, and the spirit returns to God who gave it" (Ecclesiastes 12:7 NIV). "And the Lord God formed man of the dust of the ground; and breathed into his nostrils the breath of life; and man became a living soul" (Genesis 2:7 KJV).

Humans readily identify with their physical selves, the exterior layer of their beings that allows them to engage life in the natural environment. These skills provide access to a plethora of delightful experiences. When trouble arises, those who are guided by world-centeredness and ego-centeredness rely on earthly assets and resources to resolve their issues. They revel in the offerings of the world and are driven by egotistical impulses. They reject the need for God.

The natural person does not accept the things of the Spirit of God, for they are folly to him, and he is not able to understand them because they are spiritually discerned. (1 Corinthians 2:14 ESV)

The decision to expand and grow beyond our natural capacities arouses our senses and creates a distinct awareness that something exists that is far more profound than the five-sensory worldview. This represents in earnest the beginning of our quest for oneness with God and wholeness with self and others. So we invite Jesus Christ into our lives.

> If you confess with your mouth that Jesus is Lord and believe in your heart that God raised him from the dead, you will be saved. For with the heart, one believes and is justified, and with the mouth one confesses and is saved. (Romans 10:9–10 ESV)

Our souls are the essence of who and what we are. In Genesis 46:26–27 (KJV), we see individuals referred to as souls.

> All the souls that came with Jacob into Egypt, which came out of his loins ... were threescore and six; and the sons of Joseph, which were born him in Egypt, were two souls.

The answer to who am I resides in the nonphysical aspects of our being all of which fall within the purview of the soul. The lifelong process of growing whole begins with a decision to raise the energetic level on which the soul functions. Our emotions, the sum of our experiences, desires, intellects, intentions, and thoughts are by-products of the soul. The struggles between good and evil, love and hatred, and right and wrong take place on this level. At the beginning of this process, we engage the natural environment through the levels of world-consciousness and ego-consciousness, and the genesis of our worldview is horizontal. We selfishly concern ourselves with how circumstances and events affect us personally. As reconciliation and realignment between the physical and the spiritual take shape, the soul binds these two dimensions together and we adopt a more Christ-centered lifestyle.

With the indwelling of God's Holy Spirit, we begin to function on a higher level of consciousness, but we are still controlled by the world and ego rather than fully committing our lives to God. At this stage of our Christian walk, conflict and confusion continue to permeate our existence because our inner and outer selves are not yet reconciled. The consciousness of the body, soul, and spirit is not in alignment.

> The sinful nature wants to do evil, which is just the opposite of what the Spirit wants. And the Spirit gives us desires that are the opposite of what the sinful nature desires. These two forces are constantly fighting each other, so you are not free to carry out your good intentions. (Galatians 5:17 NLT)

As we continue to grow in faith, worldly influences and egotistical desires diminish and no longer dominates us. Our worldview shifts, and we draw conclusions and make decisions based on a belief in the Lord's divinity and supremacy. We embrace our standing as children of God and commit ourselves to the fullness of our faith.

While we connect to God in myriad ways, the spirit is our primary communication channel. Through prayer, meditation, conversation, personal and corporate fellowship, service, and other means, we establish and maintain a relationship with our Creator. God enters the spirit thereby making it holy at the point of salvation. This connection, the Holy Spirit, makes it possible for us to navigate life in ways that move us closer to oneness and wholeness. The genesis of our worldview shifts from horizontal to vertical. We now concern ourselves with how our circumstances and events fit into the metanarrative of biblical teachings. We are acquiring additional knowledge, understanding, and wisdom to support spiritual growth. We are better able to discern good from evil and right from wrong.

During a client session several years ago, Stan, a Christian, asked me a stunning question: *"As grown-ups, don't we get to decide what is right and wrong for ourselves?"* The answer to his question is no. The roadmap for our lives is clearly laid out in the Bible. With spiritual guidance and a growing faith, this truth becomes clear. Our connection to the ever-present God patiently nudges us in the right direction and keeps us from veering off course. But when we falter, grace and mercy are there to redirect and help us self-correct.

The principles of oneness and wholeness are that reconciliation must take place on the individual and corporate levels alike. We must first resolve discrepancies between our tripartite nature of body, soul, and spirit, and then we must align our lives with the Christ-centered consciousness of the Holy Spirit and commit to the guiding light of His will rather than ours. We cannot accomplish this transformation without God and without divinely inspired and unconditional love. When we learn to view the world through the lens of love and sacred purpose, life gets so much better!

When Jesus descended from heaven, He took on a human persona. During His earthly ministry, He taught us how to effect the transformation from physical to spiritual. He made it clear that love was the only pathway. God is pure love. So if we want to mend our broken relationship with Him and reconnect, we must love our way back.

Multidimensional Unity

Our tripartite human nature is complex. We receive input and send output from each of these three aspects of our being. Five-sensory, worldly inputs and outputs are predominantly physical, and they are experienced through the body's ability to hear, see, smell, taste, and touch. Multisensory, ego-centered inputs-outputs are predominantly emotional, psychological, and social and are experienced through the soul. These encompass the heart, mind, gifts and talents, personality, self-awareness, will, and everything else about us that is not physical.

The body is continuously receiving and sending inputs and outputs to the soul and spirit from every dimension of our being. These dimensions provide the framework by which we experience, interpret, and navigate life. The dimensions include the creative, cultural, emotional, environmental, financial, intellectual, mental, physical, social, spiritual, visionary, and vocational aspects of who we are. The spirit is either sacred and holy or secular and worldly. The sacred, holy spirit is governed by Christ-centered inputs and outputs while the secular, worldly spirit is governed by ego-centered inputs and outputs. Our worldview is the result of this complicated, ongoing, input-output communications process.

We engage life in a variety of ways and from different perspectives. To function at peak level, every aspect of our being must be aligned, balanced, and working in harmony with the other. This heightened level of reconciliation can occur only in the context of God's perfect will.

Illustration 1 on page 42 depicts the tripartite nature of humankind; it is a visual representation of the body, soul, and spirit in their broken states. On this level, misalignment, imbalance, disharmony, and separation dominate every aspect of our being. Illustration 2 depicts the Twelve Functional Dimensions of Humankind; it is a visual representation of the aspects of our being through which we engage life. Ideally, when the body, soul, and spirit and their functional dimensions are aligned, balanced, and harmonized, we experience wholeness. While we realize this utopia is unattainable in the earthly realm, the closer we get to this functional state, the more joy-filled our lives become.

Everything that happens to us affects the whole person. Nothing occurs in a vacuum. For example, if I am penniless and unemployed, my mental state is tenuous. I might not have the emotional strength to fellowship and otherwise engage socially. If my heart is broken, I may be so distracted that I fail to catch an easy pass to win the football game. When I experience bouts of depression, my job performance will suffer. If my outlook on life is controlled by fear and discontent, my creativity and ingenuity are out of balance. If life's circumstances bring me to my knees, I cannot continue to be the leaning post others have grown accustomed to.

When life happens, we are affected on every level of our being. As a result, we must take a whole-person approach to our spiritual brokenness. When the doctor admonishes us to reduce the stressors in our lives, we must realize that this is a complicated directive. A demanding job or a wayward teenager are obvious stress points that can adversely affect our physical health, but the soul and the spirit are impacted as well. These same sources of stress can reduce our creative capacity and cause us to make unwise financial decisions like going on spending sprees. We are more prone to emotional upheaval. In extreme cases, we may even lose hope and give up on God.

Whatever we are feeling either positive or negative affects us as individuals and has universal implications. The energy level on which we function can lower or raise others' spiritual energy. Our intentions, thoughts, words, and deeds affect people in myriad ways. Think about a time when you interacted with someone whose kindness immediately lifted your spirit. The process of growing whole requires us to manage our lifestyles in ways that acknowledge and respect the spiritual implications of oneness with God and wholeness with self and others. When we operate in the spiritual space of compassion and love, we elevate everyone's energy frequencies, including our own. When we decide to function on this higher level, we move closer to a Christ-centered lifestyle.

From the perspective of growing whole, illustrations 1 and 2 are useful in several ways.

1. Alignment, balance, and harmony in and among every aspect of our being is vital to wholeness.
2. Multidimensional interconnectedness is a critical by-product of growing whole.
3. Each of the twelve functional dimensions represents a different input-output category, but every experience permeates them all.
4. When we raise the energy level on which we function individually, the corresponding positive impact is universal.

The Tripartite Nature of Humankind™

(Spiritual Brokenness)

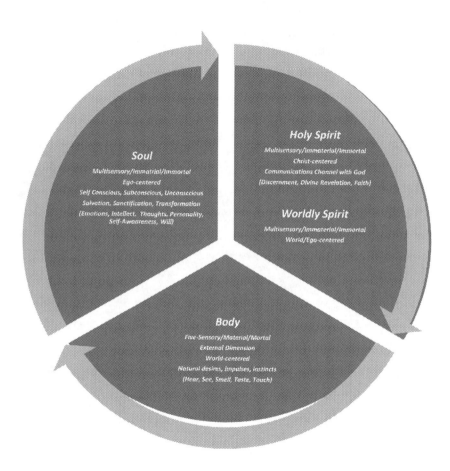

Soul
Multisensory/Immatrial/Immortal
Ego-centered
Self Conscious, Subconscious, Unconscious
Salvation, Sanctification, Transformation
(Emotions, Intellect, Thoughts, Personality,
Self-Awareness, Will)

Holy Spirit
Multisensory/Immaterial/Immortal
Christ-centered
Communications Channel with God
(Discernment, Divine Revelation, Faith)

Worldly Spirit
Multisensory/Immaterial/Immortal
World/Ego-centered

Body
Five-Sensory/Material/Mortal
External Dimension
World-centered
Natural desires, impulses, instincts
(Hear, See, Smell, Taste, Touch)

The Tripartite Nature of Humankind™

The Twelve Functional Dimensions of Humankind™

(Spiritual Wholeness)

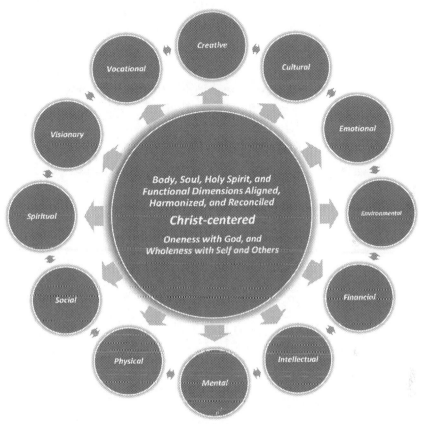

The Twelve Functional Dimensions of Humankind™

The Twelve Functional Dimensions of Humankind

Following is a summary of the twelve functional dimensions of humankind. From the perspective of growing whole, they are interconnected and work in unison with the body, soul, and spirit.

1. **Creative Dimension**

The creative dimension represents a diverse range of pursuits including artistic expression, economic innovation, and problem solving. Here, we learn how to turn imaginative ideas into reality and use our gifts and talents to make the world a better place. We blaze new trails and explore uncharted territory. We tap into our creative genius, which leads us to amazing discoveries and interesting ways of solving problems. We utilize our internal and external resources to contribute to the greater good. We embrace new strategies and repurpose old materials and ideas. From the perspective of growing whole, we view longevity as an opportunity to discover exciting ways to serve others while expressing our unique personalities.

We were created with recreation in mind. The desire to add value by improving processes, making something more beautiful, or providing an outlet for our passions is one of the strongest human impulses. Nothing is more invigorating than transforming a vision into a finished product; this makes life exciting. When we are lost in creative pursuits, we lose track of time, we forget our troubles, and we can often feel the divine presence of God. These moments of bliss offer us glimpses of the true meaning of life.

Devoid of creative outlets, we may wither away and even lose the will to live. In this low-energy state, life shifts to autopilot and we simply exist. As we age, the pace of life slows. While this is a natural occurrence that should be celebrated, there must be some level of urgency that catapults us out of bed each morning. The meaning of life and its corresponding sacred purpose is deeply embedded in the creative dimension of our being. In 1 Kings 3:16-18 we see an example of King Solomon using his creative genius to solve a tricky court case. Two prostitutes came to him, both claiming the baby that accompanied them was theirs. Since there was no witness to the circumstances supporting their claim on the baby Solomon was faced with deciding which woman was telling the truth. When he offered to split the baby in two and give one half to one and one half to the other the hearts of the two women were exposed. Rather than stand by and let her son be killed, the mother pleaded for his life and offered custody to the other woman. It became clear to Solomon who the real mother was and who the imposter was. King Solomon used his creativity to properly administer justice in this case. This is a great story about the wise use of the creative dimension of our being to resolve conflict. Consistent fidelity to and humble awareness of the lifelong need to be creative move us closer to wholeness. The blessing of longevity expands our hearts and minds to give our creativity a place to thrive. Growing whole requires us to continuously seek fulfilling and insightful ways to glorify God.

> We all have different gifts, according to the grace given to each of us. (Romans 12:6 NIV)

2. Cultural Dimension

The cultural dimension is where we learn to appreciate and respect individual and group uniqueness and diversity. All cultures contribute to the world's rich tapestry. Much-needed healing occurs when we recognize and accept the wisdom and rituals of our own culture and then extend those sentiments to the broader human community.

An unexpected benefit of longevity is letting go of the uninformed, egotistical need to inflate the contributions of one culture to the detriment of others. The dangerous human conditions of evil, greed, hatred, lust, and pride permeate all humanity. Every culture has its share of good, bad, and ugly, and when we outgrow the false narratives about one culture being superior to or less than another, we move closer to wholeness. When we learn to respect ourselves and our own culture as well others and their cultures we magnify the divinity that is within us.

Growing whole requires us to accept that we have cultural presuppositions about the nature of reality. This is one of the reasons corporate worship is so important. As we listen to our spiritual leaders and to one another we embrace the wisdom of the Holy Spirit in our Christian development. As we increase our awareness of the cultural and historical settings in which God has providentially placed us we gain the knowledge and understanding that is required to love and serve God by loving and serving each other.

> My brothers and sisters, believers in our glorious Lord Jesus Christ must not show favoritism. Suppose a man

comes into your meeting wearing a gold ring and fine clothes, and a poor man in filthy old clothes also comes in. If you show special attention to the man wearing fine clothes and say, "Here's a good seat for you," but say to the poor man, "You stand there" or "Sit on the floor by my feet," have you not discriminated among yourselves and become judges with evil thoughts? (James 2:1–4 NIV)

3. Emotional Dimension

The emotional dimension offers us the spiritual space to objectively examine the full range of feelings from fear and hatred to unconditional love and the deeply rooted motivations behind them. We actively pursue self-awareness and learn how to cope with the challenges and stressors that present themselves. We all have scars, and those scars have compelling stories. Emotional wounds require us to take an active role in determining what happened, accept our part in creating the wound, and pray to God for forgiveness and healing. Sometimes the difficult situation is of our own creation. When this is the case we must admit our iniquity and accept the consequences for our behavior. Psalm 51 is David's personal confession of adultery and murder and his plea for cleansing. There is no justification for what he did, and he does not try to cast blame on anyone or anything else. He took responsibility for his mess, and he genuinely expressed remorse. This vivid example of man's repentance and God's forgiveness offers comfort to the collective human spirit.

We process the concerns and experiences related to aging in the emotional dimension. If we look forward to what this new stage might bring, we harness the positive energy required to continue the important work of refining the unfinished self. Growing whole requires us to find the courage to pursue authenticity and integrity. In part, this involves letting go of who we think we were, releasing the identities and roles of our younger years because they are no longer necessary, and embracing who we are right now. Every stage has unique growth opportunities, and for me, the thought of being a guiding light to help shape worldviews about aging and spiritual growth offers invigorating possibilities.

Do not be anxious about anything, but in everything by prayer and supplication with thanksgiving let your requests be made known to God. And the peace of God, which surpasses all understanding, will guard your hearts and your minds in Christ Jesus. (Philippians 4:6–7 ESV)

4. Environmental Dimension

The environmental dimension is where we learn to take personal responsibility for the health and welfare of the natural resources God has blessed us with. A deep and abiding appreciation of and respect for nature moves us closer to our spiritual essence. This includes appreciating and respecting our natural surroundings, living in harmony with the environment, and doing our part to preserve its resources. Knowledge of God and His works are found in understanding plants and animals and the delicate, interwoven, and intricate web of life. Job 12:7-10 reminds us that the animals, birds, fish, and plants have something important to teach us. Christians have a sacred responsibility to the earth and the creatures in it. In Genesis 1:26-28 God gives man dominion over the earth, but this is not a license to exploit it merely for human pleasures and purposes. God expects us to live in harmony with nature. As stewards of the earth we must internalize that all of creation belongs to God, not us. We have been granted permission to use nature for our basic needs but not for selfish exploitation.

As we age and continue to grow whole, we can see God in every aspect of nature and its abundant resources. We are duty bound to be good stewards of God's bountiful and magnificent natural environment.

The earth is the LORD's and the fullness thereof, the world and all that dwell therein, for he has founded it upon the seas and established it upon the rivers. (Psalm 24:1–2 ESV)

5. Financial Dimension

The financial dimension is where we acquire the skills to manage our economic resources. We align our consumption habits with short-term and long-term asset protection goals. When our lifestyle exceeds our assets, we undermine efforts toward economic solvency. Controlling finances requires a serious commitment to budgeting, debt elimination, saving for emergencies, and retirement planning. Growing whole requires a determination to share our resources with those in need and to support individual and group efforts to glorify God.

Scripture has a lot to say about material possessions and money. They are important issues because our attitude toward them directly reflects the condition of our hearts, our relationship with God, and our desire to fulfill sacred purpose. In Mark 10:18 Jesus had an interesting encounter with a rich man who asked him what he must do to inherit eternal life. Jesus responded by advising the rich man to sacrifice his earthly wealth and follow Him. When he heard Jesus' response the rich man went away disheartened. Wealth and privileged positions can be emotional obstacles to pursuing sacred purpose. Growing whole requires us to internalize that God is the source of everything and we should seek His counsel in all things, including the management of our economic resources.

> Honor the Lord with your wealth, and with the first fruits
> of all you produce. (Proverbs, 3:9 ESV)

6. Intellectual Dimension

The intellectual dimension represents the lifelong pursuit of knowledge. It includes a willingness to accept and apply reliable data and newly acquired inputs to solve problems, optimize daily living, and increase production. Continuous improvement, active pursuit of scholastic achievement, and expansion of cultural appreciation and awareness are examples of opportunities to grow intellectually. Knowledge is the foundation for understanding and wisdom. When we know better, we usually do better. To live well and age well, we should be eager to learn new concepts and skills and expand our academic capacity. The intellectual dimension encourages involvement in creative and stimulating mental activities. Balance in this aspect of our being includes keeping our mind active, staying abreast of current events, and participating in activities that challenge the brain. Growing whole requires us to actively seek knowledge and wisdom with the full understanding that all good and perfect gifts come from God.

> The heart of the discerning acquires knowledge, for the
> ears of the wise seek it out. (Proverbs, 18:15 NIV)

7. Mental Dimension

The mental dimension is the area of our being where we learn to cope effectively with activities and events of daily living. We strive for inner peace, serenity, and tranquility. We quiet our minds so we can hear God speak to us, and we open our hearts to receive and act in accordance with His instructions. We focus on being productive, contributing to society, and serving others. When we encounter challenges and stressors that are beyond our capacity to cope, we seek professional assistance and engage our spiritual resources through prayer and meditation. Growing whole requires us to guard our minds. An agitated mind cannot manage the thought processes necessary to embrace and engage life from the vantage point of mental wellness. Today's fast-paced world can be stressful. Medical professionals warn us that stress is a risk factor for heart disease and strokes. As we grow spiritually we learn to consult the Bible when problems present themselves. We learn that the Bible is more than a holy book, it is a practical guide for dealing with the ups-and-downs of life. We accept that the ebb and flow of challenging situations are a natural part of the human experience. We comprehend that efforts to live our best lives require us to be alert and sober minded, strengthen our defenses against ungodly influences, and stand firm in our faith.

> The mind governed by the flesh is death, but the mind
> governed by the Spirit is life and peace. (Romans 8:6 NIV)

8. Physical Dimension

The physical dimension reflects our ability to maintain a healthy quality of life that supports the successful accomplishment of routine activities without undue stress or fatigue. Balance in this area also includes being active, eating healthy foods, getting sufficient sleep, paying attention to the signs of illness, and seeking assistance when needed. The physical dimension is the vessel through which the other eleven dimensions flow. Within the space of our earthly bodies the vibrational energy fields that make us who we are overlap and affect each other in profound ways. While the dimensions have their own distinct functions they continuously send messages back and forth to each other. The physical body brings these messages to our awareness when we are heartbroken, filled with excitement and happiness, or we are grieving over the loss of a loved one. To achieve the internal and external balance and harmony that is required for wholeness we must become adept at understanding the various messages moving through our bodies. Memories of everything that has ever happened to us are stored somewhere in the body and affect us even if we are not aware of their existence. Growing whole requires us to appreciate and take care of our bodies to ensure they are acceptable to God.

> Therefore I urge you, brothers and sisters, by the mercies of God, to present your bodies a living and holy sacrifice, acceptable to God, which is your spiritual service of worship. And do not be conformed to this world, but be transformed by the renewing of your mind, so that you may prove what the will of God is, that which is good and acceptable and perfect. (Romans 12:1–2 NAS)

9. Social Dimension

The social dimension includes a strong, supportive network of trusted friends and family. Over time, we become amazingly proficient at differentiating between true, authentic relationships and superficial, selfishly motivated ones. As we age, these distinctions become increasingly more important and critical to our overall well-being. The complex experiences and understandings that support conscious aging heighten our senses and quickly discard inappropriate alliances and associations. People enter our lives for a multitude of reasons, some as transients and others as permanent relationships. The social dimension of our being gives us the tools we need to distinguish one from the other. Growing whole requires us to care for, encourage, and fellowship with each other. Whether the relationship is transitory or permanent, there is a divine reason for the interconnection. There is something we need to learn. The challenge for each of us is to treat every human-to-human engagement with respect, even when we sense the presence of evil. While we must be prudent and protect ourselves from potential harm, what if the reason for the two souls meeting is to lead the individual to Christ?

> And let us consider how to stir up one another to love and good works, not neglecting to meet together, as is the habit of some, but encouraging one another. (Hebrews 10:24–25 ESV)

10. Spiritual Dimension

The spiritual dimension is rooted in a strong sense of meaning and sacred purpose. It manifests itself in several ways including establishing a lifestyle that reflects the character and image of God, living well, and growing whole rather than simply growing old. Balance and growth in this dimension represents a commitment to Christian principles and adherence to the practices of divinely inspired unconditional love and Christ-centeredness. Growing whole requires us to vigorously pursue meaning and sacred purpose. It requires us to establish beliefs, guiding principles, and values that help give godly direction to our lives. It requires us to activate our faith by loving God, ourselves, and others. When we volunteer, for example, we demonstrate our spirituality through fellowship and social responsibility, and we contribute to society.

The spiritual dimension is the entryway to awareness and enlightenment. Growth in this dimension occurs exponentially as we align our inner and outer selves.

> Blessed are those who hunger and thirst for righteousness, for they shall be satisfied. (Matthew 5:6 ESV)

11. Visionary Dimension

The visionary dimension allows us to establish realistic goals and to create a life that supports their accomplishment. In this dimension, we can look beyond the present, see the future we desire, and make the adjustments necessary to live in integrity and truth. No matter our age or stage, we should have a clear vision for our lives that supports sacred purpose. The visionary dimension of our being encompasses developing the skills to discover fresh insights about the way things are and cultivate different outlooks on what can be. Growth in the spiritual dimension requires us to regularly re-examine the assumptions on which we base our understandings of reality, identify areas that we might consider from a different perspective, and re-frame the conversations about issues that impact lives and contribute to the common good. In this dimension we pursue solutions that promote fairness and justice. Growing whole requires us to have spiritual vision and to add value to the human experience.

> And the LORD answered me: Write the vision; make it plain on tablets, so he may run who reads it. For still the vision awaits its appointed time; it hastens to the end—it will not lie. If it seems slow, wait for it; it will surely come; it will not delay. (Habakkuk 2:2–3 ESV)

12. Vocational Dimension

The vocational dimension requires the diligent pursuit of professional endeavors that fulfill and support our desired lifestyle. While actively employed, growing whole requires us to exercise our administrative and leadership skills in ways that glorify God by treating coworkers and those we serve with respect. It also requires us to find creative ways to fulfill sacred purpose. The book of Nehemiah gives us a peek inside the personal memoirs of a great leader. There is no mistaking his style. He was an organizer and a pragmatic administrator. These attributes probably had a lot to do with him rising to a top-level position in the Persian empire, one of the greatest in the history of the world. While serving as a cupbearer to King Artaxerxes of Persia Nehemiah received some disturbing news about the deplorable conditions in Jerusalem, his ancestral homeland. After fasting and praying he decided he would share his concerns with the king and ask permission to help rebuild his beloved city. He used his administrative skills and his position to serve his people and glorify

God. Once we retire, the vocational dimension expands to include how we interact with others as we pursue hobbies, volunteer, and embrace our status as wise elders. Growing whole requires us to utilize our vocational skills to improve the collective human condition whether actively employed or enjoying retirement.

> For the gifts and the calling of God are irrevocable. (Romans 11:29 ESV)

Three Stage Process to Address Unresolved Pain

Growing whole rather than simply growing old is a decision to alter the current trajectory of your life. If you do nothing and keep breathing, you will grow old. If you envision something better in your future than what you have now, there is no magic wand to wave; you must act. Prayerfully invite God to participate with you on an internal journey of discovery and resolution. Before you can step into sacred purpose, you must do the inner work required to cleanse and purify your soul. There may be years of betrayal, bitterness, lost opportunities for love, pain, heartache, roads not taken, and unrealized dreams of could-haves, should-haves, would-haves and if-onlys. Unresolved issues weigh you down like a cement block and prevent you from realizing your potential. There may be intentions, thoughts, words, and deeds that breed feelings of guilt and regret. There may be abuse, addiction, or benign neglect.

Spiritual cleansing is the act of taking a hard look at yourself and realistically assessing the quality of your life from the perspective of meaningfulness and Godly purpose. Though extremely unpleasant, it is a vital prerequisite to addressing unresolved pain. This cleaning occurs in three stages. Stage one is self-examination, stage two is self-exploration, and stage three is discovery and resolution. You can undertake this spiritual cleansing exercise alone, you can ask an accountability partner to participate with you, or you can seek the assistance of a life coach or therapist.

Stage One: Self-Examination

1. Begin each session with prayer and contemplation. For this exercise to work, you must be brutally honest and willing to take responsibility for your contribution to any problems you identify. Clarify your goals and set your intention. *What are you trying to accomplish? What would you like to see happen by completing this exercise?* It is important that you are clear about why you are engaging in the process.

2. Find a quiet space that allows you the freedom and privacy to fully consider any source of emotional, mental, or physical pain. Make notes as issues are revealed to you. These notes will contain valuable information you can use during current or future sessions.

3. Ask deep and probing questions about each issue that arises. This is the most important component of self-examination. Do not move forward until you have clarity about what you are experiencing and why. Honor your emotions, and allow the time necessary to engage them completely. If you need to cry for thirty minutes, do so. If you need to pray, meditate, or punch a pillow, do so.

Stage Two: Self-Exploration

4. Give yourself the emotional and mental space to explore every aspect of each issue that arises. Be compassionate and nonjudgmental. Forgive yourself and your perceived offenders before moving forward. Let go of any feelings of anger that you harbor about the issue. When you forgive, anger subsides and you make room for internal peace.

5. Do not rush the self-exploration stage. You have probably accumulated sizeable amounts of unresolved pain over the years. It will take time to appropriately address all your issues. It may take several sessions to completely empty out. Take a break if you begin to feel overwhelmed.

6. With courage, face every issue that springs forward. You may be surprised by some of the sources of pain that reveal themselves to you. Continue to explore by asking deep and probing questions.

If you begin to feel uncomfortable, breathe deeply and slow the process down.

Stage Three: Discovery and Resolution

7. You will know when the self-examination and self-exploration stages are complete. First, you will feel lighter. The weight of years of damage will be lifted from your shoulders. Second, you will experience emotional exhaustion. Third, the exhilaration of newfound freedom will overwhelm you. Perhaps for the first time in your life, the chains that bound you and stunted your spiritual growth will be broken.

8. By the time you reach the discovery stage specific actions you need to take to support resolution should have been revealed to you. If nothing comes to mind, ask yourself, *What do I need to do to move forward and leave this pain behind? What am I getting out of continuing to hold on to this issue? Am I honestly seeking resolution, or do I want to remain stuck here?* Pray for guidance, then identify your plan of action. Maybe you need to apologize, seek coaching or counseling, work diligently to improve certain relationships, or pray for the peace that comes with acceptance of realities you cannot change.

9. Engage this three-stage process for every unresolved issue you identify. Do not take shortcuts. You might consider incorporating it into your newly informed lifestyle as issues arise in the future.

10. Close each session with prayer and meditation. Thoughtfully consider everything that happened throughout the experience. Be grateful for the opportunity to gain valuable information and insight. Give yourself a mental pat on the back because you are one step closer to growing whole.

New awareness may have emerged about your behavioral and thought patterns that do not serve you well. Be honest about what you discovered. If it matters, admit it. Do not try to tell yourself that something is unimportant if your feelings say otherwise. Remember, your emotions are the keepers of important information about you. They paint undeniably accurate pictures of the internal forces at work in your life.

Using a journal, record your hurts, anger-inducing triggers, and efforts to expand and grow. Always try to pinpoint the cause of any emotions you feel. Simply by engaging in the process of capturing your feelings in writing, you gain valuable insight, knowledge, understanding, and wisdom. If beyond the process of self-examination, self-exploration, and discovery and resolution you continue to feel pain from situations in your past, you may have deeply repressed emotions that require professional assistance. If this is the case, do not procrastinate. Find the help you need.

Chapter 3 Important Points

- The doctrine of the Trinity is foundational to the Christian faith. There is one God who eternally exists as three persons, the Father as Creator, the Son as Savior, and the Holy Spirit as Comforter.
- Human life is part of the metanarrative of the story of creation. As a result, meaning and purpose are embedded in all humanity.
- Alignment, balance, and harmony are necessary for you to thrive, find meaning, and pursue sacred purpose.
- Humans are tripartite beings—body, soul, and spirit.
- Every life experience affects you in every dimension of your being.
- Multidimensional interconnectedness is a critical by-product of growing whole.
- The twelve functional dimensions of humankind include the following aspects of your being: creative, cultural, emotional, environmental, financial, intellectual, mental, physical, social, spiritual, visionary, and vocational.
- An important component of growing whole is a commitment to regular self-examination, self-exploration, and discovery. This process is helpful for addressing unresolved pain.
- Get in the habit of journaling.

4

ESTABLISH A PERSONAL RELATIONSHIP WITH GOD

When the righteous cry for help, the Lord hears and delivers them out of all their troubles. The Lord is near to the brokenhearted and saves the crushed in spirit. Many are the afflictions of the righteous, but the Lord delivers him out of them all. (Psalm 34:17-19 ESV)

We live in a self-serving and egotistical world. Too many of us routinely put our desires, interests, and needs ahead of anyone or anything else. From a secular perspective, we are taught that money, position, power, and prestige are worth obtaining. While none of those things is necessarily bad, ruthless pursuit of them is. From a spiritual perspective, we are taught that compassion, humility, love, and having a servant's heart and a personal relationship with God are worth obtaining. Outside the context of the creation story, the importance of being in fellowship and relationship with God and being led by the principles of a Christ-centered lifestyle is easily misunderstood and undervalued.

Creation and the Fall

The overarching story of humankind is one of second chances. A once-perfect bond between God and His children fell apart because of selfish, shortsighted disobedience. This relationship breach was of severe consequence so much so that all subsequent events and experiences of life are rooted in this stark reality. God's kingdom story is largely about fellowship and relationship. It is also circular; there is no beginning or ending.

Humankind entered the kingdom story with God creating a being in His image. The drama that unfolds as revealed to us in the Bible is the greatest story ever told. Initially, humans lived in direct fellowship and relationship with God. Milestones of the kingdom story include creation, a perfect relationship with God in the beautiful Garden of Eden, disobedience, a relationship breach, the fall from grace, a strategic redemption plan, and ultimately, a reconciled, perfect relationship with God in heaven. It is clear from the beginning that fellowship and relationship are important aspects of God's character.

The Bible includes myriad stories about everyday people who played notable roles in the metanarrative of the kingdom story. Much like our own, their lives reflected accomplishments, aspirations, disappointments, drama, and dreams. Like us, they were flawed, and they made their share of missteps. They went about their daily routines until there was a holy calling. Some, including David, fully embraced their sacred purpose, while others such as Jonah, went to great lengths to avoid theirs. Some, including Joshua, executed their sacred purpose with dignity and precision, while others such as Aaron veered off course and brought tragedy to the people they led. Some callings, including Esther's, were short term. In risking her life to bring the king a message, she served her sacred purpose as God's instrument of deliverance for the Jews in Persia. For others, including Moses, it took decades to complete their sacred purpose. The exodus from Egyptian slavery to the Promised Land lasted forty years.

Some had the insight to see and appreciate the big picture. Others never fully understood the profound gravity of their calling, yet they willingly took risks and sacrificed their lives to respond to God. Some were more noble; others were deceitful. With each story, though, we can clearly see how these biblical characters either helped or hindered. The one thing these fascinating stories seem to have in common is that they were told through the lens of fellowship and relationship. The interactions of one person to another regardless of the circumstances seems to be the focus.

These stories carry contemporary messages. The spirits of the people whose lives are reflected in the Bible speak to us. They left important clues we can apply to our lives in ways that benefit the common good. Their stories generously offer us the gift of hindsight. I fell in love with the Bible when I learned to view its stories through the lens of fellowship and relationship. Let us consider a few details of two lives that affected human history in pivotal ways.

The pinnacle of God's creation was humankind, to whom He gave dominion over everything else. Original man was named Adam and original woman was named Eve. God gave them a beautiful garden, Eden, to occupy, tend, and enjoy. They had plentiful fruits and vegetables, but God made it clear that one tree was off limits. This was the Tree of the Knowledge of Good and Evil. God warned them that the penalty for disobedience was death.

The relationship between God, original man, and original woman was initially harmonious. Over time, though, this special divine-human bond was broken, and conflict and division erupted. Adam and Eve chose to disobey God by succumbing to Satan's temptation to eat the delicious fruit from the forbidden tree. This single act of disobedience introduced sin into the world; it changed their lives forever and changed the course of history.

The harmonious relationship was severed. Suddenly there was disharmony between humankind and God and between man and woman. As God had previously warned, disobedience brought death in two forms—physical and spiritual. While their physical bodies continued to exist, they were immediately alienated from God, which resulted in their spiritual death. They were kicked out of Eden, and they no longer had personal communion with God.

Adam and Eve had a perfect life in a perfect paradise, yet they wanted more. They willingly forfeited the opportunity to have eternal bliss for a few moments of forbidden pleasure. Their greed ushered in disastrous consequences including broken relationships, death, violence, and wars. The ills that have plagued humankind since the fall can be traced back to that fateful day of disobedience in the Garden of Eden. The element of sin was introduced into the human equation, and it continues to define the human condition in the twenty-first century.

The Strategic Redemption Plan

Despite the dire circumstances, we see God's unconditional love and forgiveness right away. He set in motion a strategic redemption plan to repair the damage caused by human disobedience. Jesus Christ would play a major role in the redemption plan through His sacrifice on our behalf. In the ultimate act of unconditional love, He assumed personal responsibility for our conversion. In doing so, He gave us a pathway to oneness with God and wholeness with self and others. The damaged, broken pieces of our souls could then be repaired. Through His death, He gave us life.

Redemption offers myriad benefits including eternal life, forgiveness of sins, adoption into God's family, joy, peace, and the indwelling of the Holy Spirit to guide and comfort us. Redemption frees us from sin's bondage and its consequences, and it paves the way for us to reconcile our broken relationship with God. Reconciliation must occur before the process of growing whole can begin.

Reconciliation

Growing Whole is a story about reconciliation. At our core, we are spiritual beings witnessing life from a fundamentally physical perspective. Within the boundaries of this duality, reconciliation must occur. Herein lies one of the major reasons for our earthly existence. Many elements of our spiritual and physical essence are not harmonized; they are often at war with each other resulting in disagreement and dysfunction. Becoming one with God, ourselves, and others is our life work.

Since the breach, we have been on a course of deficit-driven correction. Because of the fall, we are disconnected from our source, and the loneliness and pain of this isolation are our constant companions. We crave a relationship connection that we are hard wired to need yet are incapable of realizing on our own. By offering a pathway to a restored fellowship with Him, God provides a permanent remedy for our spiritual brokenness. The two-step process for restored fellowship and relationship includes salvation and then sanctification.

Salvation

Salvation, a gift from God, is not something we earn through good works or positive attitudes. While these are important cornerstones to Christianity, salvation is available only through faith in Jesus Christ. God generously offers His grace and mercy once we confess our belief in Jesus's death and resurrection, repent, and place our trust in Him. In effect, we accept God's conditions of repentance and place our faith in Jesus as Lord. Once we make a conscious decision to accept the biblical explanation of the Trinity of God, Jesus Christ, and the Holy Spirit, God graciously bestows salvation.

With this gift of salvation, we immediately become a member of the body of Christ. The process of growing whole can then begin. We no longer rely solely on our own physical prowess, natural gifts, talents, or senses to navigate life. We shift our focus from the secular to the sacred. As our newly established relationship with God strengthens, we learn to rely on His Word to encourage, guide, nourish, and protect us. With prayer, meditation, and spending one-on-one time with Him, we continue to grow closer. We fellowship with other Christians who offer encouragement and support.

> God saved you by His grace when you believed. And you can't take credit for this; it is a gift from God. (Ephesians 2:8 NLT)

As a child, I often heard the elders in my community church say, "I'm working out my soul salvation." Until I became a serious student of the Bible, I did not really understand the depth of those words. Once we are accepted into the family of Christ, we spend the remainder of our lives growing whole. The spiritual imperative to expand and grow nudges us away from worldly pursuits toward higher callings such as serving our sacred purpose, healing our wounds, learning to love as God loves, and reconciling our broken spirits.

Sanctification

Growing old and growing whole are not the same. With every breath, the aging process continues, but the transformation from brokenness to wholeness resides in the territory of willful and deliberate soul sanctification. The relationship breach resulted in dysfunction on three levels—human to God, human to self, and human to human—and reconciliation must take place on each of these levels.

Once salvation occurs, the lifelong process of sanctification begins. We are set apart by God for His purposes. Through the work of the Holy Spirit, our sinful nature loses its control over us and we are gradually molded into the character and image of God. We shift our attention from world-centeredness and ego-centeredness to a Christ-centered lifestyle. As we grow beyond the salvation experience, we are slowly being transformed from the physical to the spiritual. Essentially, this purification process takes place in our hearts, which are within the sacred territory of the soul. Sanctification is the bridge that makes it possible for us to no longer be of the world though we are still in it.

The sanctification process occurs in two stages, immediate and ongoing. First, when we experience salvation, sanctification begins. As believers, we are immediately set apart from nonbelievers. Second, through a close, lifelong partnership between us and the Holy Spirit, we are transformed into committed followers of Christ.

Growing whole is an integral part of sanctification. The basic tenets of love and unity are deeply embedded in the process of growing whole. God is love, and if we expect to emulate Him, we must do so in this same context. When we decide to grow whole, we unleash powerful forces of spiritual energy that orchestrate our lives to help us fulfill this holy commitment. The character traits we need to acquire and the lessons we need to learn become available to us in divine order. Purification and transformation from the physical to the spiritual begin to take shape, and we lose our appetite for worldly pleasures and treasures. Life morphs into its true meaning in the form of sacred purpose.

Sanctification is at once individual and corporate. On the individual level, God's redemptive work takes place deep in our souls. Through prayer and meditation, our personal relationship with God strengthens. Through putting our faith in action and living and breathing sacred purpose, we grow beyond knowing *about* God to knowing Him intimately.

On the corporate level, the body of Christ supports us in so many ways. Fellow believers worship with us, pray for and with us, serve as role models, and hold us accountable when necessary. They challenge us to step outside our comfort zones, and when we are called to do something that stretches our capacity, they encourage us. Believers check on us when we are sick and shut-in. They mourn with us when we are brokenhearted, and they empathize and sympathize with us when we need compassion. They are loving and supportive. They teach us and allow us to teach them. They are kind and forgiving. This mutually beneficial relationship strengthens our faith and lifts our spirits.

Spiritual Transformation

From a spiritual perspective, life has no beginning or end; it simply transforms and transitions. Our brief time on earth was always known, and our celestial existence was from everlasting to everlasting.

> Even as he chose us in him before the foundation of the world, that we should be holy and blameless before him. (Ephesians 1:4 ESV)

From a physical perspective, life officially begins at conception, when breath enters the body. At a predetermined date and time, the breath is withheld, and we return to our ever-present spiritual essence. We are liberated from a world of limitations, and we can see God with utmost clarity. The blinders deeply embedded in the contours of our earthly worldview are removed, and everything finally makes sense. Our gifts and talents, our blunders and our moments of light, our labor, and our periods of rest—all culminate when we are rewarded with the blessing of transition.

Early in His ministry, Jesus delivered a powerful message that would later become renowned worldwide as the Sermon on the Mount. Shortly after He called His first disciples to follow Him, He began to teach them about how their lives could serve as examples for others. He painted a picture of what a believer's lifestyle should be like in practical terms. The spiritual and moral principles He espoused left little room for misinterpretation. The basic tenets of Christianity were included in His message on that fateful day.

He started with a reminder of God's blessings. He challenged traditional interpretations of Old Testament law, and He stressed the need for His disciples to grow up and live like the kingdom servants they had become. He taught them how to pray and how to be in fellowship and relationship with themselves and others, and He clarified that forgiveness was a critical component of their faith walk. He admonished His disciples to refrain from criticizing and judging others. In a simple, practical guide for behavior, Jesus encouraged them to live by the golden rule—treating others the way they would like to be treated.

Jesus focused on salvation, reconciliation, and reunification. He entered the world in a way that was sufficiently common so everyday people could identify with His message. His lowly appearance signified humility and made it clear that a bottoms-up movement was underway. A complete transformation in the lives of His followers was about to unfold. His physical presence on earth marked the beginning of a revolution that had been set in motion before the foundation of the world. Everything that was previously accepted had to be reimagined and considered from a deeper, less worldly, and more spiritual perspective.

God spoke clearly and decisively through Jesus, who made salient points with fascinating yet down-to-earth parables—earthly stories with heavenly meanings. His tone and rhythm made His words relatable and easy for His followers to comprehend. Those who continually rejected His message, though, were left in a state of spiritual blindness and wonderment. When you think about Jesus's unique delivery style and the unusual message He conveyed, it becomes clear why the biblical account of history is the greatest story ever told.

We receive information from secular and sacred sources. Secular knowledge, understanding, and wisdom are acquired through reliance on our five physical senses. This information can be beneficial to efforts toward growing whole as long as it comports with our Christian teachings. Sacred knowledge, understanding, and wisdom are revealed to us in scripture and become an integral part of our being through the indwelling of the Holy

Spirit. As we are transformed from secular beings to sacred beings our five physical senses are elevated to the status of five spiritual senses.

Through the gift of discernment, we learn to distinguish between biblical truths and false teachings. Spiritual transformation requires us to abandon false beliefs. The problem we face is that false teachings are not unique to secular input. Not all information presented under the umbrella of Christian teaching is Bible based. Some of the information available to us from religious teachers cannot withstand the test of comparison to scripture. As we are transformed from our worldly ways to a Christ-centered lifestyle, we must become adept at assessing the validity of information presented to us.

The relationship breach that resulted from sinful disobedience set in motion circumstances and situations that we know as the human condition. The guiding principles of growing whole acknowledge our broken spirits and offer a pathway back to oneness with God. Christians readily acknowledge Jesus Christ as the architect of their reunification efforts. Those of us who choose this pathway have certain milestones that serve as guideposts, all of which rely on an unshakable faith in the Trinity. Through faith and God's grace, we receive the gift of salvation, which is the necessary first step toward reunification. Once saved, we become active participants in the quest to experience the fullest extent of the promises of God. Our efforts to grow whole must include a revolutionary transformation from a world-centered and ego-centered existence to a Christ-centered lifestyle.

Spiritual transformation is complex and multifaceted. It requires us to put God first in every aspect of our lives. This is a serious commitment that morphs into a lifelong journey toward wholeness. It extends far beyond salvation and regular participation in our Christian rituals. It requires honesty and sacrifice on levels we are not comfortable going. Without God's guidance and support, we are unable to love as He loves or live as Christ taught us to live.

Spiritual transformation demands that we consciously discard the negative, unconscious brainwashing and ideologies passed down to us from our ancestors and other cultural influences. It relies heavily on personal introspection and a willingness to face the character flaws and destructive behaviors that have become a normal part of our lives. We must learn to ask probing questions, challenge our long-standing beliefs, and examine everything against the gold standard of unconditional love. Spiritual transformation means replacing old, nonproductive habits with new, productive ones that honor God and position us for implementation of sacred purpose.

Spiritual Growth Plan

Living well means successful management of the important events of our lives. Whether these events are expected and predictable or unexpected and unpredictable, planning and preparation are necessary to help ensure success. A key component to growing whole is sustained spiritual growth.

We appreciate the benefits of having a roadmap to guide us toward realization of goals. There are many types of plans, but regardless of the subject, their purpose is to guide, inform, preserve, and protect us.

- They guide our efforts to set goals and priorities.
- They keep us informed and gauge progress.
- They preserve our right to make decisions about our lives, and they record our intentions.
- They protect us from undue exposure by helping ensure sufficient preparation.

The Spiritual Growth Plan (Plan) is an excellent tool to support manifestation of your intention to grow whole. At a minimum, your Plan should include the following components.

1. **Statement of Purpose**. What is your overarching goal? (Example: To cocreate a lifestyle that reflects the character and image of God.)
2. **Personal Vision Statement**. Draw a mental picture of what your short-term and long-term spiritual lives look like. Have fun dreaming and envisioning, but be realistic and practical. Write this statement in present tense. (Example: I am sitting on my balcony enjoying a cup of coffee and engaged in my daily spiritual practice of praying, meditating, and communing with nature. I am feeling especially grateful for my health and the overall well-being of my

family and friends. I volunteer to serve meals at a homeless shelter, and I am involved with the youth ministry at my church. I am actively working to build positive relationships with fellow church members whom I do not know. I regularly attend services and I am a committed tither.)

3. **Objective Self-Assessment**. Describe your spiritual life. It is important to be brutally honest. You cannot grow closer to God if you are unwilling to admit the present condition of your spiritual life. (Example: I pray, meditate, and read the Bible as often as I can, but my hectic schedule makes it hard for me to commit to a regular time. I attend church services one or two Sundays each month. I am involved in a great community service project that I feel good about, and I work with the married couples ministry. I support my church financially as best I can, and my husband and I include discussion of a specific scripture during our daily thirty-minute walks.)

4. **Strategies to Strengthen Spiritual Practices**. List specific steps you will take to support your vision statement. (Example: Develop a consistent Bible reading plan, ask God's help in dealing with my low self-esteem issues, spend more time in nature, pray and reflect more, join a Bible study group, connect with fellow believers, attend church services more regularly, get involved in a ministry so I can put my faith into action.)

5. **Impact of Sacred Purpose on Lifestyle**. Describe how you will incorporate sacred purpose into your Christ-centered lifestyle. (Example: I believe sacred purpose means using my gifts and talents to serve God, my family, and my community. I will accomplish this by spending more one-on-one time with God. I will give my spouse and my children the undivided attention they deserve when I come home from work. I will leave the concerns and job-related stress behind when I walk out the door. I will not bring work home from the office. I will volunteer to become a reading tutor at my child's school.)

6. **Personal Life Code.** The life code is the basic framework for how you will implement your overarching goal in the statement of purpose. The primary reason for the code is to draw an invisible

line in the sand, a mark beyond which you simply will not go. It should include the principles and guidelines for your life. (Example: I will not engage in activities or discussions that are demeaning or hurtful to other people. I will work diligently to minimize the influence of worldly pleasures and treasures on my life. I will be guided by the biblical principles of love of God, self, and others. I will be honest, and I will use my gifts and talents in service toward the common good. I will find creative ways to live out my sacred purpose. I will not be guided by selfish, egotistical needs, and I will set my intention to reduce any fear-based emotions that hinder my efforts to grow whole. With God's help, I will cocreate a Christ-centered lifestyle.)

7. **Civic and Community Involvement**. Identify your level of sustained participation in efforts to address local issues of concern. (Example: I will support local initiatives that serve the needy. I will educate myself about approved programs and monitor their implementation. I will vote, attend town hall meetings, and take other steps to become an informed citizen. I will support my church in its outreach efforts, and I will volunteer my time in support of these activities whenever I can.)

I spend an inordinate amount of time trying to better understand the human condition from a spiritual perspective. I realize that our level of knowledge, understanding, and wisdom is too often one dimensional, and as a result, we are often unable to see God at work in our lives. When we view the world through the lens of a Christ-centered lifestyle though, clarity and enlightenment give us a peek into immortality. Meaning and sacred purpose are sufficiently complex that our capacity to grasp their depth and robustness is limited.

I do not believe God intends for us to receive the fullness of His character and image while we remain in the earthly realm. I do believe, however, as we become more Christlike, glimpses of heaven are revealed to us. With development and implementation of a personal spiritual growth plan, we continue raising our level of consciousness and our natural ways are supernaturally transformed.

Chapter 4 Important Points

- A critical component of growing whole is establishing a personal relationship with God.
- The overarching story of humankind is one of second chances.
- Initially, humans lived in direct fellowship and relationship with God. This once-perfect bond between God and man was severed because of disobedience.
- The relationship breach was of severe consequence, so much so that all subsequent events and experiences of life are rooted in this stark reality.
- Despite the serious breach, God provided a means of reconciliation. This redemption plan includes the gift of salvation and sanctification.
- Salvation is a gift that is only available through faith in Jesus Christ.
- Once you are accepted into the family of God, your world-centered and ego-centered lifestyles are gradually transformed into a Christ-centered lifestyle.
- The pathway back to oneness with God is through the lens of unconditional love.
- The spiritual growth plan is an excellent tool to support manifestation of your efforts toward growing whole.

5

DEVELOP A CHRIST-CENTERED LIFESTYLE

So then, just as you received Christ Jesus as Lord, continue to live in him, rooted and built up in him, strengthened in the faith as you were taught, and overflowing with thankfulness. See to it that no one takes you captive through hollow and deceptive philosophy, which depends on human tradition and the basic principles of the world rather than on Christ. (Colossians 2:6–8 NIV)

The Heart: The Center of Human Life

We live from the heart, the center of human life where our intentions, thoughts, words, and deeds intersect to form our worldviews. Our sense of fairness, justice, reason, self, and the deeply held motivations that drive us reside in the heart. Compassion and love flow from the heart. Choices and decisions that affect the quality of our lives are developed and nurtured in the heart. It fuels life and is the reservoir of our convictions and desires.

From a physical perspective, our anatomical hearts sustain us. This fist-sized powerhouse performs specific functions like moving blood through the body and supplying oxygen and nutrients to the tissues. It is shaped like an upside-down pear and is located under the rib cage. It has a measurable size, specific functions, a unique shape, and a defined location. From a romantic perspective, the heart that epitomizes love and affection has no resemblance to the anatomical heart. This iconic pictogram is what we envision when we think about the word *heart*. Its origins are difficult to determine, but there are several interesting theories. Some believe it is shaped like ivy leaves, which are associated with fidelity. Others contend the shape is patterned after parts of the human anatomy including breasts and buttocks. Still others suggest it is molded in the form of the silphium plant, which once flourished on the North African coastline. The ancient Greeks and Romans used this plant as birth control, medicine, and food seasoning.

From a spiritual perspective, our hearts offer valuable inputs that influence our worldview and move us closer to a Christ-centered lifestyle. The spiritual heart is a catalyst for understanding lifelong meaning and sacred purpose. It is the fundamental essence of who God intends us to be as individuals and as a species. It permeates our bodies and minds, and it cannot be contained by parameters that define size, function, shape, or location. It has an undeniable, all-knowing presence that has the power to transform lives and alter the course of history.

Whether we engage life from the perspective of the anatomical heart, the romantic heart, or the spiritual heart, we are in the territory of formation and transformation. Proverbs 4:23 (ESV) reads, "Keep your heart with all vigilance, for from it flows the springs of life."

Our hearts derive their character from our belief systems, choices, emotions, and experiences. Life happens, and when it does, we have the free will to act and react. How we use our creative genius to form a lifestyle that supports the internal and external layers of our being will directly impact our quality of life. How we respond to the divinely designed events that mold us is a critical component of wholeness. In that sacred space, where intentions breed thoughts and focused thoughts fuel actions, lies the divinely inspired formula for holy transformation from world-centeredness and ego-centeredness to Christ-centeredness. All this occurs in the territory of the heart.

Out of our hearts flow the rivers of purity or impurity, good or evil, and love or hate, whichever we decide. No doubt heartfelt choices are some of the most consequential decisions we will ever make. The truisms of our lives do not flow into us from external influences; they flow out of us from the depths of our souls through the consciousness of the Holy Spirit. This is where matters of the heart are received, processed, and transmitted. Growing whole is an inside-out job, and it requires an unshakeable confidence that the God of the universe has chosen specific experiences to move us closer to sacred purpose.

The Practical Implications of Growing Whole

When we commit to a Christ-centered lifestyle, we are in effect setting our intention to live in accordance with the teachings of Jesus Christ. We are making a conscious choice to engage in ongoing efforts to turn life as we know it upside down. We are embarking on a journey of no return. The human heart is designed for fellowship and relationship. When we love others, we have a strong desire to be with them. We gauge the strength of this love by how often we think about them, the amount of time we spend with them, and the level of emotional energy we expend on them. These same parameters apply to our relationship with Jesus Christ. If we love Him as we profess to, our thoughts, time, and energy should reflect that.

The term *lifestyle* is best described as the way we live. It reflects tangible and intangible attributes such as attitudes, behaviors, beliefs, habits, interests, living conditions, opinions, and values. If we have committed ourselves to a Christ-centered lifestyle, that should be apparent in our daily lives. Every intention, thought, word, and deed should glorify God. We make decisions based on an awareness of our faith and our choice to participate in the kingdom story. We avoid the drama of worldly discord and entanglement. We spend time in prayer and meditation. We consider every decision in light of its eternal significance. We bridle our tongues and use our words for good rather than evil. We honor God with our first fruits. When we fall, we seek forgiveness, get back on our feet, and keep moving forward. We learn to love as God loves. We are humble and are willing to serve. Despite trials and tribulations, we keep our eyes on meaning and sacred purpose. We take responsibility for our messes. We avoid hypocrisy and judgment. We assume the character and image of God. When adversity, betrayal, death, disappointment, pain, and suffering come—and they will—we endure, persevere, and push through even though our hearts are broken.

When life happens, we seek blameless resolution by asking probing questions to separate allegations, feelings, and opinions from facts. *Do our actions match our emotions, thoughts, and values? Can we embrace our life mission and find joy in the valleys as well as on the peaks? Are we able to derive comfort from the knowledge that enduring the lows will give us the strength we need to fulfill our mission? Do we know who we are and why we are here? Can we use our gifts and talents to create a legacy of love and compassion despite egotistical temptations to do otherwise? Do we have the courage to hold ourselves accountable when we veer off course? Can we tell our stories in a manner that serves as a pillar of hope for future generations? Do we have sufficient humility and fortitude to self-correct and apologize for our missteps? Is there enough space in our hearts to love beyond selfish desires?* These are just a few of the questions we must ask and responsibly answer as we pursue wholeness.

Habitual Transformation

To fulfill our life work and realize our sacred purposes, we must be in continuous growth mode. Stagnation is not an option. God wants us to grow spiritually. He expects and requires us to grow. He tells us in 2 Peter 3:18 (ESV), "Grow in the grace and knowledge of our Lord and Savior Jesus Christ."

We humans are creatures of habit. Our daily activities are essentially the same year after year. We find comfort in routine even if there is no goal or vision. In some ways, we are addicted to the monotony that accompanies repetition. While the dullness of habit can strip us of our passion, we willingly sacrifice the potential for vitality in favor of the familiar. We go through near-robotic motions giving little thought to why we do what we do. We waste untold hours on mediocre activities that have little or no lasting value beyond immediate entertainment or gratification.

Periodically, we consider altering our course and dream of a different lifestyle, but unless we are committed and determined, doubt soon creeps in and stifles the momentary desires. The initial excitement wanes and morphs into fear of the unknown. Far too often, we succumb to that fear, hesitate, and abandon our dreams in favor of the familiar discomfort we tolerate.

As we are transformed, we exchange old, negative patterns for new, positive ones. The Holy Spirit guides us as we slowly establish a new way of living. Thankfully, God is patient and does not abandon us despite our waywardness. Instead, with grace and mercy, He gently guides us toward oneness with Him and wholeness with ourselves and others.

Expansion and growth require an awareness that people choose to avoid. It is not easy to face our most basic and least pretentious selves. Here, in these unpolished, wounded areas of our being, the view is not pretty. It takes commitment and courage beyond measure to change negative habits and elevate our spiritual energy. We are creatures of habit. Consider for a moment your daily routines and rituals. We blindly repeat the patterns we have become accustomed to, giving little thought to whether they serve us well. If we realistically expect to resist the temptation to backslide or revert to our old habits, we must replace them with new ones.

Making the Decision to Change

The simple yet powerful act of deciding to change unleashes certain desires in us that stoke the flames of creativity and move us closer to a higher consciousness. There is a crispness and freshness to shifting course and disturbing routines. Something happens in the brain that sends a message of excitement throughout the body. Our emotions are stimulated, and we are ready to redirect our energy.

From a spiritual perspective, the transformative value of a decision to change is profound. The nature of choice is complex and far reaching. We make countless decisions every day from the moment we wake up until we fall asleep. Our choices range from small and inconsequential such as deciding which dress to wear or what to eat to significant and consequential matters such as whether to marry or remain single, to go to college or learn a trade, to become a doctor or a politician, and so on. Each of these options presents far-reaching opportunities and challenges and will result in rather different lifestyles.

Whenever we are faced with a consequential decision, rather than following the desires of our hearts, we should discern the will of God, who promises, "I will instruct you and teach you in the way you should go; I will counsel you with my eye upon you" (Psalm 32:8 ESV). When we rely on God to guide our decision-making process, we can trust that the choices we make will align with His will. God blesses our decisions when we glorify Him and reflect His character and image. When our choices promote fairness and justice, kindness and humility, God is pleased. When we choose love over hatred and good over evil, God blesses our decisions. When our choices are faith based, He will give us the wisdom to do what is right.

Following is an inspiring story about a father, his three sons, and a golden dog. The sons are given a task by their father, which is specifically designed to test their character.

Once upon a time, there was a wealthy and wise king known for his flawless administration. He ruled his subjects with care and fairness. People regularly brought their problems to him with high hopes, and he never sent them away disheartened. His heart of compassion and wise counsel gave his subjects comfort and security.

In time, he began to worry about who would take care of his kingdom after his death. He was blessed with three sons who were loyal, obedient, and respectful, but he decided to test their character by presenting them with an unusual challenge to help him decide who was most worthy to be king. He gave his three sons a hundred gold coins each, and he gave them one year to use them however they chose. Then he said, "Whoever brings me a golden dog shall inherit the throne."

The three sons set out with their gold coins. The eldest went to the city and rented a palace for himself. Then he hired some men and sent them out to find a golden dog. After a few weeks, the men returned empty-handed. By the end of this process, all his gold coins were spent.

The second son started lending money to people at low interest rates and earned significant profits. He used his money to hire the local goldsmith to make a golden dog.

The youngest was the most loyal and the wisest. He bought a small house for himself in an area of town where the poorest and neediest people lived. He invested his money in a business and reaped heavy profits. He chose to use his financial resources to significantly improve the quality of life for the townspeople. He employed several of them. He built hospitals to serve the sick and schools to educate the children. He also built a community center and a library. He invested in local roads and parks. His goal was to help them become self-sufficient so they could sustain their new lifestyle once he departed. The town was bustling with positive activity and energy. The people were thriving in ways they had never before envisioned.

A year passed, and the three sons stood in front of the king. The eldest gave nothing while the second gave him a golden dog. When the turn of the third son came, he said, "Your highness, please accept this dog made from cotton. I ask you in all humility not to underestimate the special appeal of this dog. I have crafted it with my own hands. The hard work, toil under the hot sun to grow this cotton, and the labor put in by me and my fellow companions are worth their weight in gold."

The genuine feelings and heartfelt words of the youngest son brought the king to tears. He always felt a kinship to the struggles of everyday people. His humble beginnings contributed to his compassionate heart. He never forgot how he struggled for food, clothing, and shelter before fate offered him a pathway out of poverty. He understood that in addition to strong administrative skills, compassion was an essential character trait for the future king. Well deserved, the throne was given to the youngest son, the one who possessed the heart of gold.

Like these three sons, we are often tested by our heavenly Father. Although He already knows the choices we will make when tested, He gives us the opportunity to discover certain truths about ourselves. The tests or trials we undergo appear in various forms. One of the reasons God tests us is to reveal the condition of our hearts. *When given a task, the question for us is, will we follow the desires of our hearts or will we discern the will of God?* He wants us to make the right choices but He will not force us to do so. In the ESV we see the following contrasting references to the condition of the *heart*.

> The heart is deceitful above all things, and desperately sick: who can understand it? I the Lord search the heart and test the mind, to give every man according to his ways, according to the fruit of his deeds. (Jeremiah 17: 9-10)

> The good person out of the good treasure of his heart produces good, and the evil person out of his evil treasure

produces evil, for out of the abundance of the heart his mouth speaks. (Luke 6:45)

Conscious Choice

The book of Joshua tells the story of the dramatic conquest of the Promised Land. Realization of this dream resulted in the fulfillment of God's commitment to Abraham to give Canaan to the Israelites. In his later years, Joshua called the elders, chiefs, judges, and officers together and spoke to them one last time. His words of wisdom reminded the Israelites of their historical relationship with God, and he cautioned them to remain faithful and avoid idol worship. He wanted to make sure their decision about whom to serve was the result of conscious choice rather than benign default. He admonished them with these words.

> Now fear the LORD and serve him with all faithfulness. Throw away the gods your ancestors worshiped beyond the Euphrates River and in Egypt and serve the LORD. But if serving the LORD seems undesirable to you, then choose for yourselves this day whom you will serve, whether the gods your ancestors served beyond the Euphrates, or the gods of the Amorites, in whose land you are living. But as for me and my household, we will serve the LORD. (Joshua 24:14–15 NIV)

Joshua framed his last message to his people in a format that left no room for misunderstanding. In this scenario were two divergent paths. The Israelites were reminded of their option to worship the idols their ancestors had worshiped in Mesopotamia and Egypt or to worship the Lord. In his speech, Joshua made two things clear. First, the choice was theirs to make. Second, he and his family had already made their choice. This impactful story ends with the Israelites choosing to serve the Lord.

I am reminded of another biblical story about conscious choice. Again, the Israelites were the audience, but the speaker was the prophet Elijah. This story begins with the final showdown between the God of Israel and a false god named Baal. Elijah asked, "How long will you go limping between two different opinions? If the Lord is God, follow him; but if Baal, then follow him" (1 Kings 18:21 ESV).

Because the Israelites did not answer Elijah, the ending to this second story is less clear. I imagine they saw no harm in remaining silent. Maybe they wanted to hedge their bets, to keep their options open. But by saying nothing, they were in effect making a conscious choice. By refusing to declare their loyalty to God, they were dishonoring Him and forfeiting an excellent opportunity to be the spiritual giants they were called to be.

There are several lessons to be learned from these two stories. When the Israelites honored God and kept His commandments, He provided for and protected them. When they defied God, they suffered dire consequences. The contemporary lesson for us is similar. When we honor God by pursing meaning and sacred purpose, He blesses us. When our lifestyle is Christ-centered, we reap the benefits and we experience joy and spiritual abundance. When we dishonor God we suffer needlessly.

The Consequences of Choice

Similar scenarios play out in the lives of countless people daily. Like the Israelites with Elijah, we often ignore the question of who or what we serve. We claim the benefits of acceptance into the family of God, but we shy away from the responsibilities of being His children. We keep one foot in the secular world; we keep our options open just in case. We pray, we fellowship with other Christians, and we even tithe, but we cannot seem to bridle our caustic tongues. We praise Him loudly and often, yet we cannot find the time to check on the sick or volunteer to feed the hungry. We are consistently the first to enter the sanctuary for church services and the last to leave, but our haughty disposition is demeaning and hurtful to our fellow worshipers. We enjoy the God-given benefits of our gifts and talents but see no need to show our gratitude by serving the common good with them. We lose ourselves in religious formalities all the while avoiding the truth about where we stand on the issue of who or what we serve. The process of growing whole, though, requires us to declare our intentions and to set them in the direction of holiness. We must draw a line in the sand beyond which we will not go.

Our choices have consequences. When we consider how our decisions affect our efforts toward growing whole and developing a Christ-centered lifestyle, we must look beyond the options and consider the long-term effects of each. *Are we willing to let go of our negative attitudes in favor of a positive worldview? Are we ready to be inconvenienced and pushed out of our comfort zones as we are called to serve God's people? Are we serious about growing into a Christ-centered lifestyle?* When presented with a choice, we should ask questions and seek clarification. We should evaluate all options and their possible consequences.

There is an ethical component to every consequential choice we make. When we are selfish and fail to consider how a particular decision may affect others, we run the risk of hurting people we care about and damaging relationships. Everyday choices such as which route to take to work or which news channel to watch are inconsequential and have little impact on anyone other than us. When the choice affects others though, we have a responsibility to be compassionate and thoughtful. *Is the choice we are about to make fair? Is it just? Does it help or hurt? Does it move us closer to our sacred purpose?*

A drop of rain hitting a pond will send out ripples. Let us imagine ourselves as drops of rain. Every consequential choice has a ripple effect either negative or positive. Everyone in our spheres of influence and ultimately the universe is impacted by the decisions we make, the ripples they create. When we become aware of this awesome responsibility, life assumes an entirely new meaning and sacred purpose blossoms.

Several years ago, Debra, a young coworker, shared a concern with me. She had decided to go back to school to become an attorney. She had already secured a part-time job with a law firm, and she was excited about the lucrative future she envisioned. She felt pangs of guilt though because her favorite aunt, a devout Christian, had chastised her and warned her about the consequences of her choice to become an attorney. Her aunt believed that her desire to make money would compromise her faith. According to her aunt, "People with money forget about God." Debra asked me, *"Do I have to be poor to serve God?"* We discussed her dilemma, and I suggested she look at the issue from the twofold perspective of love and sacred purpose.

Regardless of our professions, we are here to serve God's kingdom by serving our fellow humans. Jesus commands us to love Him, ourselves, and others; that is the gold standard that should guide our lives. With God's blessing, we have the freedom to make choices that move us closer to realization of the meaning and sacred purpose of our existence. We also have the freedom to make choices that move us closer to realization of our personal and financial goals and objectives. We can serve God's purpose and enjoy some of the fruits of our labor as well.

There is nothing wrong with attaining success and reaping financial rewards. We do not have to relinquish personal ambition to enjoy a Christ-centered lifestyle. If there is a problem, it is a problem of the heart rather than a problem of success. When our material possessions become more important to us than God, we have created false idols.

The Bible is clear that we cannot serve two masters. King Solomon was extremely wealthy. Mary Magdalene had sufficient financial means to help support Jesus's ministry. Abraham was wealthy, and so was the virtuous woman mentioned in Proverbs. We receive God's gracious bounty through our hard work. He tells us in Proverbs 10:4 (ESV), "A slack hand causes poverty, but the hand of the diligent makes rich."

Faithful, steady efforts build character while building wealth. Through toil, we experience the dignity that accompanies an honest day's work, and we gain the spiritual benefits of gratefulness. We also gain the knowledge, understanding, and wisdom necessary to support our efforts toward growing whole.

There are many contemporary examples of wealthy people who love and serve God by supporting the ministries and missions of their places of worship. I understand and appreciate the concern expressed by Debra's aunt. This is a common dilemma that must be resolved in deeply personal ways. However, wealthy people are not the only ones who serve idols; we are all subject to idol worship, so we must remain prayerful and vigilant about the potential for veering off course and backsliding. This is an area that requires continuous self-examination.

The Power of Setting and Activating Holy Intention

The value of setting intention applies to every aspect of your life. You can set your intention to have a productive day, or learn a new skill, or successfully manage your stress level. If you have a public speaking engagement and you are tense, activate your intention to be calm and give the speech of your dreams. If you want to strengthen your prayer life, set this as an intention and then spend more time reading your Bible and praying.

There are many creative strategies to setting intentions. Some people record their intentions in journals while others declare them in front of the mirror each morning. Still others write them on note cards or ask people to be their accountability partners. Affirmations and vision statements are other ideas for setting intention. If any of these strategies work for you, great. But the real power of setting intention lies in the awareness of choice. Once you are empowered by the realization that with God's blessing you can choose to be who and what you want to be, you become a formidable agent for change. After prayer and deliberation, set your intention and then act. You begin to experience the positive energy associated with this decision. When you are clear about what you want to cocreate in your life, you will almost immediately reap the spiritual and therapeutic benefits of the decision.

God has blessed each of us with a personal point of power that is uniquely ours, a point at which we are our most effective selves. Many of us experience this blessing as being in the zone. When we tap into this eternal, free-flowing resource, we are elevated to a higher level of consciousness that touches our souls. The point of this blessing though is to support sacred purpose, not to be self-serving. When God looks at us, He sees the potential for the greatness He bestowed on us. Just as God does, good fathers know their children. They know their strengths as well as their weaknesses. These fathers expect their children despite their human weaknesses to use their gifts and talents to realize their fullest potential. When they do, their fathers smile. The same is true when God looks on us. As a loving Father, He expects us to use the gifts and talents He blessed us with to realize our enormous capacity to glorify Him. Blessings are not designed for our own selfish benefit, however. When we offer our best in service to others, we activate holy intention, and our Father smiles.

Manifestation of Intention

When our intentions are holy, we blossom in ways that support growing whole. This means that for intentions to serve sacred purpose, they must be in alignment with God's plan for our lives. My prayers regularly include a petition to God for His guidance in setting my intentions for the day. Being the natural planner that I am, I am mindful of my tendency to sometimes move too fast. I pray daily for the discernment to know when to act and when to wait patiently to hear the voice of God. When my intention is not aligned with His intention for my life, it is not holy. I have learned that at some point, He will let me know this in no uncertain terms. When this revelation occurs, I am remorseful, but I am also at peace.

There are many energy forces in the universe that affect us but none quite as profoundly as intention. Living well requires us to consistently question the holiness of our intentions. At our core, we are spiritual energy, and within this continuously vibrating field, intention takes root. Life as we know it originates from intention. Our conception, birth, and death are inextricably connected to intention. The story of creation is a story of intention. How we live and where we live are inflection points that signify intention. Whom we love and what we hold dear are key indicators of intention. Our thoughts, words, and deeds are manifestations of intention.

Thoughts

> Finally, brothers, whatever is true, whatever is honorable, whatever is just, whatever is pure, whatever is lovely, whatever is commendable, if there is any excellence, if there is anything worthy of praise, think about these things. (Philippians 4:8 ESV)

Our thoughts are powerful beyond measure. Their energy forces can strengthen or weaken. They can dignify or disrespect. They can repair or cause further damage. They can reconcile or irreparably sever. They can build bridges or tear them down. Thoughts are the primary influencers of our worldview, which is the lens through which we see the universe and everyone and everything in it. In many ways, we are the product of our thoughts, and our quality of life directly correlates with the quality of those thoughts.

Positive thoughts bring us closer to wholeness while negative thoughts sabotage efforts to realize meaning and sacred purpose. When we shift our thoughts from negative to positive, the process of growing whole takes root. As we work diligently to develop a Christ-centered lifestyle, one of our biggest challenges is replacing negative, fear-based thoughts with positive, love-based thoughts.

There are numerous biblical examples of how changing the way we think can improve our capacity to discern what is good, what is just, and what is right. One such example is this.

> Do not conform to the pattern of this world but be transformed by the renewing of your mind. Then you will be able to test and approve what God's will is-his good, pleasing and perfect will. (Romans 12:2 NIV)

There is a wealth of credible information to support the undisputed value of positive thinking. Norman Vincent Peale was an American minister and author best known for his efforts to proclaim positive thinking as a practical means for Christians to improve the quality of their lives. He told us in *The Power of Positive Thinking* (1952) that with faith, positive thinking, and prayer, we could overcome any problems or obstacles. This outstanding best seller challenges people of faith to integrate certain principles related to positive thinking into their daily practices and draw on their higher power to heal wounds.

From a spiritual growth perspective, when we eliminate negative thoughts about ourselves, we move closer to oneness with God and wholeness with ourselves and others. *But what about our human tendency to harbor negative thoughts about others?* A Christ-centered lifestyle requires us to address this shortcoming. Many of us have encountered mean-spirited people whose negative energy frequency immediately impacts us adversely. If we are not careful, they will bring our previously positive energy frequency down to their level in short order. *How do we effectively handle such an encounter?* This may not be the best strategy, but I generally excuse myself from this type of situation as quickly as possible. If I remain in their presence, I am likely to react in ways that fall beneath my personal code of conduct. Once the negative stimulant is removed, I can think through the experience with compassion and seek blameless resolution.

The first awareness of intention is often a thought that enters our stream of consciousness. The thought serves as an early indicator or an internal stirring that has not yet revealed itself. The thought gives us an opportunity to assess and dispose of the idea if it does not support our spiritual growth efforts. If we allow the thought to linger, it can gain emotional traction and activate the power of intention.

Words

> In the beginning was the Word, and the Word was with
> God, and the Word was God. (John 1:1 ESV)

"Sticks and stones may break my bones, but words will never hurt me." I used this childhood chant on occasions when someone made a statement that insulted me or called me a name. It was one of my favorite comebacks. I would say it loudly and with much attitude to display my resilience and strength while dispelling notions of hurt. But verbal bullying often crushed my spirit.

Words matter to us. They can convey messages of goodwill, inspire, and offer hope. On the other hand, they can cause heartache, make people feel insignificant and unimportant, and influence them to act in ways that violate their principles. When we direct harsh and insulting language toward others to control, demean, frighten, or humiliate them, we are guilty of verbal abuse. Low self-esteem and a general sense of unworthiness is often the result of being exposed to regular dosages of the blatant disrespect inherent in your willingness to verbally abuse someone emotionally attached to you. From the perspective of growing whole, we must remain mindful of the awesome power of the tongue. The seeds of oneness with God, self, and others cannot gestate in the negative energy of hurtful words.

Words matter to God. The Bible has a lot to say about words and the power of the tongue. In the ESV, we see the following references to *word*.

And God said, "Let there be light, and there was light." (Genesis 1:3)

By the word of the Lord the heavens were made. (Psalm 33:6)

On the day of judgment people will give account for every careless word they speak, for by your words you will be justified, and by your words you will be condemned. (Matthew 12:36–37)

Lying lips are an abomination to the Lord. (Proverbs 12:22)

Since you have been born again, not of perishable seed but of imperishable, through the living and abiding word of God; for all flesh is like grass and all its glory like the flower of grass. The grass withers, and the flower falls, but the word of the Lord remains forever. And this word is the good news that was preached to you. (1 Peter 1:23–25)

Death and life are in the power of the tongue. (Proverbs 18:21)

Growing whole transforms us in myriad ways including how we use words. The words we speak and those we allow others to speak in our presence reveal the condition of our souls. Loving words honor God, and they bind us in fellowship and relationship. Kind and thoughtful words are a rare treasure in a world where people expend inordinate amounts of their time in harmful, trivial, and useless chatter.

Deeds

Remember Tyler Perry's movie *Mr. Good Deeds*? It is the story of a successful, wealthy businessman named Wesley Deeds, who is jolted out of his scripted life when he meets Lindsey, a down-on-her-luck single mother who works on the cleaning crew in his office building. When Deeds offers to help her get back on her feet, the chance encounter sparks a relationship that adds flavor to his otherwise mundane life. While the rags-to-riches tease of this movie is unlikely to materialize in real life, the essence of the story offers far more than entertainment. The plot of one human being stepping out of his comfort zone to aid another is inspiring. I enjoyed the movie from a spiritual perspective, and I appreciated the wholesomeness of the message. Once Deeds sets his intention to help Lindsey, the quality of her life changed in myriad positive ways.

In the Sermon on the Mount Jesus describes how those who have decided to follow Him are called to demonstrate the nature of God and His kingdom through the character of their own lives.

> You are the light of the world. A city set on a hill cannot be hidden. Nor do people light a lamp and put it under a basket, but on a stand, and it gives light to all in the house. In the same way, let your light shine before others, so that they may see your good works and give glory to your Father who is in heaven. (Matthew 5:14-16 ESV)

As Christians we are God's ambassadors. We are His representatives in the earthly realm and we are called to love, live by Godly standards, and have compassion. We demonstrate His character through our thoughts, words, and deeds. We tell the kingdom story in myriad ways through simple, human acts of sacrificial love.

The Bible tells us to support those who need our help and consolation, commune with those who desire to know more about Christ, and let our spiritual lights shine in ways that magnify God's greatness.

The impact of good deeds is far more profound than simply satisfying the material or physical needs of others. People who are hurting need emotional and spiritual support. Acts of kindness can lead the recipients to encounters with God, who is pure, unadulterated love. Good deeds are manifestations of that love which spring forth in ways as simple as a smile, a word of encouragement or as miraculous as saving someone's physical life or leading them to a reconciled relationship with God.

During His time in the earthly realm Jesus offered us many profound examples of good deeds. He healed the sick, gave sight to the blind, cast out unclean spirits, raised the dead, purified diseased bodies, comforted the broken hearted, and restored sanity. He used His power over the physical universe to introduce His followers to the spiritual realm.

His good deeds gave authority to His words, they softened hearts, and they modeled what was possible through faith for future Christian leaders.

Humility

> Do nothing from selfish ambition or conceit, but in humility count others more significant than yourselves. Let each of you look not only to his own interests, but also to the interests of others. (Philippians 2:3–4 ESV)

The foundation of biblical wisdom is humility before God and one another. There is no better example of humility than the life of the suffering servant, Jesus Christ. Despite His equality with God, He set aside His heavenly privileges, descended to earth, and assumed a life of human servitude. The implications of this degree of sacrificial love are impossible for us as mere mortals to comprehend. Even for serious students of theology, His story is almost unbearable and unthinkable. Meaning and sacred purpose are seen throughout His ministry as He was singly focused on salvation, sanctification, reconciliation, and reunification. In the end, He endured the degradation and humiliation of crucifixion, a punishment reserved for the lowliest criminals. His was the most profound lesson in humility in history.

Humility is a core value that brings out the best of what it means to be human. It is the perfect antidote to arrogance, greed, and pretentiousness. Along with laudable virtues such as compassion, empathy, forgiveness, and gratitude, a humble spirit is one of the most admired of all character traits. When we put the needs of others ahead of ours, something remarkable takes place in our souls, our hearts and minds expand exponentially, and we begin the systematic removal of negativity and fear-based energy.

The face of humility is complex. It has many interrelated components including ethical, intellectual, psychological, interpersonal, and theological. From an ethical perspective, we can readily admit our shortcomings and work diligently to address them. We acknowledge and respect the dignity of others, and our mindset is one of continuous improvement. Intellectually, we understand that others have expertise in areas where we are lacking, we embrace teachable moments, and we possess the insight to self-correct. Psychologically, we resist the temptation to self-promote and we have balanced, modest egos. From the interpersonal perspective, we listen empathically, we are sympathetic to opposing views, and we are concerned for the well-being of others. Theologically, we do not consider ourselves above anyone else, and we understand our place in the world.

Humility does not require us to deny our gifts and talents, but it does require us to acknowledge God as their source. One of the most endearing and heartwarming stories in the Bible is when God asked King Solomon if there was anything he wanted. Despite his greatness, the king humbly asked for the wisdom and knowledge to govern his people. God was pleased with his response because it acknowledged his human weakness and admitted the need for divine intervention.

> The reward for humility and fear of the Lord is riches and honor and life. (Proverbs 22:4 ESV)

Humbly Seek Assistance When You Need It

Stephen, a former coworker, was an outstanding employee well known for his accuracy, dependability, kindness, and productivity. These qualities led management to appoint him as team leader of an important department-wide special project that would take three years to complete. For the first year, he met his timelines and milestones, and management was impressed with his leadership skills. Then something happened that no one expected. Stephen would disappear from the job for several hours at a time, and his supervisor could not reach him by phone. Over a six-month period, his performance level dropped from "above average" to "needs improvement." His absenteeism rate skyrocketed, and his error rate increased significantly. Eventually, his supervisor gave him a performance improvement plan that included termination if he failed to meet specified standards.

When I met him, that was his situation. Management was unaware that his personal circumstances had changed drastically. His father had been in a terrible car accident that left him temporarily paralyzed and dependent on Stephen. To help make ends meet, Stephen took on a second job that also required him to work long hours. He was exhausted most of the time and simply could not keep pace with the heavy demands of both jobs.

Thankfully, he followed my advice and discussed his situation with his supervisor, who generously agreed to take on some of his duties. Working together, they met critical project completion dates, and Stephen managed to make amends for the damage to his professional reputation. Rather than continuing to utilize dishonest strategies to manage an unmanageable situation, he faced his gloomy reality and then took ownership for his poor handling of it.

During our time together as coach and client, Steven learned an important lesson. When our actions impact others in a material way, we have a responsibility to be honest with ourselves and with those affected. Life happens, and none of us knows where trouble lies. But our code of conduct must always be to put the needs of those who depend on us ahead of ours. No matter how dire the circumstances, usually, when we humbly ask for help, willing assistance avails itself.

Emotional Integrity

Emotional integrity—internal and external harmony—is another important prerequisite for oneness with God and wholeness with self and others. Five-sensory, multisensory, and multidimensional unification must occur before we can fully experience the holiness of emotional integrity. As the kingdom story continues to unfold, whether our days in the earthly realm help or hinder matters is to a great extent up to us.

Emotional integrity demands that we face painful facts about ourselves. Many disasters we encounter are of our own creation, and we must be willing to take responsibility for that. The *Who am I?* question has little to do with external circumstances; it is entirely in the realm of our inner workings. No matter who we are, the good, the bad, and the ugly will find us at some point. Our response to each of these will determine whether growing whole will occupy prominence in our life stories.

Finding the Courage to Face Our Demons

Have you spoken with people whose hypocrisy and insincerity were blatantly apparent? When body language, facial expressions, and voice tones do not match your words, they send messages of insincerity and phoniness that undermine your efforts to communicate effectively. In this world of political correctness, many feel pressured to respond in ways they think others will support rather than finding the courage to speak their truth. When this becomes our gold standard, we lack authenticity. In its most basic form, emotional integrity means having the courage to be who we really are yet possessing the insight and fortitude to improve in the areas where growth is necessary. When our bodies, souls, and spirits function in a balanced and unified manner, we experience the holy benefits of emotional integrity.

Usually we can recognize when someone is not being sincere with us. *But can we recognize when we are not being sincere with others, or even worse, with ourselves?* I had a client who was blessed with excellent oratory skills. Ralph could stand in front of a crowd and make people believe anything he chose to communicate. He was the vice president of a major company. Over time, the questionable norms inherent in the company's culture began to influence him in unhealthy ways. While his public persona was polished and he was able to motivate his audiences to significantly improve their lives, his private life was a different story. His marriage was in shambles, and his children were in pain.

Ralph continuously expressed his desire to keep his family intact, but his actions suggested he was far more interested in his status as a company man than husband and father. The marriage eventually crumbled under the weight of two short-term adulterous relationships. As a divorced father of four, his sporadic and toxic interaction with his ex-wife undermined the safety and security of their children. He struggled to fulfill his responsibilities as a positive role model, and signs of serious dysfunction were taking a toll on those he loved.

Ralph was handsome and charming, so finding short-term infatuation and companionship was easy. For a while, he continued his pattern of superficial relationships. In the meantime, he refused to take responsibility for the adverse impact his selfish behavior was having on the children. The personal pain of his deceit, though, was evident. He loved and missed his family. The guilt he harbored was real, yet facing it would mean admitting something he simply was not ready to accept. So the family lingered in the painful status of brokenness.

When we lack the capacity to admit our messes, we delay reconciliation and hurt ourselves and others needlessly. Our valley experiences offer us excellent opportunities to grow. Emotional integrity requires us to face our problems with brutal honesty and then do our part to put the broken pieces back together. It took several months of intensive coaching before he could assume responsibility for his role in the demise of his family, seek forgiveness, and take steps to improve his relationship with his ex-wife and their children. When Ralph finally addressed his feelings of guilt and accepted the reality of his truth, he was able to reclaim the authenticity he abandoned for short-term, ill-conceived gain.

As a young girl, I dreamed of becoming an adult, living independently, and having the emotional wherewithal to resolve issues as they arose. I assumed that by the time we reached adulthood we had already learned the lessons necessary to make the right decisions and live well. But as I matured, I realized this was not necessarily the case. In truth, many adults lack emotional integrity. While we become adept at creating facades to camouflage our broken spirits and missteps, we are often devoid of the skills required for self-control and self-management. Much of the drama we find ourselves embroiled in reflects this deficiency.

We exist year after year in the mind space that someday, somehow, someone will rescue us and transform the false narratives we tell ourselves into something that remotely resembles meaningfulness. Emotional integrity requires courage. At some point, we will find ourselves wallowing in the uncomfortable messes we created. This reality comes with the human condition. Instead of apologizing and asking for forgiveness, we justify our messes and blame others causing even deeper pain. Ralph justified his affairs by blaming his ex-wife for not attending to his emotional and physical needs. Had he been authentic and honest with his wife about his feelings, he might have saved his marriage and kept his family intact.

Getting Real

No one told me I would someday face a pivotal dilemma that would forever alter my life's trajectory. There were subtle warnings—an unexplained restlessness, numbness, and a general lack of joy. From the outside, my life screamed success; I had a supportive husband, children, a nice home, community involvement, and a great career. Yet in the privacy of my internal emotions and thoughts I was keenly aware that something significant was missing. For years, I had struggled silently with this profound discomfort while I privately searched for inner contentment. Meditation, persistence, prayer, and research led me to the clarity of sacred purpose. I decided to undertake the work required for wholeness. My efforts began in earnest with self-exploration, a willingness to see myself for who I really was, and a determination to change the things about me that interfered with my deep intention of becoming a better person.

I did not like some of the things I saw when I looked within. There was an edginess about me that manifested itself in a variety of unhealthy ways. My childhood pain and youthful insecurities had led me to a heart space and mindset that did not comport with my deeply held convictions about human dignity and respect for self and others. I did not possess the emotional integrity necessary to support true growth. I outwardly displayed a smart mouth that spewed unnecessary hurt. I erroneously equated meanness as a sign of strength, and I so wanted to be perceived as strong. I had developed a habit of purposefully saying things merely for shock effect and ignoring the negative impact. I embodied an aloofness that sent unintended messages of cold-heartedness not to mention my signature rigidness that showed up as inflexibility and control.

It took years of intentional effort to grow beyond these irrational strategies to manage my relationships. I am thankful for the courage to face my burdensome, unresolved pain and reconcile the discrepancies resulting from my lack of emotional integrity. Although there is still much inner cleansing to be done, it has been a privilege to do the work required to move closer to wholeness.

Mine is a story about recognizing the critical role of God and godliness and my complete inability to experience spiritual abundance on my own. I know the difference between secular abundance and spiritual abundance because I have witnessed both firsthand. Secular abundance relies on worldly trappings such as jobs, money, power, and status to define purpose and value. Spiritual abundance embodies unconditional love and all its miraculous manifestations. Seeing the world through the eyes of Christ-centeredness, compassion, endearment, personal responsibility, possibility, and promise elevates our quality of life to nothing less than remarkable, and it provides an assortment of interesting opportunities for emotional integrity to flourish.

A dear friend once surprised me with this statement: "I am so sick of these fake happy people I could scream!" She had just concluded a meeting with her manager, and it seemed that throughout the meeting, the manager was quite critical of her work all the while being all bubbly and smiley faced according to my friend. She was hurt to learn that her manager was not impressed with the quality of her work, but she was also insulted at what she perceived to be her blatant insincerity. Over time, we explored her feelings in depth, and she was eventually able to take responsibility for her role in the uncomfortable situation. Once she took her focus off the manager and objectively evaluated her own work habits, she made great strides in meeting and even exceeding her performance standards.

That is a vivid example of how the perceived lack of emotional integrity can adversely affect relationships. The manager's words and her body language did not match, and she thus appeared insincere. People cannot hear your words when your actions drown them out. While neither my friend nor I had enough information to gauge the manager's level of sincerity, at a minimum, she had forfeited the opportunity to use the session as a teachable moment. Because her integrity was in question, she sent an unintended message, and any desire she may have had to counsel and encourage her subordinate failed.

My friend perceived that the manager was not acting with emotional integrity, and rather than uniting around the mutual goal of improved performance, it created an unnecessary divide between employer and employee. It is perfectly all right for a manager to chastise substandard performance, but the employer unintentionally sabotaged a golden opportunity to demonstrate her sincerity. Perceived inauthenticity is a red flag when it comes to establishing positive, trusting relationships.

Remember, every relationship offers equal potential for godliness and growth or ungodliness and stagnation. The choice is ours.

Having emotional integrity means you value and respect yourself and others. It means you have a level of self-awareness that is sufficiently healthy to give you important insight into your strengths and weaknesses alike. You comprehend there are things about yourself that need to be addressed as you progress toward enlightenment. You begin to take responsibility rather than blame outside influences. This represents a degree of honesty that opens the floodgates to sincere connections and encourages you to act honorably in your dealings with others.

When we internalize the value of honesty and noble intentions, we grow exponentially and we make room for loving relationships to thrive. Introspection is an important tool in our efforts toward self-awareness and enlightenment. No matter the situation, we must never miss an opportunity to turn inward as we search for the meaning and value of our experiences.

Personal Life Code

The road to emotional integrity requires commitment and determination. It may cause a major shift in our worldview and the way we live. We often need to baby-step our way to this ideal, and it is appropriate for us to acknowledge and respect any misgivings.

A commitment to authenticity is a major milestone along the journey toward emotional integrity. To be authentic, we must honestly evaluate situations from the inside out rather than from the perspective of someone else's expectations of us. It is not easy to transform our worldview from one of "going along to get along" to one of "*Is this something I really want to do?*" Ask probing questions to assess your true feelings and then honor those feelings by acting in accordance with the decision you make. Trust God and trust your gut. If it does not feel right, it probably is not right. Being pressured to conform or do something someone else wants us to do is a common human experience. No matter the relationship, we should not comply with the wishes of others to the point that we lose ourselves. Each of us should have a personal life code that is sacred. The more we honor the standards we have established for ourselves the closer we get to emotional integrity. Being authentic means being cognizant of that code and saying no when opportunities to violate it present themselves.

My first job out of college was with the prison system. One of my lasting memories is how often women justified participation in criminal activity because their lovers had insisted on it. This was several decades ago, and the social landscape has changed drastically, but low self-esteem and cultural influences were common explanations. Women often receive subtle messages beginning at an early age that compromise is key to successful relationships with men. While healthy compromise is natural, relationships should affirm and support rather than manipulate and pressure you to violate your core values.

Hypocrisy deals a devastating blow to emotional integrity. When we engage in behaviors or activities yet criticize others for doing the same, we become hypocrites. While others can see this character flaw, we are often oblivious to it. From a spiritual perspective, hypocrisy is the state of pretending to have virtues or religious beliefs we really do not have. Jesus openly criticized the scribes and Pharisees for this tendency throughout Matthew. One such example is this.

> So, do and observe whatever they tell you, but not the works they do. For they preach, but do not practice. They tie up heavy burdens, hard to bear, and lay them on people's shoulders, but they themselves are not willing to move them with their finger. They do all their deeds to be seen by others. For they make their phylacteries broad and their fringes long, and they love the place of honor at feasts and the best seats in the synagogues and greetings in the marketplaces and being called rabbi by others. (Matthew 23:3–7 ESV)

The scribes and Pharisees were positioned to do great harm to the Jewish people. Because they were learned in the scriptures, they occupied positions of authority and influence, but they appeared blind to their own hard-heartedness toward Jesus Christ. As a result, they were on the road to destruction and were negatively impacting others. The contradiction between what they felt in their hearts and what they outwardly displayed was strikingly hypocritical. Authenticity and hypocrisy cannot coexist peacefully. We must have the courage to pursue what is real, what is true, and what is holy at all costs.

Emotional integrity requires honesty and openness. There is value in expressing or venting and danger in suppressing true feelings. It is perfectly okay to feel the full range of emotions, but it is not okay to become abusive and explosive. Be open to exploring and fully experiencing your feelings, but be sensitive to how you impact others—particularly those closest to you—as you express yourself. Emotional integrity is not necessarily linked to chronological age or level of success; the world is full of people who have grown old but are not emotionally and spiritually mature.

I love this quote by Shannon Alder.

> When you think yours is the only true path you forever chain yourself to judging others and narrow the vision of God. The road to righteousness and arrogance is a parallel road that can intersect each other several times throughout a person's life. It is often hard to recognize one road from another. What makes them different is the road to righteousness is paved with the love of humanity. The road to arrogance is paved with the love of self.[9]

As we move through our days, we experience a plethora of emotions that run the gamut from negative and fear-based to positive and love-based. Emotional integrity requires us to be honest about what we are feeling and why and then face the truths that accompany those emotions. Through the lens of compassion and love, we find the strength to do what is required to reconcile any discrepancies between our inner and outer selves. Our bodies, souls, and spirits must be of one accord. Our intentions, thoughts, words, and deeds must be in sync if we are to give emotional integrity the fertile ground it needs to thrive. Just because we grow old does not mean we grow up. Aging does not equate to growing whole; there is nothing automatic about it. Sincere effort and energy are required for the ideal of wholeness to become a realistic possibility. When we decide to grow, we need to be clear that good intentions are not enough. We must commit wholeheartedly to the process and stay the course. We must put our whole soul in it.

---

[9] Alder, S. L. Quotes by Shannon Alder.

Chapter 5 Important Points

- You live from the heart, the center of human life.
- The heart functions from physical, romantic, and spiritual perspectives.
- Out of your heart flows purity and impurity, good and evil, and love and hate whichever you decide.
- When you commit to a Christ-centered lifestyle, you are making a conscious choice to live in accordance with His teachings.
- To fulfill your life's work and realize your sacred purpose, you must be in continuous growth mode.
- When you rely on God to guide your decisions, you can trust that your choices will align with His will.
- Choices have consequences. There is an ethical component to every consequential choice you make.
- When your intentions, thoughts, words, and deeds are holy, you blossom in ways that support growing whole.
- Words matter greatly. Kind words have the power to build bridges and tear down walls. Mean-spirited words are abusive, hurtful, and they make people feel insignificant.
- Humility is a core value that brings out the best of what it means to be human. It is the perfect antidote to arrogance, greed, and pretentiousness.
- Emotional integrity, which is internal and external harmony, is a critical prerequisite to oneness with God and wholeness with self and others.
- Everyone should have a personal life code that is sacred, a line in the sand beyond which you will not go.
- A commitment to authenticity is a major milestone along the journey to emotional integrity.

PART III

THE DICHOTOMY OF EMOTIONS

6

TRANSFORM YOUR WORLDVIEW FROM FEAR TO LOVE

Each of us has a worldview, a lens through which we interpret the universe and everyone and everything in it. Our worldview affects how we understand and make sense of global events and influences how we express ourselves in the boundaries and unique design of these events. The essence of who we are as human beings—our attitudes, deeds, desires, dreams, fears, and our sense of right and wrong—forms our worldview.

The fundamentals of worldviews are determined by internal and external factors; some are sacred and others are secular. Some are biological and some are environmental. Some are cultural and others are driven by ego and personality. Even before birth and throughout our lives, relationships matter greatly as they play a critical role in how we see ourselves. These relationships also determine whether the lens through which we view the world is rooted in fear or love.

At conception, certain traits were immediately passed to us biologically from the genetic pool of our parents. The environmental circumstances of our fetal development significantly impacted who we would eventually become. Our prenatal interaction with family members for instance was a major factor in our womb experiences. *Was our home joyful and peaceful or chaotic and stress ridden? Were our parents caring and compassionate? Once born, were we exposed to chronic abuse and neglect, or were we a welcome addition to a caring and nurturing family?*

Child development experts tell us that the earliest relationships with caregivers affect brain development, academic achievement, social and emotional development, and even language literacy. Abusive and neglectful caregivers expose children to varying degrees of trauma, which can be devastating to their sense of self-worth. Strong, supportive, and loving relationships on the other hand increase children's capacity to handle negative experiences and help them develop compassion, empathy, and trust.

As we mature, we undergo refinement that is molded by the people, places, and things to which we are exposed. Family, school, church, friends, and media culture are primary influencers. Attitudes toward life and fundamental belief systems take shape during the maturation process as we begin to consider ideas and principles beyond those initially instilled in us by our original caretakers. Growing whole requires the ability to discern and discard false beliefs and teachings that do not support sacred purpose. Our worldview has profound implications for what we think about ourselves and others, the meaning of life, what really matters to us, and how we organize and orient our lives. It is all-encompassing, and it impacts every dimension of our being. As we age, we settle on certain perceived truisms that become the foundation on which we build our lives.

We experience a wide range of emotions that are either fear-based or love-based, and regardless of their genesis, emotions profoundly affect how we navigate life. If our worldview is fear-based, emotions such as anger, control, envy, greed, jealousy, resentment, and self-hatred serve as our principal guideposts. If on the other hand our worldview is love-based, emotions such as compassion, forgiveness, gratitude, and happiness inspire us and serve as catalysts for our intentions, thoughts, words, and deeds. Every aspect of our worldview is rooted in either fear or love. These two underlying emotions are mutually exclusive; one cannot exist in any meaningful way with the other.

Fear-Based Emotions

Fear is a strong emotion caused by the expectation or reality of danger. It can be warranted or unwarranted. Warranted fear is justified and helps us recognize and respond appropriately to situations that could result in harm. Unwarranted fear often has little to no basis and may be influenced by past experiences being interjected into the present situation. It is a powerfully destructive emotion that can derail dreams, dominate lives, ruin relationships, and sabotage efforts to focus on sacred purpose. At its core, unwarranted fear undermines our capacity to love.

Fear is like a vicious parasite that feeds on our hearts and minds and adversely affects our outlook. A parasite is an unwelcomed organism that attaches itself to another species and survives by feeding on the lifeblood of its host. Humans are quite susceptible to these parasitic organisms, particularly if our immune systems are weak or otherwise compromised. Parasites can linger in our bodies and cause great harm if not properly treated. The symbolism of the parasite is akin to what happens to us when we view our beautiful world through the lens of fear. No matter how much the universe has to offer, those who are governed by fear lack the capacity to appreciate its awesome wonders and lessons.

The Toltecs are believed to have been an ancient culture in central Mexico, known for their great wisdom. According to legend these mythical people dominated Mesoamerica for centuries and are credited with having shared great spiritual wisdom regarding the parasite. They believed that fear was the lifeblood of the parasite and that humans were the incubators within which these organisms gestated.

From a spiritual perspective parasites are demonic influences that attach themselves to us in the form of negative emotions and they attack us in every dimension of our being. They fester and hold us hostage to such ills as low self-esteem and feelings of unworthiness. Unresolved self-hatred, for example, takes on the characteristics of a parasite, and if left unchecked, it can undermine our ability to make basic quality of life decisions. Although he was regularly physically attacked by human opponents the apostle Paul insisted that our fight is not with people but with spiritual powers. He tells us in Ephesians 6 that we do not wrestle against flesh and blood but against spiritual forces of evil and he implores us to remain alert and vigilant against the schemes of the enemy.

Whenever a negative situation arises, it is usually rooted in fear. No matter the circumstance however, we must always try to leave room for respectful disagreement and blameless resolution. Develop the habit of questioning the genesis of your fear whenever this emotion surfaces. Probing for the root of the problem usually helps you determine whether the fear is warranted or unwarranted. If it is warranted pray and meditate for divine guidance as you seek resolution. If the fear is unwarranted, ask penetrating questions to help uncover unresolved issues that might be the culprit. *Am I fearful of rejection, fearful of failure, or even fearful of success?*

Fear of rejection can lead to unhealthy emotional detachment that limits our capacity to give and receive love. Fear of failure could result in unconsciously limiting opportunities to acquire new skills or expand our professional portfolios. Fear of success usually appears in the form of self-sabotage. We often see this phenomenon play out in the lives of celebrities and other public figures.

If our worldview is fear-based, we build our lives around negative emotions and energies. The circumstances and events that present themselves in our lives will reflect this negativity. The universal principle of karma will ensure that whatever we send out into the world will be returned to us in kind. In Galatians 6:7 ESV, the apostle Paul used an agricultural illustration to underscore his point that grace does not negate the need for moral character: "Whatever one sows, that will he also reap."

In 2 Timothy 1:7 we see that God did not give us the spirit of fear. Instead, His gifts are love, power, self-control, and sound mindedness.

Anger

> Anger is an acid that can do more harm to the vessel in which it is stored than to anything on which it is poured. (Mark Twain)

Anger is the emotional energy we generate when we feel violated, wronged, or threatened. It is a natural response to a negative experience and can serve to protect us in dangerous situations. If the anger is warranted, it can be beneficial. However, when we incorrectly perceive a cause for anger, it has the potential to be the most toxic of all the fear-based emotions.

Brittany shared an interesting story with me that caused concern. It seems she was an aggressor in a road-rage incident a few days before our coaching session. Her story was that she was in the center lane of a three-lane highway and was observing the speed limit. An impatient driver had been tailing her too closely for some time because he was blocked in and could not access either the right or left lane to pass her. At his first opportunity, he sped around her and cut sharply back into her lane causing her to hit the brakes to avoid an accident. The incident scared and angered her. She responded in kind by tailing him too closely just as he had done to her. When she could, she pulled up beside him, rolled her window down, and shouted obscenities at him. He ignored her, and that further intensified her anger.

At that point, it appeared that she had entered a dangerous stage of road rage as she continued to do whatever she could to aggravate him and get his attention. She blew her horn, pulled dangerously close to the side of his car, and got behind him and tailed him too closely when traffic hindered her other outrageous antics. She got so caught up in her rage that she persisted in following him well past her turn. She continued her aggressive driving until she caught the attention of a police officer, who pulled her over. To make matters worse, the driver she had been harassing turned around, drove past her, rolled his window down, waved, and drove off. In the end, her aggression cost her three hundred and fifty dollars in traffic violations and a mandatory defensive driving class. She was still quite angry about the incident when she spoke with me.

Brittany's initial reaction of fear and anger was legitimate. These emotions probably heightened her awareness and caused her to hit the brakes quickly enough to avoid an accident. However, what she did from that point forward was completely unwarranted. As we talked, she shared that her brother, Timothy, had been the victim of road rage several years earlier. The incident had gotten out of hand and the aggressor had attacked Timothy, who was hospitalized for three days.

During our conversation, Brittany realized how her brother's serious experience may have caused her to overreact and put herself and others in danger. She made some false mental assumptions and connected the two incidents when one had had nothing to do with the other. Once her anger was no longer needed to protect her, it became her enemy and ushered in some very destructive behavior. Hopefully, now that she is aware of what may have been the genesis of her aggression, future outbursts like this probably will not occur.

Whether an incident is real or imagined, unbridled anger can have devastating consequences. In relationships, it can cause severe pain for everyone involved. Anger itself is not necessarily the problem, and often the incident itself is not the problem either. Often, the problem is rooted in the thoughts, false beliefs, and scenarios we create. The mental stories we tell ourselves about incidents are usually based on negative experiences. When unbridled anger presents itself in our lives, we need to thoroughly explore our feelings to understand its genesis if we expect to avoid such emotional traps in the future. No matter the circumstance, we do not have the right to recklessly unleash anger in ways that endanger the lives or well-being of others.

In Matthew 5:22 ESV, during His famous Sermon on the Mount Jesus made it clear that everyone who hoarded anger was subject to judgment. When we realize the feelings of discord, we should immediately reconcile. Whether we are the offended or the offender, the goal should be rehabilitation and restoration. We begin our quest for wholeness with the intention of transforming our worldview from one that is fear-based to one that is saturated with the positive emotions that emanate from love.

At the root of all anger is fear, and when we habitually resort to this highly charged emotion, we limit options for blameless resolution. Rather than festering in this unhealthy condition, we should practice taking deep breaths, pausing, hitting the time-out button, or simply walking away. We can do whatever it takes to reduce the tension, facilitate quietness, and allow logic to enter the equation.

Give yourself enough mental space to probe certain questions. *At this moment, what am I most afraid of? Is the volatility of the situation my biggest concern? Am I desperately seeking acknowledgment of my feelings? Am I frustrated that I am not being heard? Am I afraid of losing someone I care deeply about?* Once you shift the focus from the emotion itself to its catalyst, your reasoning skills begin to generate options that make blameless resolution possible. This simple but profound strategy acknowledges the presence of fear, provides a forum for its logical expression, and offers the soothing balm of positivity and possibility.

> Whoever is slow to anger has great understanding, but he who has a hasty temper exalts folly. (Proverbs 14:29 ESV)

Control

> As your faith is strengthened you will find that there is
> no longer the need to have a sense of control, that things
> will flow as they will, and that you will flow with them,
> to your great delight and benefit. (Emmanuel Teney[10])

Control issues often stem from the need to micromanage and orchestrate others' actions and behavior. Control has many faces including domination, violence, oppression, and manipulation. If you are the controller in your group, this is an aspect of your personality that needs work.

Regardless of its focus or intent, control is rooted in fear. We are afraid that the outcome of a situation will be something other than what we want it to be as if we were anointed with special powers to discern what is best for all parties involved. We manipulate and pressure others to change so that we ourselves can avoid changing. In our minds, we have all the answers and there is no need for us to change. It reflects a sense of superiority that is completely unfounded and probably ego-induced.

Control is an emotion I identify with. Among the people who know me best—my family and my immediate circle—I was known as a controller. It took me years to recognize this about myself, and it has taken even longer for me to acknowledge it as a flaw. I told myself that my control issues stemmed from wanting what was best for everyone. The problem was that I failed to acknowledge that I did not always know what was best. I will confess to being a serious planner, and I really got carried away as I prepared for family vacations. Many of the favorite family stories are about my trying to force everyone to abide by my detailed itineraries. Invariably, a rebellious plot would ensue, and the leader of the resistance was usually my son. It seems the family often did not view fun quite the same way as I did, so they developed their own itineraries without my input! In the end, everybody had a great time, but I was the one stressed out because of my unrealistic and unnecessary need to control their activities. They ended up doing what they wanted to do, and as I reflect on that, I am glad they ignored me when my plans conflicted with theirs. Over time and through conscious choice, I have learned the beautiful gift of consensus building. I

---

[10] https://brainyquote/emmanuel_teney_105084.

am surrendering my need to control outcomes and allowing situations to unfold without my domination. Somehow, things are continuing to work out fine without my being overbearing and intrusive.

The need for control creates an unhealthy, codependent relationship that undermines the spiritual growth of all parties involved. People who have a strong need for stability, security, and predictability are more prone to relying on control tactics, but control creates only the illusion of fostering these objectives. It is humanly impossible to ensure anything, especially things as significant as stability, security, and predictability. The more we try to micromanage, the more insecure we feel because we have set ourselves up for failure by establishing impossible goals.

Control is also a deeply rooted emotion, and it takes hard work and concentration to let go of that false sense of superiority that undergirds it. By detaching yourself from a predetermined outcome, you are trusting in the power of God to do His perfect will. Pray for a pleasurable, productive experience and then have faith that things will unfold as they should. This frees you to enjoy the moments as they present themselves, and it fosters good will as everyone gets the opportunity to offer his or her input. The more we learn to rely on the very faith we profess to believe in, the more we can relax and enjoy events as they are revealed to us. When we learn to function on this level, we make room for God's miracles to show up in our lives and amaze us.

It is human nature to want to control the events that surround us and the people with whom we have loving relationships. So long as it is not excessive, our willingness to take control can serve the legitimate purpose of avoiding chaos and indecision. However, when we allow our control tendencies to morph into unhealthy character traits we undermine trust and sabotage potentially productive relationships.

Katie, one of my clients, was struggling with the adverse effects of her overbearing personality. She was a member of a special projects team that had several complex deliverables due shortly. She had served as team leader but had been demoted because her team members were threatening a mass walkout after having endured almost a year of what they reported as her emotionally and verbally abusive behavior. She described herself as a controller who within the first ten minutes of our initial meeting shared the following comments—nonstop.

I simply have to be in charge if I am going to spend my time on this project. I have been with the company for more than fifteen years and nobody on the team knows nearly as much as I do. I have spent so much money out of my pocket to finance some of the materials we needed to get the job done, and this is the thanks I get? I think it is this new lady who is creating the problem. She does not like me, and she is trying to take over. She is a friend of the boss and I believe they want to give her the job and boot me out. They are just mad because I refuse to let this newcomer tell me what to do. I cannot stand her; she has been nothing but trouble for me since she got here. They say I don't share. That's probably true. I never learned to share. After all, I am an only child, and therefore I am this way. I knew some of my ways bothered them, but I thought they liked me. They are always talking about how much they need me and how glad they are to have me on the team. So, I was shocked to find out they were threatening to leave. I guess they were just misleading me. I know they know how smart I am, and I don't see how they are going to get their work done without my leadership because I am the one with the knowledge base. I'll fix them, I plan to keep my mouth shut and let them see how much they need me.

It took me a few minutes to get my bearings after that diatribe. I did not know what to say. I had been coaching others for only seven months, and I was not prepared to handle this one. So I inhaled deeply. After asking several questions to encourage her to put all her feelings about this issue on the table, we began the hard work required to shift her focus from the team and toward herself.

As she continued speaking, I began to get a picture of who she was and what was motivating her extreme need to control. She had faced some horrible circumstances as a child and had been abused regularly. Being in control helped her avoid the feelings related to what she termed her historical victimhood. It took quite some time for her to work through her unresolved pain relating to her experiences.

Several months later, I began to see progress. Through a series of role-playing activities, she was able to visualize how her actions affected her team members, and she was effectively tackling the root causes of her behavior. She calls me periodically, and at the time of our last contact, she was still working with the same team—none of them had quit. She felt she was getting along much better with them including the dreaded newcomer. She had not regained her team leader position, but she readily expressed her understanding of management's rationale for taking their time in making that decision.

Control is one of the most pervasive aspects of fear. It disguises itself as love, wanting what is best for those we seek to control, avoiding difficult situations, and creating desired conditions or outcomes. The truth is that control is nothing more than an illusion of power. We cannot control most situations, and we certainly cannot control other people. By paying close attention to how this emotion presents itself in our lives, we can begin the necessary process of detachment, which allows us to be fully engaged in the moment. Rather than focusing on what we think a particular outcome should be, we can try to relax and enjoy the unexpected pleasures of the experience, appreciate how it unfolds, and have faith that the outcome will be what it should be.

Envy

> Take all the time and energy you waste on envy and use it to try to improve yourself. You will find you are better off and happier than you ever imagined. (Gary Rudz[11])

Envy is that terrible, distressful feeling we experience when we bear a grudge toward others because we covet what they have. It creates friction between us and those we envy, and it undermines our capacity to make progress toward growing whole. Envy causes us to think and act in irrational ways that assault our character and damage our reputation.

---

[11] https://topfamousquotes/gary_rudz_179331.

When we are obsessed about someone else's success, we make unwise decisions and jeopardize our self-respect.

Envy originates from a dark place deep within, and if left unchecked, it can result in our harboring ill will or taking hurtful action against someone. When we allow ourselves to wallow in this negative space, we invite destructive energy that can harm us. Envy convinces us that we would be happy if only we had the object of our lust.

I love Proverbs. It is a practical guide to sanctification that offers words of wisdom to assist us in our daily decision making. Perhaps more than any other book in the Bible, it shows us how to navigate the complexities of life. My daily meditations usually include a visit to verses in this book for insight and inspiration. There is always new discernment that underscores this central message: those who are moral, hardworking, and wise will reap rewards, sleep better at night, and find the success they seek. These words serve as a warning against rejecting godly wisdom and assure us that we get what we deserve. An example of one of the myriad meaningful gems is, "They will eat the fruit of their ways and be filled with the fruit of their schemes." (Proverbs 1:31 NIV)

Envy is such an insidious, crippling emotion because it keeps our focus turned outward. The redemptive work from negative feelings can occur only when we admit to their presence in our lives. If we acknowledge our feelings of envy, we can begin to work on this aspect of our personality, which needs improvement. When we find ourselves desiring someone's life rather than ours, we are on a self-destructive path that will lead to psychological discomfort and risky thoughts and behaviors. The painful discontent associated with longing for someone else's blessing can make life almost unbearable. It significantly reduces our capacity to exist in a state of peace and tranquility. What someone else has does not keep us from getting what we want. Any time the focus is outward rather than inward, we fuel fear-based emotions and channel disharmony.

We must keep in mind that our gifts and talents are divinely designed specifically to support spiritual growth. When we harbor ill feelings about the perceived blessings of others, we undermine God's will for our lives.

We live in an abundant world. There are plentiful natural and man-made resources, and they are available to those willing to apply themselves.

Focusing on what someone else has moves us away from sacred purpose. We will not find inner peace until we put these covetous feelings behind us.

The only difference between you and those you envy may be the fact that they took steps to do something special with their lives and perhaps you did not. The negative energy that accompanies envy undermines our health and does great harm to our self-image. When we are envious, we should replace that feeling with expressions of gratitude, which is a natural repellant for envy.

Envy is a difficult emotion to manage. It is hard for us to acknowledge that we are capable of harboring such a socially unacceptable attitude, and we are embarrassed to let anyone know how we feel. So we work diligently to deny, repress, or conceal our envy. If it is not properly attended to, however, it will continue to surface and inevitably consume us.

Envy is a fear-based emotion that keeps our souls in a splintered status and limits progress toward wholeness. Begrudging someone else's accomplishments elicits negative energy and takes the focus off our efforts to become our best selves. Facing that will not be easy, but it is necessary for spiritual growth. With concerted effort, we will become skilled in recognizing the warning signs of potentially destructive thoughts and behaviors. Early detection allows us to quickly shift our attitude in a positive direction. Once we take responsibility for our negative feelings by acknowledging their inappropriateness, we are well on our way to releasing them.

There is no room for envy in our efforts toward growing whole. When we give this emotion power over our lives, we invite unnecessary personal pain into our world.

God has blessed each of us with certain gifts and talents, and if we are not happy with our station in life, we can make changes. When we focus on others' assets, we negate the intended spiritual value of our unique, divinely designed assets. A commitment to spiritual transformation requires realization of certain specific milestones. Primary among them is an enhanced capacity to acknowledge the blessings of others without judgment. We cannot allow the "grass is greener on the other side" syndrome to capture our emotions, rob us of joy, and steer us away from our sacred purpose. When you allow feelings of envy to occupy space in your heart and mind, discord and disorder are your constant companions.

This insidious emotion leaves no room for the joy and peace that you pray for.

> So, put away all malice and all deceit and hypocrisy and envy and all slander. (1 Peter 2:1 ESV)

Greed

> An inheritance obtained hastily by greed will not be a blessing in the end. (Proverbs 20:21 AMP)

Greed is a complicated disease. Enough never seems to be enough. When people view the world through the lens of greed, they see it as a zero-sum game; for them to succeed, someone else must fail. Despite devastating consequences, the search for more is constant and the urge never wanes. The craving is so strong that these greed addicts will do anything in search of elusive satisfaction. The endless effort to feed the hungry addiction monster includes a willingness to betray, cheat, distort reality, manipulate, murder, and steal.

Greed personifies evil and is one of the seven deadly sins of the Christian faith. Virtually every sin begins with an unholy desire. The Bible is replete with examples of sin being rooted in greed. The love of worldly possessions makes us greedy for more, no matter how much we have. Greed is a serious character flaw that impedes our spiritual growth because it keeps us from loving God with all our heart, soul, mind, and strength. In the Parable of the Rich Fool a rich man built larger and larger barns to store his growing supply of crops and goods. Rather than use his belongings to benefit others he chose to selfishly hoard them. He reveled in the feeling that his abundant earthly storehouses would afford him satisfaction, security, and success. He died before he could enjoy the wealth he had amassed. In this parable Jesus teaches us that it is unwise to value our physical lives more than our spiritual lives.

Paul regularly spoke about the constant struggles Christians face as we battle the competing forces of our lustful human nature and our divine spiritual nature. He warned believers that the urge to do evil lurks alongside and is just as strong as the will to do right. Despite our being saved, the sanctification process is a lifelong endeavor and Satan continues to entice us as we are being transformed from world-centeredness and ego-centeredness to Christ-centeredness.

Another story about greed involves Amnon, one of David's sons, and Tamar, his half-sister. Amnon was so consumed with lust for Tamar that he deceitfully conspired with his cousin Jonadab to be alone with her. He pretended to be ill and when she brought him food he raped her. After abusing his sister, Amnon's feelings of greed and lust immediately turned to hatred and he ordered his servants to throw her out of his private quarters. Tamar's reputation was ruined. She lived the remainder of her life as a demoralized, desolate woman. When her brother Absalom found out about the crime he was furious. He plotted against Amnon and eventually had him killed.

The story of Ahab and Jezebel exemplifies how one family's greed can negatively affect an entire country. From the window of his palace, Israel's King Ahab could see a beautiful vineyard that belonged to Naboth. No doubt his palace was adorned with ornate fixtures and draped with the finest materials, yet he was consumed with greed and lust and coveted the vineyard which was off limits. King Ahab offered Naboth a handsome sum for his property, but Naboth refused to sell because he was obedient to God's instructions. When Israel took possession of the land God distributed it to the twelve tribes. Because the land represented the fruit of the nation's redemption, God required that it remain in the hands of the families to whom it was originally allotted. Naboth's refusal to sell angered Ahab. Jezebel, his wife, felt he should have access to anything in the kingdom he desired. She decided to figure out a way to give the king his coveted vineyard. She falsely accused Naboth of blasphemy, which resulted in his death by stoning. Finally, King Ahab's lust was rewarded. Theirs is a long and perverted story, which prompted significant internal conflict that plagued Israel for decades. In the end, King Ahab and all his successors were slain, and the dogs devoured Jezebel's body.

America's consumer-oriented culture makes it especially challenging to ignore the constant reminders of excess. Media messages bombard us with enticing examples of the lifestyles of the rich and famous. Boundary lines between abundance and greed are sufficiently blurry and make it a challenge to distinguish one from the other. Ornate remnants of garish wealth abound in secular and religious establishments alike. Reckless and runaway greed even undermines our government. Whether the enemies are scandalous corporations, corrupt police, or crooked politicians, vulnerable citizens suffer greatly. The unbridled desires of those in power and those seeking to usurp that power destroy dreams and provoke wars. Executive orders that separate babies from their parents and laws that offer excessive tax cuts to the wealthy make sense only to those who are comfortable with their greed. Taking health insurance benefits away from people with preexisting conditions under the guise of reducing the budget while sponsoring legislation to fund "pet projects" is shameful. But many of our political leaders justify this cruelty as good public policy.

Whether corporate or individual, the picture of greed is never pretty. Under the masquerade of a strong work ethic, company realignment, or a commitment to success, greed destroys lives, topples governments, and damages relationships. Greed is an insidious character flaw that interferes with efforts to grow. It is ego-focused and it ignores the well-being of others.

We are inundated with alluring suggestions that wealth and its trappings lead to happiness.

Our pursuit of worldly treasures does not comport with sacred purpose and does nothing to answer the pivotal question of why we are here. We must ask ourselves when our need for more money, power, or stuff will be satisfied.

A dominant aspect of greed is covetousness. *Unger's Bible Dictionary* defines *covet* as the desire for gains obtained dishonestly, the desire to have more and more and more. It involves discontent with what one has. At the root of most sin is the desire for something taboo. As previously mentioned, Eve's covetous desire for the forbidden fruit in the Garden of Eden introduced sin into the world. Since then, humankind has struggled with the demons of unhealthy desire and lust.

Most humans are guilty of greed on some level. Growing whole requires us to objectively evaluate the role of this deadly sin in our lives. Character traits and personal performance standards including ambition, determination, and an intense drive to achieve can lead to positive results that help us reach our goals, but habits or desires that interfere with spiritual growth or take our focus away from our sacred purpose can lead to undesired ends. We must remain diligent in our efforts to rein in greedy tendencies.

Greed is the antithesis of love. It obscures our view of God. We create false idols that take control of our lives in frightening ways. An unnatural focus on accumulation restricts the free flow of positive energy and undermines our efforts to restore our souls. When greed blurs our vision, we cannot see love, joy, peace, patience, kindness, goodness, faithfulness, and gentleness.

> For what does it profit a man to gain the whole world and forfeit his soul? (Mark 8:36 ESV)

Jealousy

> Jealousy, that dragon which slays love under the pretense of keeping it alive. (Havelock Ellis[12])

Similar in many ways to envy, jealousy is an intense emotion that rears its ugly head when we become vengeful because a desirable possession or an important relationship is threatened. Jealousy can present itself in all types of relationships—business, familial, friendship, or romantic. Jealousy is a common emotion particularly when love is involved. Everyone experiences this negative feeling on some level at one time or another. What we do when these feelings reveal themselves will determine whether we grow spiritually or succumb to our destructive instincts. Shakespeare's *Othello* is one of the best classic tragedies of all times. It is an excellent story about how jealousy can derail dreams, ruin lives, and even lead to murder.

Othello was a noble Black warrior in the Venetian army during the sixteenth century who had enjoyed many successes on the battlefield, but character flaws and his outsider status complicated his life. He was secretly married to Desdemona, a White woman who was the daughter of a prominent senator. When her father, Brabantio, found out about the marriage, he was furious; he refused to accept it as a legitimate union. He

---

[12] https://goodreads/havelock_ellis_98081.

convinced himself that Othello had used witchcraft to trick Desdemona into marriage.

Iago, the villain in this story, was also a soldier in the Venetian army. He was jealous of Othello's battlefield successes and his position as general. He also resented Othello's decision to promote a soldier named Cassio to the position of lieutenant. Iago coveted this position and was heartbroken when he was overlooked. Plotting revenge, Iago convinced Othello that Desdemona and Lieutenant Cassio were having an affair. Because of his jealousy, Othello ordered Iago to murder Lieutenant Cassio, who survived the attack. Othello then strangled Desdemona. Immediately after the murder, it became clear that she was innocent. Grief stricken and remorseful, Othello committed suicide. In the meantime, justice prevailed; the treacherous deeds of Iago were exposed, and the authorities arrested him.

Jealousy is a sinister emotion that includes deep-rooted feelings of anger and fear. It can cause one person to consider another as an object of possession, and it can lead to violence. No relationship can survive one individual trying to control the other. To be successful, relationships must be based on mutual respect and trust, and they must give both parties enough room to grow and thrive in ways that support them. If it reaches a point that a relationship is no longer productive, both parties must graciously accept their roles in its demise and extend best wishes to each other.

Unresolved feelings of jealousy can wreak havoc in our lives in myriad ways. When we feel insecure or anxious about losing someone we care for, we need to

1. pause long enough to analyze the situation objectively,
2. seek divine guidance before acting rashly and escalating the volatility,
3. admit to the feelings of jealousy,
4. determine their cause, and
5. develop strategies to appropriately manage these feelings.

To prevent overreaction, we must expend the time and energy necessary to resolve any feelings of ill will, determine the underlying motivation for the anxiety, and think through the ramifications of any action we might contemplate. At its peak, jealousy evokes toxic feelings that can cause us to act in dangerous ways that result in regret and remorse. Rather than dwell in this unsafe space, we should shift our attention and energy to opportunities for new and even more exciting possibilities ahead.

Objectively assess the causes of your jealousy and work diligently to put those feelings behind you. It is entirely possible that your feelings are not specific to the situation. You could be reliving a past failure you have not resolved. Be compassionate as you conduct a self-assessment to help yourself better understand your strong emotions.

If your partner has been unfaithful in the relationship your feelings of jealousy may be warranted. However, unless you are prepared for the relationship to end, you need to channel your emotions in more-positive ways. Express your feelings to your partner in a nonthreatening manner, and take the time necessary to grieve. If the offense is egregious, you might need to speak with a trained counselor who can help you sort through your feelings. Giving yourself permission to empty out and fully explore your concerns with a professional could be a relationship-saving strategy. Prayer is another powerful way to deal with hurt and disappointment. Ask God for His guidance, surrender the issue to Him, and have faith that in time, you will be released from the pain of betrayal. There is no comparison to the miracle of prayer.

After a reasonable period of mourning, however, you must find it in your heart to forgive. Remember, whether the relationship survives a violation or not, to move on with your life, you must put the experience in its proper place emotionally and shift your focus to meaning and sacred purpose.

Sometimes, we make big human errors, and when we do, we need big hearts to forgive our humanness. We cannot ask God to forgive our transgressions if we are unable to forgive others.

If a relationship is to stand a chance of survival, you must find a way to channel your emotions productively. Whether warranted or unwarranted, jealousy allows your feelings to control you, and it restricts the cooperation required for the two of you to rebuild your battered partnership.

Jealousy is such a strong emotion that if not properly addressed will eventually consume you. One of my coworkers caught her husband cheating more than thirty years ago. The marriage was dissolved shortly thereafter in a bitterly contested divorce. She was devastated to find out that he was living a double life as a bigamist. According to my coworker the other woman was younger, prettier, and thinner. Marti's emotions ran the gamut from hatred toward her ex-husband to jealousy toward the person she called her replacement wife. The problem is, she was still stuck in her feelings of hatred toward him. She had never been able to move on with her life because she had stubbornly refused to forgive him for the hurt his actions and decisions caused. She joined a church and buried herself in its rituals, but the anger, hatred, and jealousy continued to haunt her spirit and stunt her growth. Unfortunately, rather than choosing wholeness, she chose unforgiveness.

No matter what happens in life, we must leave space in our hearts for love; that is the only way we can grow beyond the negative emotions brought on by jealousy whether warranted or unwarranted. When nothing else helps, love lifts us out of deep despair and offers much needed sweet relief. Even if we are not in a space to receive romantic love, there are always opportunities to extend affection to the vulnerable all around us. For example, a child two doors down may need someone to help her with her reading assignment. Seniors in the long-term care facility around the corner would thoroughly enjoy a visitor who could bring heartfelt hugs and words of encouragement. When we look outside ourselves and beyond our pain, we can give and receive love in unexpected places and ways.

We all experience the sting of jealousy sometimes. Losing someone we love hurts deeply, but even a disappointment such as this always presents an opportunity for spiritual growth. If we can see beyond the immediate pain and envision a more fulfilling future, we can benefit from the lessons learned. If new love finds its way to us, we will be in the emotional space to receive it. People enter our lives for specific reasons and to accomplish specific purposes; there are no accidental meetings. Every relationship is by divine design, and the reasons and purposes are predetermined to help us grasp the lessons we need to learn. Not all relationships are meant to be permanent; some are intended to last a lifetime and some simply are not. Once the reasons and purposes are served, circumstances and situations of fate will find a way to sever the relationship.

Do not be critical of yourself if Mister or Miss Right did not come with a lifetime guarantee. Trust in the knowledge that every relationship regardless of its quality was meant to be. Long after it has ended, the people intimately involved in the relationship will continue to feel its effects. Do not allow emotions of jealousy toward another person to rob you of the opportunities to grow from the experiences it brought. Allow love to drown out any messages of jealousy and control.

You may never completely understand the reason for a breakup, and it is possible that there is no explanation. Maybe the two of you simply grew apart. Regardless of the circumstance, spiritual growth should be your mantra. You may not be able to see the blessing headed your way, but you can have faith that God knows who or what is best for you. Your prince or princess charming may arrive shortly. Never cheat yourself out of a dignified departure when the time comes for a relationship to end. Often we hold on not because of love but because we selfishly fear the other person doing better without us. Do not allow jealousy to hinder your spiritual growth and derail your sacred purpose.

> For where jealousy and selfish ambition exist, there will be disorder and every vile practice. (James 3:16 ESV)

Resentment

> As I walked out the door toward the gate that would lead to my freedom, I knew if I did not leave my bitterness and hatred behind, I'd still be in prison. (Nelson Mandela[13])

Bitterness, envy, hatred, and jealousy breed resentment. This insidious disease will eat away at your spiritual core and sabotage your efforts to find the joy and peace you desire. When you foster resentment, you close your heart to love and remove any possibility of realizing wholeness. A heart that repels love is void of its essential lifeblood. There should always be expansive space in the heart for love.

When we are overcome by resentment, we erect walls that shut others out and we create an unhealthy living situation. We make ourselves and

---

[13] Nelson Mandela, *The Authorized Book of Quotations.*

others miserable, and it is possible that those we resent are not aware of our strong feelings or do not care about them. It is nonsensical to expect our resentment to matter to anyone besides us. *What is the point of harboring ill feelings when no one else cares about that?*

Resentment hurts you far more than the person you resent. It makes the circumstances of life more difficult than they need to be. When you resent others, you are in effect giving them control over the quality of your life; you are blaming them for something that whether real or contrived you must release to grow. Objectively examine the reason for your strong negative feelings and take the steps necessary to eliminate the walls you have erected to house these debilitating emotions. Allow yourself to feel deeply any hurt attached to the situation that caused the feelings. Behind the resentment, you will probably discover hurt; find the courage to face it. Analyze it, assess it, and allow yourself to feel it with the goal of release and relief. Wherever you find resentment, determine the cause and set your intention to move toward internal reconciliation.

Resentment usually follows judgment. We judge others based on strong feelings we harbor, but we should not. We all have character flaws and thus have serious work to do as we learn to live well so we can age well. Our personal life code should never allow room for self-righteous judgment. If we expect forgiveness for our transgressions, we must have big enough hearts to offer this level of grace to others and leave judgment where it belongs—with God. The goal of spiritual growth becomes far more enjoyable, meaningful, and realistic when we learn to forgive early and often. Those who find the courage and strength to forgive others who have betrayed their trust and hurt them understand the therapeutic value of this holy act.

> But if you do not forgive others their trespasses, neither will your Father forgive your trespasses. (Matthew 6:15 ESV)

Self-Hatred

> When the righteous cry for help, the Lord hears and delivers them out of their troubles. The Lord is near to

the brokenhearted and saves the crushed in spirit. (Psalm
34:17–18 ESV)

Self-hatred is an almost guaranteed by-product of viewing life through
the lens of fear. It is a complicated emotion with deep roots that reflect
the serious, unresolved needs of our broken spirits. People hate themselves
for a variety of reasons. At its most extreme, addictions and other self-
destructive habits permeate our lives when we exist in the emotional space
of self-hatred. Angry outbursts, bullying, feelings of unworthiness, low
self-esteem, resentment, and other emotions that emanate from fear are
often rooted in self-hatred. Growing whole requires us to do the inside
work necessary to remove this negativity from our lives.

Our faith assures us that we are made worthy by God. When we compare
ourselves to others and allow our perception of their accomplishments,
appearance, or resources to make us feel small, we are not walking by faith.
When we are in fellowship and relationship with God, we understand that
our value is not something we earn through worldly means.

Every problem has a spiritual solution. When we adopt this mindset,
the remedy for self-hatred becomes clear. It is twofold yet interconnected;
first, we must learn to love as God loves, and second, we must decide to
grow whole. To understand how God loves, we must know something
about His character.

Scripture tells us that God is pure love and that He is compassionate
and gracious. Since we are created in His image, even with our flaws,
we have the capacity for love, compassion, and graciousness, which are
antidotes to self-hatred. As we apply these principles to our sacred purpose,
they reveal themselves in positive ways. For example, through kind words
and deeds, we activate the myriad spiritual benefits of love, compassion,
and graciousness. The receiver of these kind expressions is inspired, and
we, as the givers, are uplifted. When we serve others and take the focus
off our own woes, the positive contributions we make elevate our sense of
worthiness.

When we spend time with fellow believers, the love and support
they offer lift our spirits and remind us of our holy connection to God.
By developing the habit of helping those in need, our hearts expand and
we realize the spiritual benefit of empathy. The deeper the expressions of

love we share with the world, the more Christlike our lifestyle becomes. When we routinely function on this elevated level of consciousness, we are in effect growing whole, and we leave little room for self-hatred to fester.

> I can do all things through him who strengthens me.
> (Philippians 4:13 ESV)

Love-Based Emotions

Our worldview provides the foundation on which we build our lives; everything else rests on the shoulders of the principles embedded in it. When our worldview is based on love and includes a commitment to and belief in sacred purpose, every intention and desire that flows from us will support this guidepost.

Our attitudes, beliefs, dreams, ideas, and values that create our worldview affect us in every dimension. As we grow and learn, we have an ethical responsibility to ask probing questions and seek answers that help us to make sense of the human experience. If what we witness is inconsistent with sacred purpose, it should not become a part of our worldview. We engage the world on three levels of insight: the body, the soul, and the spirit. Input from each of these levels is important as we acquire the knowledge, understanding, and wisdom required to successfully navigate life's challenges.

When our bodies, souls, and spirits are in sync we function on our highest and best levels. Our five-sensory, multisensory, and multidimensional capacities work in harmony and they offer us our best opportunities to thrive. They warn us when we are in the presence of danger and they convict us when we are selfish and hurt others.

God is continuously communicating with us, and we receive His messages through our emotions and our multisensory spiritual capacities. God is pure, unadulterated love and any level of contact with Him is through this medium. The joyful, positive, and uplifting state of loving and being loved is a critical component of the Christian faith. From a spiritual perspective, the essence of what it means to be human in the context of the temporary earthly realm and the eternal heavenly realm must be explored through the lens of love and sacred purpose.

The stark contrast between fear-based living and love-based living is undeniable. When we choose love over fear we transcend the limitations inherent in the human condition and we elevate our levels of awareness to the promises embedded in the kingdom story.

> Let us look briefly at four love-based emotions that help define what it means to grow whole .

Compassion

> Compassion asks us to go where it hurts, to enter into the places of pain, to share in brokenness, fear, confusion, and anguish. Compassion challenges us to cry out with those in misery, to mourn with those who are lonely, to weep with those in tears. Compassion requires us to be weak with the weak, vulnerable with the vulnerable, and powerless with the powerless. Compassion means full immersion in the condition of being human. (Henri J. M. Nouwen[14])

Compassion is that mysterious, deep sorrow that one human being feels for another who is stricken with misfortune. Compassion arouses in us a strong desire to alleviate others' suffering. When we feel compassion, we honor the sanctity of humanity and we are compelled to put others' needs ahead of ours. Compassion requires us to lose ourselves in the righteousness of the moment, and in doing so, something miraculous touches our souls and moves us in the direction of growing whole.

Compassion is the one emotion that connects humanity and transcends the self-centeredness and the superficial barriers we erect to withhold love. It permeates religions, spiritual practices, and economic, racial, and social layers of separation. It forces us to concentrate on the commonality of humanity rather than cultural, ethnic, or physical differences. In this world, God put billions of human beings who possess millions of characteristics, some shared by others and some uniquely individual. Every decision God

---

[14] https://goodreads/henri_nouwen_303173.

makes is perfect and purposeful. Embedded in the contours of His perfect will is the requirement that our compassion extends to all humanity.

At their core, all human souls have the same basic needs and desires. We dream of opportunities to self-actualize, and we weep with sorrow when tragedy engulfs us. No member of humanity is more significant than any other. Our differences are by divine design; they make life far more interesting and intriguing, and they give us important clues about the mysterious and unique nature of our sacred purpose. When we see every human being through the eyes of compassion, we expand our hearts and magnify the divinity in us.

Nowhere is this more evident than during natural disasters or other traumatic emergencies. Something magnificent happens to us when we see someone in trouble. At that moment, we are not thinking about culture, ethnicity, gender, or race; we focus on the situation and what we can do to help. We function at our best when we acknowledge the common cry of human despair and exemplify selfless compassion through our humane actions. Once the immediate threat subsides though, we are often content to revert to familiar habits and patterns that isolate and sabotage our progress toward growing whole.

Compassion is a willful act that involves feeling the pain and suffering and to some degree making a conscious decision to assist. Compassion expands the heart well beyond feelings of love, and it connects one individual to another soul to soul.

Compassion springs forth from our capacity to appreciate and be grateful for all that is. Life is precious, and when we internalize this in deeply felt ways, we receive the best of what each moment offers. When we are compassionate, we please God.

No earthly presence better exemplified compassion than Jesus Christ. The essence of His ministry was love and compassion.

> Then Jesus went about all the cities and villages, teaching in their synagogues, preaching the gospel of the kingdom, and healing every sickness and every disease among the people. But when he saw the multitudes, he was moved with compassion for them, because they were weary and

> scattered, like sheep having no shepherd. (Matthew 9:35–36 KJV)

Seeing the world through the eyes of compassion includes being compassionate toward ourselves. When we suffer, it is important for us to face our pain and without judgment offer ourselves kindness, understanding, and spiritual discernment. Character flaws and imperfections are integral to the shared human experience, and we overcome feelings of unworthiness by facing painful situations, objectively assessing our role in their causes, and taking the necessary steps toward reconciliation.

Self-compassion and self-pity are vastly different emotions, and we need to be mindful of how they vary. Self-pity is egocentric, usually results in unnecessary drama, and restricts our capacity to see the suffering of others. Wholeness encourages self-compassion as an effective healing strategy. When we learn to be kind to ourselves, we can do the same for others.

> Bear one another's burdens, and so fulfill the law of Christ. (Galatians 6:2 ESV)

Forgiveness

> An eye for an eye only ends up making the whole world blind. (Mahatma Gandhi[15])

We have all felt the sting of an egregious offense at one time or another. Words and deeds can attack us, violate our sense of safety and security, and crush our self-esteem. Depending on the severity of the offense, it can take us years to recover from the damage we do to ourselves and others intentionally or unintentionally.

Making the decision to forgive when you are harmed is one of the hardest and most complex spiritual tests you may ever encounter. Your instinct is to recoil in a self-protection mode and respond from the fear-based vantage points of bitterness, resentment, and revenge. The more

---

[15] https://brainyquote/mahatma_gandhi_107039.

severe the offense, the harder it is to forgive; but healing requires a willingness to let go.

On May 13, 1981, an angry gunman attempted to assassinate Pope John Paul II by shooting him. Sometime later, the pope aroused the emotions of the world as he issued words of forgiveness for his would-be assassin. In forgiving his enemy, the pope etched a powerful, unforgettable image of grace that made indelible impressions on our hearts and minds when he said, "The act of forgiveness is the first and fundamental condition so that we aren't divided and placed one against another like enemies."[16] In 1983, the pope visited his would-be assassin in prison. Following a private conversation, they emerged as friends, and in 2000, Pope John Paul II requested a pardon for his shooter.

To forgive, we must release negative emotions attached to someone or something. When we resent rather than forgive, we create negative energy. Ephesians 4:32 (ESV) requires us to "be kind to one another, tenderhearted, forgiving one another, as God in Christ forgave you."

When we are slandered or assaulted, we can harbor bitterness, resentment, and revenge or decide to embrace forgiveness. Forgiveness begins with one person facing another. What comes out of this interaction will impact the offender and the offended alike. God created us to live in harmony with each other, and when relationships are violated, barriers are erected and the opportunity for harmony is severed. Forgiveness benefits us much more than it does the person we are bitter and resentful toward. To experience the joy of spiritual abundance, we must learn how to forgive.

Forgiveness is an expression of love that comes from a holy place deep in our core. It supports spiritual growth, and it is a commonsense approach to life. Medicine and science are in general agreement that the stress of not having a forgiving spirit is profound. According to Deborah Finley, unforgiveness undermines our health in myriad ways: "Unforgiveness is the leading cause of many physical ailments, including hypertension, ulcerative colitis, and toxic goiters."[17] Unforgiveness negatively affects our health in other ways. A compromised immune system, obesity, and

---

[16] *Pope John Paul II and His Message of Forgiveness* (Loyola Press).

[17] Finley, Deborah. *What Your Future Holds and What You Can Do to Change It.* (2007).

depression are medical challenges associated with harboring resentment and unforgiveness.

Scripture tells us that harboring bitter contention in our hearts will result in disorder and evil. God commands us to walk in love, and we cannot love if we cannot forgive. The directive from Christ to "love your enemies and pray for those who persecute you" (Matthew 5:44 ESV) forces us beyond our human comfort boundaries and into the spiritual dimension of our being. Logically, we know it is more blessed to forgive than to be forgiven, but it is often hard to forgive when someone has caused us pain and sorrow. It requires us to go deep inside ourselves and rely on the Holy Spirit to guide our efforts. When forgiveness is humanly impossible, we can begin a quest for divine assistance, inspiration, and intervention through prayer and reliance on the promises of God.

Betrayal and other horrific infractions are far too common, and the damage reverberates throughout the universe. Yet in the resonant words of Pope John Paul II,

> Forgiveness can purify memory, it can travel through time and history, breathing life into the killing fields, into the collective souls of nations, and into the lives of its brutalized citizens. No less than any nation, the country of an anguished heart also cries out to forgive and to be forgiven. Personal betrayal can cut as deeply as a machete. Forgiveness can offer hope for these intimate woundings of the soul.[18]

The following is a story of such extreme pain and sorrow that it will break your heart. Despite the agony, there are glimpses of forgiveness in it that give me hope this family will find peace.

When I met them, Mitchell and his family were still dealing with the crippling sting of a broken relationship that had occurred eleven years earlier. His family was ripped apart when his wife, Beatrice, began a new life with someone else. She left their three children, who ranged in age from eighteen months to six years. Mitchell had to figure out how to move

---

[18] *Pope John Paul II and His Message of Forgiveness* (Loyola Press).

forward with his life in spite of his heartache and his new role as a single parent.

Six months after his wife left, Mitchell suffered a massive heart attack and spent several months in recovery. He was unable to care for his children, and temporary custody was granted to their maternal aunt. In time, Mitchell recovered and reestablished his family. They struggled, but they managed to continue with their lives.

After nine years of absence, Beatrice started making overtures suggesting her desire to return to the family she had abandoned. Initially, Mitchell vehemently refused to allow her near the children, but over time and with the help of professional counseling, they communicated more effectively and were beginning to deal with some of the closeted issues that had driven a wedge between them years before the breakup. His hatred toward Beatrice was beginning to subside, as he was learning to forgive her for the pain she had caused their family. The three children were deeply wounded, however, and some of their scars may never heal.

At his request, I recently participated in a therapist-led visit with Mitchell and the children. I was overwhelmed by the pain and agony that permeated the room. Their broken hearts were crying out for healing as they spoke of lost possibilities and the unending torture of Beatrice's absence. The daughter appeared to be the most damaged. The loss of her mother had punctured her soul, and she was stuck in a place where it was hard for love to penetrate. The oldest son appeared to have forgiven his mother to some extent. He was cautiously optimistic about visiting with her. I have no idea what will become of this severely wounded family. It will take years of hard work, and still, reconciliation may never be possible. Despite the gloom, though, there are glimmers of hope.

Each member of the family must find a way to forgive whomever they consider their offenders to be. If they do not, they will not be able to liberate themselves from their painful past and will suffer endless torture of victims who cannot grow beyond the anguish caused by betrayal.

From a spiritual perspective, there are many lessons to be learned by each of them as they struggle to release themselves from being hopelessly stuck in a cycle of pain and revenge. Mitchell and the children have erected a wall secured by the strength of discontent and unforgiveness. Because of fear, they are hesitant to open their hearts to Beatrice. In the meantime, she feels insurmountable guilt for having abandoned her family. The relationship with her new love did not survive the guilt and remorse, and with the benefit of hindsight, she can face reality. She caused extensive damage to her husband and children, and the hurt may never completely subside. Although the family has ample reasons not to forgive, if they do not, they will forfeit any opportunity for love to enter their lives.

The essential point of our lives is to learn the lessons of love and to express them in ways that support sacred purpose. Forgiveness is the foundation on which we build our blueprint for growing whole. Each of us is an integral part of the divine oneness of God's unconditional, universal love. When one of us harbors resentment, we all suffer. When one of us forgives, we make the world a better place for all.

> For if you forgive others their trespasses, your heavenly
> Father will also forgive you. (Matthew 6:14 ESV)

We hurt each other daily. From the beginning of history, we see the brutality of one person's actions against another. With the killing of Abel by his brother, Cain, murder was introduced into the human equation. Unfortunately, brutality is an unavoidable by-product of the overarching human condition of sin. From the sting of unkind words to personal betrayal, to mass genocide, forgiveness is essential. From the centuries-old rivalry between Arab and Jew to America's Civil War and family feuds that poison generational relationships, we see glaring examples of the severe damage unforgiveness can render. As hard as it is to forgive, for Christians, no offense is too egregious to warrant unforgiveness. On the cross, Jesus said, "Father forgive them, for they do not know what they are doing" (Luke 23:34 NIV).

The personal decision to forgive, to let go of the resentment we harbor against an offender, is one of the most endearing of all the human characteristics. When we no longer feel the need to punish or exact restitution and revenge, we release our souls from the prison of restless discontent.

Gratitude

> Counting our blessings can transform melancholy into cheerful mass; laughter and joy are expressions of praise and thanksgiving for life's glories. When looking at the glass that symbolizes our life, we can view it as half full or half empty. The choice is ours. When we feel gratitude for our experiences, it becomes easier to see the good that always exists. (Sir John Templeton[19])

I recently participated in a ceremony with familiar rituals I had witnessed many times before. That time, though, it was vastly different. My siblings and I buried our mother. I said goodbye to someone I had been physically connected to since conception but bound to spiritually forever. God always intended that I would be the offspring of the earthly parents He gave me, and their lives were orchestrated in ways that made the union possible that produced me.

My emotions were running the gamut, but when I thoughtfully considered these two people and the vital roles they played in my life, more than anything else, I was grateful. Everything that happened to me while in their care was designed to teach me the lessons I would need to manage the meaning and purpose of my life.

My parents were strict, but my mother was the disciplinarian. I spent years resenting that part of our relationship. It took me several decades to really understand who she was, why she disciplined me as she had, and how her experiences had impacted the decisions she made. When I got serious about growing whole, I realized I harbored unsettled feelings toward her that required resolution. I initially ignored this awareness because I had no idea how to address the dull, nagging pain, but what started out as a spiritual nudge grew into an overwhelming mandate to reconcile.

With the assistance of prayer and meditation, I wrote my mother a letter expressing my feelings. Once I started writing, years of bottled-up emotions poured onto the pages. That self-exploration and purging was very therapeutic. Once I had emptied out, I faced a decision about what to do with the letter—mail it to her and run the emotional risk of rejection

---

[19] https://azquotes/john_templeton_14517.

if she did not acknowledge it, or hold onto the letter and be content with the purging. I decided to mail it.

Something magical happened a week later. She called me, and we talked and cried and reminisced for hours. In the end, we listened and accepted each other's sincere words. I realized the story I had told myself about my mother was not at all how she felt or who she was. I gained a more accurate picture of this woman whose womb I had gestated in and how the totality of our relationship fit into the story of human life. I could finally evaluate our experiences from a vertical rather than a horizontal perspective. I had interpreted our disconnection as unworthiness on my part. I had been so focused on the singular me and how I felt that I had not considered her emotions and realities. It took a deep dive into a closet that contained piles of unresolved pain to uncover the love we genuinely had for each other and allow it to shine through unobstructed.

Since that divinely inspired encounter, our relationship blossomed in ways I could never have imagined. I am so grateful to God for giving me the courage and insight to share my feelings with her. I am so grateful I gave her a chance to offer me her version of our story. I am so grateful I was blessed with the opportunity to explore our unique mother-daughter relationship more fully. I am so grateful that God placed me in the care of the parents He chose for me.

There are many pathways to wholeness, which at its core is oneness with God, self, and others. Whichever route we take, let it be paved with generous portions of perpetual gratitude. When we see the world through the lens of love and sacred purpose, we surrender our hearts, minds, bodies, souls, and spirits to gratefulness, which is, in reality, the primary gateway to spirituality.

Through the lens of gratitude, we see beauty, joy, and love. We see big-picture meaning and sacred purpose. We gain a level of knowledge, understanding, and wisdom that raises our consciousness far beyond the five-sensory dimension. Our worldview is elevated to a heart-centered space that supports spiritual growth, and we become role models and wisdom teachers for what is just, right, and true. This is the space where love thrives and wholeness resides.

Early in my coaching relationship with a client in her mid-twenties, we were engaged in deep conversation one morning about gratitude and its benefits. Her history was filled with challenges and disappointments resulting from the near-lethal combination of abandonment, abuse, and addiction. Her mother was a crack addict who had passed her around to anyone who was willing to babysit while she pursued her next high. As a result, Cassie was exposed to unspeakable atrocities that were revealed little by little over time as she shared tidbits of her life with me. Seemingly devoid of emotion, she would detail examples of evil that broke my heart each time I heard how one human being's callousness could inflict such indignities upon another. There are so many aspects of life, meaning, and sacred purpose that I do not understand, but I know that she and I crossed paths so I could learn from her far more than she learned from me.

At the time of our conversation, she had no idea who her father was; the only one in her family she felt remotely attached to was her maternal grandmother. We met as coworkers who were generations apart, but a bond of mutual admiration and workplace friendship quickly materialized. Initially, she did a fairly good job of masking her extensive unresolved pain, but as I got to know her better, her dulled but constant agony became more apparent.

During our conversation one morning, she noted that I talked frequently about a lifestyle of gratitude but indicated that she had few examples of things to be grateful for. The experiential benefits of gratitude at least on the conscious level were alien to her, but she was sufficiently curious about how living in a state of perpetual appreciation could manifest itself in her life. As it turned out, that was the root of our attraction to each other and probably the primary reason our souls connected. As our bond strengthened we engaged in untold deep conversations about spirituality and the meaning and purpose of life.

No matter the valley experience, when we consistently employ the sacred spiritual practice of perpetual gratitude, we move to a higher level of consciousness and get closer to the meaning and sacred purpose of life. The lesson is not in the disappointment itself but in the fruits of the spirit we fertilize and nourish when we tackle our disappointment with the knowledge, understanding, and wisdom of gratitude. When we do this, no matter the outcome, we grow.

Over time, her worldview softened and she was able to expand the lens through which she saw her life; she made room in her heart for the blessings she had previously ignored. Sometimes, when life hurts so badly that it crushes us, we find it hard to allow ourselves the luxury of fully embracing the moments of abundance. We are so poised for the next crippling blow that we miss the sweet relief of euphoria. No matter how bad things get, God's amazing universe will offer us blissful respite from time to time as long as we keep the eternal flames of faith burning and hope deeply embedded in our psyches.

Despite her sordid family history and the dysfunction she had endured Cassie was blessed. For starters, she was the poster child for health and stamina. She was strikingly beautiful, she had a great personality, and she was quite book smart. She had ample reason for bitterness, but instead, she was warm and caring. She exuded a level of sympathy that attracted people, and she was adored by our coworkers. She was an interesting breath of fresh air in an otherwise monolithic work environment.

By the time I met her, she had two degrees and was working on a doctorate. She was an accomplished professional with a promising future, but she was not as impressed with herself as I was. I once asked her to describe herself to me, and she mentioned none of these remarkable assets. While she did not see herself as a victim, she feared giving herself permission to acknowledge the conquering spirit she displayed. She struggled to relax and let her emotional guard down long enough to give herself the accolades she had clearly earned despite formidable odds. Her self-image was so tattered that I found it hard to understand how she managed to survive and even thrive with little or no support system. Our relationship as client, coach, and workplace friend served both of us extremely well, and our spiritual bond brought forth untold mutual benefits.

After years of a beautiful connection I still cherish, she received an outstanding job offer and relocated to Oregon. We kept in close contact for a while, but gradually, time and distance took its toll. I hear from her occasionally, and I am happy to report that she is a successful wife, mother, woman of strong faith, and forensic psychiatrist.

I mention Cassie now because she forever altered my understanding of the role of gratitude in my spiritual growth. At the time I met her, I considered myself a serious student of the intricacies of multisensory and multidimensional awareness. I had fully embraced the tenets of the religious faith that I was born into, and it was no longer merely a ritualistic exercise steeped in tradition. It had evolved into my chosen way of life, and as a result, it was woven into my body, soul, and spirit. Although I was never a Bible thumper, Cassie met and befriended the version of me that was already fully committed to the Christian faith. From a theological perspective, I thought I fully understood the benefits of a life focused on gratitude as the root of my spiritual discipline. This youngster, with all her unresolved pain and youthful naivete, raised my level of awareness and helped me crystallize my deep feelings about the importance of gratitude.

At some point during my formative years, I erected an emotional barrier that bridled my capacity to express feelings of insecurity for fear of appearing vulnerable and weak. Cassie taught me so many valuable life lessons. She held me accountable and challenged the validity of the stories I told myself to justify the unnecessary aloofness that had become an indelible part of my personality.

When we allow our true feelings to burst forth, sit with them long enough to understand and appreciate their genesis, and put them in their rightful place based on where we are on our current growth trajectory, we flourish exponentially. We expand our hearts by leaps and bounds, and we heighten our sensitivity for the plights of others.

Gratitude flows freely when life is good—when we land that coveted job or meet the person of our dreams or lose ten pounds. When mothers or fathers check in with their children and find out that all is well with them, we feel great. We are thankful, we sing praises, and we celebrate our good fortune. *But what do we do when life hurts? What about when we are forced to live with the relentless, nagging ache of losing someone we love through divorce? How do we find ways to exemplify gratitude when we cannot seem to move through the stages of mourning when death robs us of the emotional and physical closeness of our dearly departed? How do we seniors remain grateful when society cherishes youth and vibrancy? What about when chronic aches and pains are the bane of our existence? How do we handle feelings of inadequacy? What do we do with unhealthy levels of anger, envy, and jealousy? How do we move forward when our sordid past haunts us?*

Life's difficulties and its litany of tragic events offer constant reminders that pain and pleasure are equal-opportunity emotions. Just when we hurt so badly that life feels unbearable, something remarkable happens to lift our spirits and soothe our souls. When our valley moments seem insurmountable, a baby's antics, a funny joke, the smell of a delicious peach cobbler, or a gentle reminder that all things work together for our good presents us with respite. When we learn to lose ourselves in these precious moments, life becomes an exciting adventure filled with great expectations, meaning, and sacred purpose.

Gratitude is the perfect antidote to pain and suffering. I am still mourning the recent loss of my brother. Sometimes out of nowhere, a sharp pain pierces my heart and brings tears to my eyes. Knowing that I will never see his face or hear his voice again is a bitter pill to swallow. So when I find myself in this state of sadness, I quickly shift the internal dialogue to the fun times he and I had as children and our devilish attempts to aggravate my mother and my older sister. As I mentioned, my parents were strict, and they did not allow us to freely mingle with other neighborhood children, so my siblings and I were each other's best friends.

He was the first sibling to leave our close-knit band of six, so we are still struggling to adjust to life without the physical presence of our second family patriarch. He had assumed that critical role after the death of my father. He never called ahead to let us know he was coming to visit. The first awareness was usually a strong banging on the door. The arrival of his fun personality almost always guaranteed laughs and jovial fellowship. We siblings and our children and their children would gather near him and hang on his every word. While we cannot replace his fun-filled antics, whenever there is a gathering, someone invariably leads us into a conversation about him and his favorite stories. These moments summon feelings of gratitude for those of us who are blessed to share his bloodline and familial bond. The joy of gratefulness replaces the pain of loss as we reminisce and invite his spiritual presence to comfort us.

Something as routine as the rising of the sun or the emergence of the moon at dusk offers us the opportunity to gratefully seize the moment and express thankfulness. Our time on earth is precious and should never be taken for granted. No matter our age or stage, life is short, and every breath has meaning and value. I am at my best when I live in the present and consume all that it offers. This state of mind and way of life supports me when I go through deep valley experiences.

I am reminded of a time when my heart was broken into a million pieces and life felt almost too unbearable. My father, who was also my friend and mentor, had a massive stroke, and his doctor called my siblings and me together to suggest we say our goodbyes. The extent of the damage coupled with his age and preexisting health conditions, the doctor surmised, made it humanly impossible for him to survive. My knees buckled upon hearing this dire prognosis; I found it hard to keep my presence of mind and remain standing. My immediate instinct was to run down the hospital's hallway to make my way outside. When life hurts, I find therapeutic respite when I leave the crowd and pray and meditate in private. Intense agony instantly took up refuge in my aching heart. That was one of the most frightening moments in my life.

Thankfully, my father survived this scare, and he lived another thirty years. His road to recovery was arduous and wrought with extreme challenges. I can still see him struggling to pick up a spoon to feed himself. He could not walk or talk or carry on any of the activities of daily living that we take for granted. I still marvel at the strength and fortitude it must have required for him to engage life on vastly different terms, embrace his new normal, and refuse to succumb to self-pity and depression. As his primary caretaker, I had a ringside seat that offered me glimpses of miracles that lifted him from the wheelchair he loathed to the self-sufficiency he craved. He persevered and worked his way back to a life of independence and vitality. Watching him graduate from invalid status to mobility and the capacity to manage his activities of daily living was a life lesson that opened my heart and connected me to my spiritual roots in ways I still cannot explain.

Yes, gratitude softens agony, but it offers us so much more. It is a state of mind and a way of life. It taps into our private reservoir of divinity, and it elevates us to levels of unspeakable joy in ways nothing else can. Our emotional and mental health status improves, and we are more productive personally and professionally. We are kind and caring, and we are motivated to strengthen relationships that materially affect our happiness.

Regardless of age or status people who consciously count life's blessings are more joyful, exhibit a positive outlook on life, and are far more engaged in the high-level energy of hopefulness. Fellowship matters greatly, not just being in the company of other living organisms but appreciating and feeling connected to them. Whether in the presence of another individual or a stately oak tree with sprawling branches that seem to defy gravity with their gracefulness, a thankful heart elevates us. Whether it is a starlit night or the moon peeking over a mountaintop, the feeling of being connected to something greater than us is fertile soil that breeds gratitude.

When life burdens us with toxic thoughts and emotions such as envy, greed, or jealousy, when pain caused by others weighs us down, when we are exhausted by the challenges of life, we can summon the internal power of gratitude to rescue us. It is one of our most potent weapons, and it permeates every dimension of our being.

Historically, gratitude resided in the domain of morality and was dutifully drilled into us by the clergy, but science now acknowledges that its benefits exist outside the context of religion. Its emotional and social implications are evident in all walks of life. When we are grateful, we behave in ways that support group harmony, we move ourselves closer to the great commandment to love the unlovable, and we exhibit goodwill toward others. Gratitude allows us to care deeply, freely share our possessions with others, and grow in ways that benefit us and the universe.

When we exist in a state of perpetual gratitude, we are far less committed to the idea that material wealth brings happiness. As a youngster, I dreamed of getting a good education, working hard, and amassing wealth. I often felt that having more money to buy more things would bring me more happiness. While shopping served as therapy for me during my young adulthood, I came to realize it was a two-edged sword. The pleasant moments were short lived, and the mounting bills and high interest rates on my credit cards became sources of stress. Money does not buy happiness, and purchasing a new dress does not hold a candle to the exhilaration of living in a space immersed in gratefulness and thankfulness.

Journaling is an excellent way to grow in gratitude. Over the years, I started several journals. I never developed this as a part of my routine, but even my intermittent attempts afford me moments of sheer joy when I stumble upon one of the many journals I tucked away here and there. They offer irreplaceable insight into who I was at specific moments in my life, and when I read them, I am reminded of the innate value of journaling as a disciplined practice. Although I remain inconsistent, I journal more frequently now, and I recommend this as a routine part of personal development rituals. When we see our burdens, challenges, and opportunities through the magical eyes of gratitude and the immeasurable benefits of hindsight, life offers us a level of joy that provides much needed respite.

Gratitude is perhaps the most passionate and transformative source of energy in the human psyche. When it is integrated into our lifestyles, it is experienced in multisensory and multidimensional ways that lead us to true alignment with God. When we see the world through the eyes of gratitude, life is good and continues to get even better as we grow and expand our hearts to include myriad blessings bestowed upon us through the aging process. The gift of years can be sweet, exciting, and invigorating provided we allow ourselves to release the unresolved pain that binds us. With the release, we become more conscious of our spirituality and our sacred purpose.

God's exceptional gift of life is the ultimate expression of His all-encompassing, everlasting, and unadulterated love for us. It is up to us to make the most of this precious gift by relying on our faith to guide the earnest pursuit of our high callings. Embedded in this pursuit is gratefulness and thankfulness. When our worldview includes these two extremely relevant elements, life has meaning and is filled with lofty purpose. We are required as beneficiaries of the purest form of love to learn how to pay this blessing forward by caring for and serving others. This is what the gift of life is all about. As we explore the gamut of how meaning and sacred purpose show themselves in the individualized boundaries of our humanness, we grow spiritually. As we embrace the responsibility to use our unique gifts and talents to serve others, our hearts expand. In the context of this reality, there is unlimited potential that can be realized only when we see the universe and everything in it through a lens of gratitude.

> Give thanks in all circumstances, for this is the will of
> God in Christ Jesus for you. (1 Thessalonians 5:18 ESV)

Happiness

We all want to be happy. No one chooses misery, but realizing and sustaining the coveted state of constant glee is nearly impossible.

I recently read an article that included a litany of things people could do to summon happiness such as listening to music, visiting friends, dancing, and singing. I enjoy all of these, and they do lift my spirits, but I have come to appreciate the distinct difference between situational happiness and interpersonal happiness.

When I am in the company of people I love and respect, I am happy. When I taste my daughter-in-law's banana pudding, I am happy. A great movie, or traveling to exotic places, or spending time communing with nature are pleasurable experiences that elicit situational happiness. If the external circumstances surrounding these examples change, my level of happiness is instantly adversely affected. Interpersonal happiness, on the other hand, is a spiritual experience. It is rooted in the basic human need to belong and is realized through fellowship and relationship building. When we give and receive love, when we feel needed and appreciated, when we comprehend that we are part of something greater than ourselves, or when we have strong social connections our level of happiness is far deeper than situational. The strong bonds of closeness offer us a sense of worthiness and inspires creativity and ingenuity.

When life has meaning and we are contributing to the common good happiness abounds and we enjoy a general sense of wellbeing. God's holy intention of happiness is available to everyone, but there is no generic route to arrive at this state of being. We all have unique starting points, so our journeys are tailored to who we are and the spiritual lessons we need to learn. We were born to fulfill a sacred purpose, and our experiences are designed to bring us in contact with teachable moments. Unfortunately, these moments are not always pleasant, but there is always a valuable lesson to be learned.

It breaks my heart to hear that someone has been mistreated. I do not fully understand but I no longer question the fairness of the universe. I accept that we are enclosed in our unique multisensory and multidimensional packages by divine design. None of it is accidental. We are exactly as we should be at this moment. When we see our lives as teachable moments, we can objectively assess our situations from the perspective of meaningfulness and purpose. Only then are we able to experience interpersonal happiness.

We should exist in a continuous state of self-assessment. *Is the inner me in harmony with what the outer me presents to others? If not, will my disharmony and dishonesty prevent me from contributing to the overarching goal set forth in God's commandment to love above all else? Can I embrace the moment and find solace and enjoyment? Can I make the most of the gift of life? Am I on track to learn the necessary life lessons to be a positive change agent in my circle of influence?* Our happiest moments come when the response to questions such as these is a resounding yes. No matter how dire the present situation might be, when we are at peace with ourselves and others, our emotional integrity and happiness will offer wise counsel and support us as we move through life's valley experiences. When we insist on living in love, happiness will reign.

As a youngster, I was constantly searching for a part-time job because I had this strong internal drive for independence and I saw earning money as the quickest path to achieving it. This aggravated my mom immensely because we lived in a rural area and she incurred the inconvenience of transporting me to and from these jobs usually in the city. It aggravated my dad for a different reason; he thought my quest for money and independence would compete with his dream of my going to college. Each of my menial, low-paying jobs paid huge dividends though in terms of lessons learned, which I carry with me today. Despite my parents' concerns, I remember being happy with my jobs. I wanted to earn my independence.

My mom had a serious germ phobia, so our house had to be nearly spotless all the time. Having younger siblings, I was skilled in the art of caretaking and housecleaning. Armed with my impressive resume as an experienced babysitter and maid, I successfully convinced people to hire me. From my limited perspective, I was utilizing my skills and making my dream of independence come true. Although intermittent and short lived, the menial jobs offered me a sense of self-worth. The external stimulus sufficiently rewarded the internal drive, and for a few brief moments, it brought harmony to this teenager whose worldview was limited and perhaps too focused on making money. The lifelong lesson of this story is that no matter how misguided my parents considered my dream to be, I was at peace with my decision because it came from a place deep in me. As a result, authentic contentment and happiness were my rewards.

Years later as I was leading a workshop session a participant asked me, *"How do I suddenly begin to expect happiness when all my life I heard negative voices telling me I was a nobody who would never amount to anything?"* That was an outstanding question. No doubt it is initially hard to shift the internal dialogue that shapes our worldview and also plants seeds of unworthiness. The psychological shift from bracing for the worst to expecting happiness is a process that takes significant effort and time. Hurt people hurt others. The damage thrust upon us by damaged people is often generational and rooted in familial relationships. At some point though, we must find the courage to replace the negative voices with conversations that support our self-worth and dignity. As we move closer to a Christ-centered lifestyle, spiritual wholeness slowly replaces the negative voices.

Happiness is glaringly intentional. It is a choice we make that changes everything for the better. When we engage in activities, experiences, and thought processes that are pleasurable and satisfying, we invite happiness into our lives. At the moment we decide that we deserve to be happy, something remarkable begins to take shape deep within us that elevates every dimension of our lives. With prayer, a deepened fellowship and relationship with God, and a commitment to service, we can find happiness in unexpected places. When doubts reappear, we can push them away with feelings of gratitude and positive thoughts. Eventually, we will reprogram our subconscious minds to accept rather than sabotage the happiness that presents itself to us. The secret to happiness is desiring it, expecting it, manifesting it, nurturing it, and showing gratitude when it appears. By giving it enough space to grow and thrive, we choose contentment, wellbeing, and wholeness.

> Delight yourself in the Lord, and he will give you the desires of your heart. (Psalm 37:4 ESV)

Chapter 6 Important Points

- Your worldview is the lens through which you interpret the universe and everyone and everything in it. The fundamentals of your worldview are determined by internal and external factors.
- You experience a wide range of emotions that are either fear-based or love-based.
- If your worldview is fear-based, you are guided by negative emotions such as anger, control, envy, greed, jealousy, resentment, and self-hatred.
- Fear-based emotions have the power to derail dreams, dominate lives, ruin relationships, and sabotage efforts to focus on your sacred purpose.
- If your worldview is love-based, you are guided by positive emotions such as compassion, forgiveness, gratitude, and happiness.
- Love-based emotions have the power to move you closer to a Christ-centered lifestyle.
- Happiness is intentional. It is a conscious choice you make that changes everything for the better.
- You can reprogram your subconscious mind to accept rather than sabotage opportunities to experience happiness.
- When life has meaning and you are contributing to the common good happiness abounds and you enjoy a general sense of wellbeing.
- God's holy intention of happiness is available to everyone.
- Happiness is experienced from a situational or interpersonal perspective. Situational happiness depends on circumstances and events. Interpersonal happiness is a spiritual experience. It is rooted in the basic human need to belong and is realized through fellowship and relationship building.
- With prayer, a deepened fellowship and relationship with God, and a commitment to service you can find happiness in unexpected places.
- When you decide that you deserve to be happy something remarkable begins to take shape deep within you that elevates every dimension of your life.
- The secret to happiness is desiring it, expecting it, manifesting it, nurturing it, and showing gratitude when it appears. By giving it enough space to grow and thrive, you choose contentment, wellbeing, and wholeness.

7

LEARN TO LOVE AS GOD LOVES

God commands us to love above all else. The process of growing whole relies heavily on our heartfelt capacity to love as God loves—unconditionally. As we learn to love unconditionally and implement our newly acquired skills, the quality of our relationships will noticeably improve, and God's Word will be revealed to us in new and creative ways. One of our greatest challenges as Christians is to apply the emotional experience we enjoy in the sanctuary on Sunday mornings to our lives on Monday through Saturday. Unconditional love is not an emotion; it is a spiritual practice. It is an action phrase. It is the practical application of God's Word.

Unconditional Love

While feelings related to emotional love come to us naturally, unconditional love does not. Through spiritual growth, this type of love begins to take root in our hearts. Fellowship and relationship quality is significantly enhanced, and we require more of ourselves. For example, when our emotions devolve into a negative space, we can choose to linger there or evaluate the situation through the eyes of love. We can ask ourselves, *What is the cause of my ill feelings? What part did I play in creating the situation that led to my present discomfort? What steps can I take to find the answers I seek?* By taking this compassionate approach, we open our hearts and minds to the possibility of blameless resolution. No matter the challenge, loving without judgment will always produce the most desirable outcome. We can employ this same strategy to any circumstance. It does not matter if the issue at hand is individual and personal or corporate and public. Blameless resolution demonstrates godly love, which is unconditional.

The human spirit cries out for continuous growth. We have a moral imperative to express love through fellowship and service and to allow our experiences to transform us from physical, egotistical selves to spiritual, Christ-centered selves. All growth is rooted in this glaring reality. As we age, the lessons we receive and retain are tailor made to support individual growth and development in ways that promote oneness with God and wholeness with self and others.

Sacred purpose begins with a commitment to unconditional love. There is no expectation here, and there are no demands. There is no selfishness, fear, or need to control. Unconditional love is the generous outpouring of our best to the universe always for the greater good with no particular motivation other than the purest expression of care and compassion. When we learn to love on this level, we have grown beyond the normal human emotions that stem from romantic love, enduring love, familial love, and even self-love.

Unconditional love springs from the God in us, the Holy Spirit. It is the single most important medium of our transformation. It is the essence of who we are and why we were born. Through our various expressions of unconditional love, we eagerly explore possibilities, realize our potential, and begin to fulfill our sacred purpose. When our view of the world encompasses emotions on this elevated level, we expand the collective human experience and thrive in spiritual abundance.

Unconditional love is the deepest and highest of all types of love. Rather than a feeling, it is a state of being. Some of the character traits of this love are benevolence, commitment to serve others, compassion, kindness, sacrifice, and selflessness. Unconditional love is a lifestyle; it permeates our worldview and is the truest definition of God's love for humankind. The sacrifice Jesus Christ made on the cross for us is the ultimate example of unconditional love.

The biblical story of David and Jonathan is a beautiful example of this Christian principle. We see the mandate to love your neighbor as yourself in 1 Samuel 18:1 (ESV): "As soon as he had finished speaking to Saul, the soul of Jonathan was knit to the soul of David, and Jonathan loved him as his own soul."

Later in this same chapter, we see Jonathan stripping himself of the regalia that distinguished him as crown prince and giving them to David. He willingly shared his robe and his armor including his sword, bow, and belt. At one point, Jonathan even warned David of King Saul's intention to kill him. These heart-wrenching gestures of selflessness present Jonathan as a man who understood his sacred purpose as demonstrated through his unconditional love. When we study the relationship between David and Jonathan, we can see sacred purpose revealing itself in myriad ways.

During Jesus's time on earth, the Jews had created and accumulated hundreds of laws. By some accounts, they numbered more than six hundred. Certain religious leaders tried to distinguish between major and minor laws while others argued that they were equally binding. Jesus's response to the question of which of the laws was the greatest clearly demonstrated the relationship between unconditional love and sacred purpose.

> And you shall love the Lord your God with all your heart and with all your soul and with all your mind and with all your strength. You shall love your neighbor as yourself. There is no other commandment greater than these. (Mark 12:30–31 ESV)

We learn what unconditional love means through relationships—our relationship with God, our relationship with ourselves, and our relationships with others. We are not capable of realizing and expressing unconditional love without holy assistance. We learn to love unconditionally by first wholeheartedly giving and receiving the emotional love that naturally flows from one human being to another.

Think about the number of times you use the word *love* in a day. Sometimes, we say, "I love pizza," "I love your dress," "I love my parents," and "I love you" with little emotion and often without giving any thought to the profound importance of the word. Clearly, the love we have for pizza and the love we have for our parents are not the same, but both statements could be true because they represent different nuances of the concept of love. For centuries, poets, musicians, and psychologists have attempted to define love with varying degrees of success. For me, the following verse is the gold standard for the definition of love.

> Love is patient and kind. Love is not jealous or boastful or proud or rude. It does not demand its own way. It is not irritable, and it keeps no record of being wronged. It does not rejoice about injustice but rejoices whenever the truth wins out. Love never gives up, never loses faith, is always hopeful, and endures through every circumstance. (1 Corinthians 13:4 NLT)

Love is far more than a warm and fuzzy feeling; it is a decision to give our best to someone or something. Unconditional love functions on an even higher level. It requires forethought, holy intention, and selfless sacrifice. Jesus referred to unconditional love in various ways throughout His ministry. Practically speaking, it gives rather than receives, it does not keep score, it means putting the welfare of others ahead of our comfort, and it is the model for Christian living.

Tucked in every true love story is our first glimpse of unconditional love, which comes from the essence of our humanity, our souls. God is unconditional love, and the lesson He most wants us to learn is to care for Him, for ourselves, and for each other deeply and generously offer fellowship and service. Unconditional love flows from the Creator directly to our souls. There are no rules, stipulations, or qualifiers, and there is no way to earn unconditional love. God loves us unconditionally no matter our station in life. If we simply open our hearts and minds and allow Him to show us the unadulterated beauty of His unconditional love, the promised-land experience of spiritual abundance will flourish.

Learning to love unconditionally is a complex, lifelong process that requires focused attention and intention. Romantic love, enduring love, familial love, and self-love are necessary precursors to unconditional love. Each of these types of love has specific lessons for us to grasp as we move closer to appreciating and understanding love on the deepest and highest level.

Romantic Love

Romantic love is perhaps the most exciting and most passionate of all the various types. Do you remember the feeling of ecstasy you experienced when you found who you considered to be the one for you? It felt like you were floating. Life was completely blissful. Everything was perfect, and nothing could bring you off that cloud. The butterflies in your stomach and the quickened heartbeat when he or she walked through the door were normal occurrences during the early stages of the relationship. The two of you were almost inseparable, and whenever you were apart, you spent hours dreaming about the next time you would be together. Romantic love is beautiful, magical, and awe inspiring. This glimpse into ecstasy is a precursor to what is available as we grow in love and expand our hearts and minds beyond the physical dimension.

But romantic love can be a two-edged sword. The decision to fall in love with someone should be considered with sacred purpose in mind. Otherwise, lust can falsely imitate love and cause great pain and suffering. For example, David's adulterous relationship with Bathsheba led to murder and generations of severe family dysfunction. Samson's passion for Delilah led to his eyes being gouged out and imprisonment.

Under the umbrella of romantic love, we see versions that run the gamut from innocent and naive fairytale love to the lifetime commitment of love expressed in a marriage. We often get lost in romantic fairytales about goddesses and their loving gods who rescued the object of their affection from danger. Marital bliss soon followed, and they lived happily ever after. We used our imagination to become the god or goddess, and it was hard sometimes for us to distinguish between our realistic world and our fantasy world. Fairytales offered early glimpses into the unknown world of romance.

One of my favorite modern fairytale love story heroes is Shrek, a green ogre who discovers that the scheming Lord Farquaad has invaded his beloved swamp with hundreds of different creatures. Shrek set out with a loud, obnoxious donkey to persuade Farquaad to give his swamp back. During the negotiation, an interesting deal was made between them. Farquaad, who wanted to become the king, sent Shrek to rescue Princess Fiona, who was waiting for her one true love. Once they head back with

Fiona, though, it becomes apparent that she and Shrek are falling in love. In the end, they marry and produce several little Shreks.

Over the past eighteen years, I watched this movie and its sequels with my grandchildren, and I still get lost in the romantic backdrop every time. As I observed them being swept up in the movie, I realized that my grandchildren were learning about romantic love much the same way I had—by way of books and TV and their happily ever after themes. Fairytale love stories offer children a harmless illusion of love and in many instances serve as the catalyst for their dreams of becoming gods or goddesses or even eventually falling in love.

Enduring Love

Over time, romantic love evolves into enduring love. On this level, love has a much higher calling than butterflies and quickened heartbeats. Enduring love demands effort beyond emotional expressions. Eventually, the butterflies depart, and the flutters are replaced with much deeper connections. This supernatural strengthening of fellowship between two people lasts sometimes for decades. The promise of permanence and the feeling of loving someone who loves you back is enhanced by a sense of worthiness.

Enduring love is not hormone-driven or motivated by passion, nor is it related to the thrill of purchasing a new dress or the excitement of accomplishing a major milestone. This type of love grows deeper and stronger with time. It overlooks human flaws and missteps. It reveals itself in unexciting, everyday experiences such as sitting with your partner as they wait for a doctor's appointment or offering encouraging words when life hurts. Enduring love does not care what you look like and is forgiving and flexible when necessary.

Enduring love is willing to bear all things, and it perseveres even during the worst circumstances. It is patient beyond compare, and it quietly tolerates life's disappointments and storms. When you suffer, enduring love shares the pain and offers hope and support. Even when there are few options to remedy the situation and all hope seems lost, enduring love persists. The biblical story of Abraham and Sarah reveals their enduring love for each other and for God as they awaited the fulfillment of His covenant promise. The epitome of this type of love is manifested in God's giving of His Son as a sacrifice for mankind's redemption.

Familial Love

Examples of familial love include husband and wife, parent and child, sibling, cousin, and other significant relationships that may not be connected by bloodline but are bound by care, compassion, and conscious decisions to share in each other's lives.

Many of today's family structures are complex and multifaceted and often bear little resemblance to the simpler nuclear model that includes husband, wife, and children. Nonetheless, the contribution, individual and societal value, and significance of the family gives it a special status unmatched by any other human-to-human relationship. Healthy familial love is deep, far reaching, and critical to the emotional wellbeing of its members. Our sense of self-esteem and self-worth is to a great extent determined by family bonds that are strong, respectful, loyal, and unbroken and are characterized by acceptance, affection, and attachment.

I have finally slowed down enough to really enjoy people who have been an intimate part of my life from the outset. My siblings and I resemble each other physically and in our mannerisms, voice tones, value systems, health challenges, and thought processes. I must have known this all along, but the blessing of longevity gives us the time to fully appreciate and explore each other's nuances in new and exciting ways. I am having fun rediscovering the revered strength of bloodline connections, and I am reveling in the reality of this lifelong spiritual bond that is uniquely ours.

As children of parents who were both loners, we too are loners by nature. We enjoy people while we are in their presence, but in general, each of us prefers solitude and being alone with our thoughts. As expected, we left our childhood home and established families, engaged in careers, and made contributions to society. Yet as our lives have circled back around and we are getting reacquainted, I am amazed at the extensive similarities that remain intact. Life experiences and time have changed us in many ways, but in the ways that really matter, we are fundamentally who we were as siblings running around in the backyard playing hide-and-seek. Family trees have deep roots that support expansion and independence, yet the bonds are so intimately interwoven that no amount of time or distance can weaken them.

The role of wife and mother has taught me so much about familial love and its amazing durability and strength. I married my childhood sweetheart, so we grew up together all the while pursuing our careers and parenting three wonderful children. Along the way, we have said and done things that have offended each other, but the seriousness of our commitment and the depth of our love has brought us to spiritual oneness.

With the birth of each of my children, my heart expanded in ways I did not know was possible. Our firstborn came into my life ten months after marriage at the young age of twenty. I still had so much growing up to do, but through trial and error, she taught me many of the intricacies of motherhood. In fact, I believe she taught me as much about life and what really matters as I taught her. Spiritually, she is an interesting mix of her parents. She is strong willed and independent like me, and she values emotional and social interconnectedness like her father. Like both of us, she is quite assertive, internally motivated, and results oriented.

When our second child was born, I was more mature, and I better understood the role of motherhood. Our son is so much like his father that I can hardly find me anywhere. The personality, physical features, thought processes, and worldviews of the two of them are so similar. He was his own person from the beginning, and while he was always well mannered and respectful, he taught me that despite our many "counseling" sessions that he was intent on doing things his way.

I was a seasoned mother by the time our youngest arrived. For the most part, she enjoys being the baby in the family, and her demeanor and personality are perfectly suited for that status. As I am, she is more aloof and less socially connected than her siblings are. She abided by the rules, and she was far more focused on scholarly pursuits than her sister and brother were.

I marvel at how they—the only three people in the universe with their unique gene pool—can have distinctly different personalities. Their pursuit of meaning and sacred purpose reflects these differences in amusing and interesting ways. I am so proud of how much they love and respect each other. During extremely rare disagreements, they are spiritually broken until they reconcile, and their loyalty to each other is absolute. My husband

and I are blessed with five grandchildren each of whom has expanded our hearts even further. My roles as wife, mother, and grandmother have given me firsthand experience with learning to love as God loves.

Friendship Love

The version of love that is embedded in true friendship is one of God's greatest gifts. This special bond is rooted in genuine acceptance, caring, and respect. Friends are loyal to each other; they enjoy each other's company, they teach, encourage, share burdens and secrets, and they correct each other when necessary. The special chemistry friends share is a jewel of immense spiritual value. The opportunities for spiritual growth that friends offer each other make it one of the deepest and strongest human bonds.

In the delightful biblical story of Ruth and Naomi, we find a rare combination of deep friendship and loyalty. On the surface, the only thing these two women appeared to have in common was the fact that Ruth had married one of Naomi's sons. Their cultural, ethnic, and religious backgrounds were different, and their age variance spanned two generations. When you look deeper into the relationship though, it is easy to understand their rare bond of love, which seems to have been built on mutual suffering. Both had lost everything when their husbands died. With no men to rely on, they learned to depend on each other for safety and survival.

At one point, Naomi urged Ruth to go back to her homeland. But Ruth said,

> Do not urge me to leave you or to return from following you. For where you go, I will go and where you lodge, I will lodge. Your people shall be my people, and your God my God. Where you die, I will die, and there will I be buried. May the Lord do so to me and more also if anything but death parts me from you. (Ruth 1:16–17 ESV)

Self-Love

Embedded deep in self-love are the critical components of self-compassion and self-esteem. Learning to love yourself is required before your splintered soul can begin its healing process.

Nobody knows our deep secrets better than we do. Much of what we keep in the cluttered closets of our souls is there for good reason. There are things about us that we do not want anyone else to know, not even our most intimate partners. The rawness of this private view often leads to feelings of regret and remorse and can hinder our efforts to reconcile broken relationships. Learning to love ourselves despite our messes is an important step in our efforts to grow whole.

Self-love requires forgiveness. We learn to forgive others by forgiving ourselves. Over the years, we added layers of façade to the false personae we created to hide our true selves from the world. As we peel those layers away, something quite spiritual happens—we become more compassionate and loving toward ourselves and others.

Self-love requires courage. Facing the deep secrets of our pasts is no easy task, and it is not for the fainthearted. Courage is an important attribute of good character we all desire but many lack. Whether enjoying a good Bible story about Moses leading his people out of slavery in Egypt or a fairytale about Shrek rescuing Princess Fiona, we love examples of courage. When we find the courage to confront the fears that haunt us, we demonstrate self-compassion and we raise our level of self-esteem through self-love.

Once you learn to love yourself, your spiritual energy level rises and messages of love freely flow from you to others, to the universe, and to God. The Bible assures us that we please God when we love. The karmic effect of love is infinite. The more we love, the more love we receive. As this love takes root and blossoms, we get closer to understanding and expressing unconditional love. Our attraction to love is so strong because we were created as revelations of God's love. When our love expresses itself in ways that support joy, peace and harmony, we elevate our spiritual energy and we become cocreators of unconditional love.

God's Love in Us

God's love for humanity is unconditional. It is without limitation and it has no boundaries. It is love all by itself because God's nature is pure love. Creation is the ultimate demonstration of God's unconditional love. Christ dying on the cross to offer us a pathway back to oneness with God is the ultimate demonstration of unconditional love. The Holy Spirit residing in us and comforting, guiding, and teaching us is the ultimate demonstration of unconditional love.

The process of growing whole is filled with opportunities to learn to love as God loves. As we assume traits of the character and image of God, we become more Christlike and our lifestyle is transformed in ways that mirror the divinity in us. God is involved in every aspect of our lives, and the more we rely on His guidance, the easier it is for us to experience His presence.

Janet, a former coworker, was known to have serious anger issues. She retired five years ago and quickly became a couch potato. Even before the advent of the COVID-19 pandemic, she chose to spend her time week after week in almost total isolation. The highlight of her day was watching reality shows on TV. She tried to convince herself that this do-nothing pattern was a sufficient postretirement life strategy.

Over time though, the isolation became too much for her to bear. She was lonely, and she started to display signs of depression. Her condition worsened to the point that her children became extremely concerned. They eventually intervened and sought the professional help of a therapist to address the unresolved anger and the suspected depression. She was diagnosed with major depressive disorder, but after about seven months of therapy, she was feeling better. She had acquired new skills for coping with her anger, and she was proactively addressing her depression through strict adherence to a multidisciplinary treatment plan.

One day during a phone conversation, Janet confided in me that she had experienced periodic hallucinations and had gotten dangerously close to committing suicide. In her words, "I could see the dark clouds slowly closing in on me telling me to end my life." She is a woman of strong faith, and throughout her treatment, she fasted, meditated, and prayed. She is certain she heard the voice of God one evening telling her to read seven scriptures repeatedly for seven days. Although she appreciated the professional help she received, she is convinced that God intervened on her behalf and saved her life.

To show her gratitude, she became a volunteer at a local hospice. While she still indulges in her reality shows, she does not allow that guilty pleasure to interfere with her volunteering. She is happy, and her life has new meaning; her sacred purpose is manifesting itself in rewarding ways. According to her, she has not thought about suicide since she became a volunteer.

The God of love created humanity with the expectation that we learn to love as He loves. In a broken world, our mission is to do the work required to transform our hearts in ways that reflect His love in us. Jesus made it clear that no other commandment surpassed the mandate to love. Learning how to live out this directive is a lifelong pursuit that is uniquely individual and often complex. Just as we are strategic about reducing stress to protect our physical health, we should be equally strategic about increasing love to protect our spiritual health. The free-flowing energy of unconditional love elevates our experiences and reminds us of our connection to God. As we earnestly continue efforts toward growing whole, the miracles that spring forth from love reveal themselves in amazing ways.

There are so many opportunities to express God's love in us, but here are some ideas that come to mind. I encourage you to add your favorite examples to this list.

- Forgiving someone who hurt you deeply.
- A wife giving up on fixing her husband and accepting him for who he is.
- Friends bringing a paralyzed man to Jesus, and when they could not get close because of the large crowd, cutting a hole in the roof and dropping him down at Jesus's feet (Mark 2:1–12).
- Admitting when you are wrong and saying, "I'm sorry."
- A husband thinking his wife is beautiful after sixty years of marriage.
- Spending quality time with someone who needs a friend.

- Never giving up on wayward sons or daughters yet finding the strength to hold them accountable and administer tough love when necessary.
- Telling her the dress does not make her look fat when she asks.
- Rejoicing when others are happy and mourning when they are sad.
- Cuddling a baby.

Chapter 7 Important Points

- Growing whole relies heavily on your capacity to love as God loves—unconditionally.
- Unconditional love is the deepest and highest form of love.
- The character traits of unconditional love include benevolence, commitment to serve others, compassion, kindness, sacrifice, and selflessness.
- You learn to love unconditionally by experiencing and expressing human, emotional love. Examples include romantic love, enduring love, familial love, friendship love, and self-love.
- God's love for humanity is unconditional.
- The process of growing whole is filled with opportunities to learn to love as God loves.
- Jesus Christ made it clear that no other commandment surpassed the mandate to love. Christians are required to love God totally and without conditions and love others as themselves.
- The free-flowing energy of unconditional love elevates your experiences and reminds you of your holy connection to God.
- There are myriad opportunities to express unconditional love.
- The human spirit cries out for continuous growth. You have a moral imperative to express love through fellowship and service and to allow your experiences to transform you from a physical, egotistical being to a spiritual, Christ-centered being.
- God commands you to love above all else.

PART IV

LIFE GETS BETTER

8

CONSCIOUS AGING

So we do not lose heart, though our outer self is wasting away, our inner self is being renewed day by day. For this light momentary affliction is preparing for us an eternal weight of glory beyond all comparison. (2 Corinthians 4:16–17 ESV)

Conscious aging is essential to lifelong vitality and wellbeing. Old age is not an affliction thrust on those of us who have survived for seven-plus decades. It is not an excuse to abandon our creativity, curiosity, or our sense of adventure and discovery. The universal, God-ordained responsibility to find meaning and sacred purpose applies to every stage of life and there is no age restriction. Old age is in fact a well-earned status that should be received and revered with a sense of gratitude and thankfulness. As we identify unique ways to embody and embrace our true roles as wisdom teachers, life offers exciting and previously unforeseen opportunities to serve.

I regularly hear elders say that they have earned the right to do nothing if they choose. I agree and disagree. At this golden age, we have tolerated and toiled, and we have given so much of ourselves that sometimes it feels there is nothing left to give. We have endured and turned the other cheek to maintain harmony and peace. We have earned the right to engage life at a slower pace and we have earned the right to attend to some of the items on our bucket lists.

I agree that do-nothing days are a welcome relief and that we should indulge ourselves in this satisfying luxury periodically. But I disagree that this should become a way of life for those who reach the sacred stage of elderhood. As seniors who are blessed with longevity, there is no spiritual justification to simply rest on our laurels. We do not have permission to settle into a state of self-centered lingering and lounging. Far too much has been invested in us, and when we consider the human condition, we see there is much work to do. We must pay forward some of our blessings.

We elders are in a unique position to make positive contributions by unleashing the sage wisdom we have accumulated. The spiritual growth mandate requires commitment and engagement with the expectation that we continue to glorify God through service to humankind.

There are stimulating outlets for the academic and experiential knowledge and skills we possess. Life lessons have endowed us with foresight, insight, and hindsight and well-honed talents that can help reframe the conversation about aging. Gone are the days when elders should allow themselves to be unwittingly marginalized in what looks like a youth-oriented world. It is incumbent on each of us to make our presence and value known in ways that contribute to the common good and move us closer to oneness with God and wholeness with self and others.

Conscious aging is a decision to remain engaged and continue to grow. It involves taking deliberate steps to live productive lives while successfully coping with the challenges inherent in this stage of our journey. Conscious aging means having a plan to ensure success.

To some extent, aging is an automatic, biological process that occurs without attention or forethought. As long as we breathe, we will age. It is possible to never delve into the personal, community, and corporate implications of longevity beyond the knowledge that you are just another day older. Embedded in each stage of life from birth to death are obstacles and opportunities that depending on how we respond to them define us and expand or restrict our growth.

Conscious aging requires us to develop a contemplative spirit and a willingness to engage life on a higher level than most people are inclined to do. It requires us to examine our lives and do the inner work necessary to let go of vestiges of earlier versions of ourselves that no longer serve us.

Humans are five-sensory, multisensory, and multidimensional beings. We experience life on so many integrated levels simultaneously that it is hard to know which dimension we are operating in at any given time. Since everything is infinitely and intimately interconnected, it really does not matter which dimension is dominant at the moment. The major benefit to understanding that we experience life from varying perspectives is the innate comprehension of the need for synchronicity. Everything that happens in our lives affects all aspects of our being. For example, a physical illness could have psychological, emotional, social, or financial implications for life balance and long-term safety and security. A financial setback will affect our emotional wellbeing. If our vocational skills are no longer relevant in the workplace, our sense of self-worth and intellectual value may be undermined.

We live in a world that is sufficiently transparent, but our youthful attitudes and views often drown out the subtle, long-term messages. As we age, the simplicity of life comes more clearly into focus and we begin to understand that God's spiritual essence permeates everything—events, nature, people. To see Him though, we must be in a heart space and mindset of elevated consciousness. Our sincere commitment to continuous personal development moves us closer to this functional level. Those who are committed to the idea of aging consciously rather than aging by default refuse to tolerate a mediocre existence or spend time lingering in thoughts about unrealized dreams, unresolved feelings, or "what-ifs." We hold ourselves and others in our circle of influence accountable for accepting nothing less than the best of what we have to offer. Even in our most private moments our Christ-centeredness must prevail and we must insist on noble pursuits such as authenticity, meaningfulness, and living on purpose for purpose .

One of the few guarantees in life is that change is continuous and inevitable. Everything and everyone we know and love will change whether we like it or not. While change comes easier for some than it does for others, how we handle change will make the difference between our living well, aging consciously, and just existing. Living well means engaging life from a love-based perspective and actively pursuing opportunities to grow.

The alternative is clear; you simply age. In this scenario, you continue to breathe and exist. You go through the motions like a zombie feeling numb and doing what everyone else in your age bracket does. You accept a quality of life that is devoid of meaning and sacred purpose. You allow complacency to rob you of opportunities to expand your vision of what is possible. You may waste energy and time gossiping about others to make your uninspired life appear more tolerable. To fill the unsatisfied holes in your soul, you continue to focus on accumulation and consumption. You never outgrow reliance on fear-based emotions such as anger, control, envy, greed, jealousy, resentment, and self-hatred. Rather than focusing on practical ways to express love and pursue sacred purpose you indulge in negativity. This is the space where you are most comfortable because you have chosen not to grow and expand your heart and mind.

Growing whole on the other hand requires allowing the transition from youth to elderhood to elevate you beyond the physical to the spiritual. The decision to morph into the multisensory and multidimensional being ascribed by destiny will affect your existence profoundly. Those who honor the sanctity of life and comprehend its meaning and sacred purpose are blessed beyond measure. They are far more likely to witness a physical world filled with exciting adventures, magical moments, and levels of joy and peace that surpass human understanding.

Conscious aging is a decision to enter elderhood with a positive attitude and a sense of eagerness in anticipation of a future filled with exciting options. We have acquired a vast reservoir of resources to draw from, and we are finally in a position to let our imagination flourish unfettered by day-to-day obligations and responsibilities of our middle years.

There is an unmistakable connection between aging and spirituality. Time offers so many invaluable lessons. The transformation from egotistical self-centeredness to humility is often subtle. Quietly and without fanfare, we evolve in ways the youthful version of us would never have considered possible. If we live to see our eighty-fifth birthdays, we will have spent a little over 31,000 days on earth. This is a blessing reserved for only a few. With every breath, new opportunities unfold, and we get another step closer to the enlightened individuals we were created to become.

> Leading up to my fortieth birthday, I started to feel a sense of loss. I bought into the popular opinion that my life would begin to spiral downhill and that my previous pattern of ascension would suddenly shift to one of descension. I believed this downward trajectory would

continue until the grim reaper found me and took me out of my misery. I allowed the worldly notion of aging to penetrate my psyche and at least temporarily hold my aspirations and dreams hostage. I forgot God's promise in Psalm 92:12–14 (NIV).

The righteous will flourish like a palm tree, they will grow like a cedar of Lebanon; planted in the house of the Lord, they will flourish in the courts of our God. They will still bear fruit in old age; they will stay fresh and green.

One day, my boss, who was about fifteen years my senior, and I were discussing my feelings of dread. He offered words of solace that helped reshape my attitude toward aging. He said, "If you live right and make good decisions along the way, life gets noticeably better every decade." I have found this statement to be profound and true; life really does get better as we age and particularly when we learn to view the world through the lens of love. Each time I think about this story, I chuckle. I cannot believe I once considered forty to be old. Moses was eighty, and his brother, Aaron, was eighty-three when they made their demands to Pharoah.

For me, one of the most challenging aspects of aging has been the irreversible nature of unrealized dreams. To fully embrace elderhood without regrets, we must confront the dimmer realities that accompany it. Whether it is the dream job, the knight in shining armor, fame, or fortune, conscious aging requires us to come to grips with the inevitable truth that some of our youthful dreams will never be realized. Many of them were never destined to be realized because they were not in alignment with God's plan for our lives. Yes, dreams matter, and big dreams matter even more; they offer hope and supply the energy necessary to give life gusto. As we age though, it becomes clearer that no matter how focused we are, some items on our bucket lists were never meant to be there.

Although we are most familiar and most preoccupied with our physical features, that is not what drives and organizes our lives. We often falsely assess ourselves and others based on superficial matters such as facial features or physiques. We sometimes unconsciously value one human being over another using characteristics such as race or gender. In terms of what really matters from the perspective of meaning and sacred purpose though, nothing could be further from the truth. Conscious aging gives us a healthy perspective on life that supports our transition from the irrelevant to the relevant, from the insignificant to the significant.

Because we engage life primarily through our five physical senses, we sometimes misunderstand their value from an eternal perspective. As critical as these natural qualities are to our wellbeing, they pale in comparison to the attributes they assume when they are infused with the holiness of salvation and sanctification. As we are transformed from ego-centeredness to Christ-centeredness our five physical senses take on the multisensory capacities that accompany the lifelong sanctification process. They are, in effect, raised to multisensory status, which includes the infusion of the Holy Spirit. The tripartite essence of humankind—the body, soul, and spirit—relies on every available asset whether five-sensory, multisensory, or multidimensional to navigate life. Everything essential to human existence and growing whole falls in this tripartite essence. We are physical and material as well as spiritual and immaterial. In between is an invisible soul that binds the physical and the spiritual together and provides the foundation for oneness and wholeness. The entirety of our being must be organized around an unshakable faith in the all-knowing, all-powerful, and ever-present God of the universe who has masterfully created us to facilitate reconciliation and reunification. He has designed our life experiences to accommodate our predetermined time in the earthly realm and the lessons we need to learn in order to successfully pursue sacred purpose.

> I will be your God throughout your lifetime—until your hair is white with age. I made you, and I will care for you. I will carry you along and save you. (Isaiah 46:4 NLT)

Conscious Aging Plan

Many of us have financial plans to protect ourselves from unforeseen expenses and shelter our assets, but few of us have a conscious aging plan (CAP), which is of equal importance. The primary purpose of a CAP is to be proactive about preserving the lifestyle of our choosing. It will help keep us focused on our long-term goals and facilitate a periodic analysis of our activities.

If you are involved in something that you do not envision having relevance in your future, consider whether it is wise to continue expending energy on it. Your CAP should be a dynamic document. Journal your progress, and make the necessary adjustments as your life's circumstances change. Life happens, and your CAP should align with its realities. At a minimum, the CAP should include the following

- **A vision statement that details what your future looks like.**

Have a clear picture that includes such elements as where you will live and how you will spend your days. *Will you live near family? If so, does that require relocation? What lifestyle changes will you need to make now to support realization of your long-term vision? Will you become a world traveler or stay close to home?* Commit your vision statement to writing and refer to it often.

- **Outstanding goals you want to accomplish.**

Brush the dust off your bucket list. Evaluate each item to determine if it is still something you want to do. Prioritize your list, and make plans to enjoy it.

- **Specific strategies for continued spiritual growth.**

Objectively assess what your long-term spiritual growth goals are. Analyze where you are now, and identify the steps you need to take to reach your goals. Determine what sacred purpose means to you, and begin work in this important area.

- **Activities that keep your mind sharp.**

Challenge your brain. Take classes, do crossword puzzles, learn chess, read more, learn a foreign language. Identify specific things you will do, and produce a timeline for doing them where applicable.

- **Options for civic and community engagement and service.**

Volunteer to support a cause you believe in. This is an excellent way to strengthen social bonds and meet people with similar interests.

- **Health and wellness strategies.**

Develop a comprehensive fitness regimen. Move more, eat right, reduce stress, educate yourself about health promotion and disease prevention, spend time with nature, stay hydrated, get appropriate amounts of sleep, and maintain a positive attitude.

- **A close-knit social network.**

Identify the activities you will engage in to stay connected with people. Take classes, join an organization, pursue interesting hobbies, become a mentor.

- **Safety and security.**

Remove hazards from your home that could cause accidents such as loose carpeting, electrical cords, space heaters, and uneven flooring. Research the benefits of a medical alert system particularly if you live alone. Consider installing a security system for your home.

The Basic Biology of Aging

I am aware of the challenges of growing older. At age seventy-two, I live at least some of these trials every day. Those not intimately experienced by me exist in the bodies, souls, and spirits of people I know and love. While I witness them secondarily, they are up close, personal, and painstakingly real.

From a practical perspective, aging appears in myriad forms. Aches and pains come out of nowhere, and for some, regular bouts of grief from the loss of loved ones are common occurrences. We are often isolated and lonely, and physical infirmities that restrict movement and challenge our sense of wellbeing have become our new normal.

Unfortunately, aging is accompanied by some unavoidable realities.

Glaring reminders of the irreversible deterioration of our bodies are plentiful. Clogged arteries, kidney malfunction, weakened bladders, are just a few.

Yielding to a long-standing need to purge a filing cabinet behind my desk, I recently stumbled upon a folder labeled Elderhood-Comedic Stories. To my glee, it contained several articles that captured some of the more common attitudes teenagers and young adults have about elders. I must share their stereotypical responses with you. It gave me a chuckle, and I hope you find this list entertaining. Attitudes among young people about old people can include these.

- Always talking about dying
- Creepy, poorly dressed, smelly, and toothless
- Economic burdens on the family
- Focused on doctor visits, illnesses, and medications
- Grumpy, lonely, and mean
- Live in the past, no futuristic vision
- Memory loss
- Poor drivers who cause too many accidents
- Sick and in constant pain
- Unable to use computers and other modern technology
- Wrinkly, scaly, and gross looking

Yes, our bodies change as we age, and we must accept that. Our experiences confirm that our hearts and joints stiffen, brain tissue shrinks, digestion slows, eyes get cloudy, hearing lessens, airways narrow, lungs restrict, teeth and gums weaken, bones become brittle, skin gets rough and wrinkly, muscles and kidneys stiffen, sex drive fizzles, immune system becomes compromised, the bladder weakens, and our hormones—well, some decrease while others become imbalanced reducing their efficiency. For example, estrogen and testosterone levels drop. Insulin and glucagon, two hormones that regulate blood sugar levels, often function less effectively.

The body undergoes many changes as we age. The subtle messages that accompany these changes remind us that our time on earth is finite. On the other hand, something exciting and invigorating is occurring. Our spiritual essence is expanding and growing in ways that can happen only with the gift of years.

The physical challenges of aging pale in comparison to what we gain, and with proper self-care, elders often avoid or certainly delay the ill effects of aging. I think that the joys of youth are overrated and the spirituality of conscious aging is underrated.

Lifetimes of accumulating knowledge, understanding, and wisdom give us insight from a vantage point that youth cannot offer. We are experienced and resourceful. Our resilience is evident by our having survived decades of challenges. We are the beneficiaries of apprenticeships from expert craftsmen who learned their trades by refining processes until they reached near perfection. We did not have technology to give us immediate answers, so we developed critical thinking skills to solve problems. We are invaluable resources, but we must see ourselves in this light before others will.

People over sixty-five make up the fastest growing population group in the world. According to the *World Population Prospects: the 2019 Revision*, by 2050, one in six people in the world will be over age sixty-five. The United States Administration on Aging reports that by 2030, there will be approximately 72 million people aged sixty-five and older in America. Communities and governments are not prepared to address the unique challenges this will bring. As the population continues to age, the twenty-first century will usher in one of the most significant social transformations in history.

Input from people who possess experiential, intellectual, and intuitive knowledge related to aging is critical to the success of public policy discussions and planning strategies. The benefit of hindsight and wisdom should never be underestimated. While science provides invaluable information about the physical world, much of the insight into the spiritual world comes with age and experience. The physical and the spiritual dimensions of life are of critical importance to elders. For this reason alone, they should be included in brainstorming sessions and subsequent proposals. In this instance, quantifiable data and qualitative information are equally important. Decision makers need our feedback, and we must be poised to respond to them effectively and efficiently.

In the second half of life, we expand our worldview to include the redemptive work of the soul. There is so much value in this work, which is waiting for a suitable outlet. Part of our story should include using the experiences unique to elderhood to improve the quality of life for future elders. Conscious aging requires a willingness to assume an advisory role as younger, less experienced administrators and managers seek our input. When we say yes to opportunities to serve, we are doing God's work. We are breathing life into the holy mission of sacred purpose, and we are also breathing vitality into our souls.

Wisdom of the Lotus Plant

> Wisdom is with the aged; and understanding in length of days. (Job 12:12 ESV)

According to Eastern tradition, the lotus is a cherished and revered flower that serves as a powerful representation of human experiences. Growing naturally in ponds, the lotus begins life rooted deep in mud and scum. To blossom, it must patiently and diligently push through the murky water until it breaks the surface.

Its growth process mirrors the spiritual journey of human souls as they push through the mud and scum in their lives in search of meaning, purpose, and wisdom. No matter whom we appear to be, deep in our souls, there is much unfinished work. For unknown reasons, creation thrust us into the world. Rather than continuing to focus on the why, I try to remain attuned to opportunities to serve. The journey through the secular world is predestined for good reason, and spiritual transformation must occur within the limitations of this circumstance.

The symmetry of the lotus plant makes it a strikingly beautiful sight. Its diversity and vibrant coloration are noteworthy. The yellow lotus symbolizes spiritual ascension, the white lotus is associated with purity, the blue lotus represents wisdom, and the gold lotus conveys enlightenment. Flower enthusiasts all around the globe enjoy its beauty. This alone is sufficient reason for it to exist, but its greatest value lies in a far deeper purpose.

In many Eastern cultures, the lotus is considered sacred. According to popular folklore, in the Hindu culture, ancient gods and goddesses sat on lotus thrones. It is one of the eight symbols of Buddhism. In fact, Buddhas are often portrayed as sitting on lotus pedestals. The ancient Egyptians revered the lotus plant believing it could resurrect their dead. It is the national flower of India and Vietnam. In Western cultures, the lotus represents the search for the meaning of life. The symbolic relevance of this flower lies in what it represents. It continues to grow despite difficult conditions; it overcomes significant obstacles during the growth process, and it experiences daily struggles. It is a symbol of beauty, enlightenment, purity, rebirth, spirituality, and triumph. By the time we see the beautiful blooms, the lotus plant has withstood grueling conditions. Each night, it is fully submerged in murky water, but it emerges each morning as beautiful and vibrant as the day before.

I liken the experience of conscious aging to the lotus plant, which is a metaphor for life. Despite the challenges, daily struggles, the sometimes murky waters, and the messiness of life, we persevere toward enlightenment. The search for the meaning of life is a cornerstone of conscious aging and growing whole. Just as the lotus breaks through and connects to the sun, once we make a deliberate and direct connection to our ultimate life source, we blossom into the beautiful flower we were destined to be.

There are many qualities of conscious aging I admire—forgiveness, gratitude, kindness, love, patience, resilience, and perhaps most important of all, wisdom. At the heart of conscious aging lies a decision to cultivate these qualities. Longevity is a privilege reserved for a small percentage of the population. Whether it is experienced as a blessing or curse depends on several factors. Aging is as much a cultural and environmental process, as it is a biological process. Global attitudes and practices differ greatly, and they significantly impact experiences related to aging. Some cultures venerate their elders while others honor and revere them. In societies where the aged are celebrated and highly respected, wisdom and life experiences are passed down and familial roots grow deep from one generation to the next. By comparison, in societies where the status of youth is idolized and elders become invisible and unimportant, family trees, legacies, and even finely honed crafts are unnecessarily deposited in graveyards as we bury our loved ones. Sage wisdom is not preserved, and future generations are denied the benefit of their family heritages.

My mother was an outstanding cook. Her God-ordained skills far exceeded what you learn in cooking classes. There were no written recipes as all the knowledge associated with her inviting, scrumptious dishes resided in her essence. She expressed her love through some of the most outstanding meals I have ever enjoyed.

Over the years, my siblings and I tried unsuccessfully to entice her to pass this exceptional gift to us but to no avail. She was not willing to share this special part of herself with anyone with the exception of periodically offering pointers to her granddaughters. I often think about the sad reality of such giftedness dying with her, but I find comfort in remembering how happy she was when we pressed her for her secrets. Much of her sense of self-worth was rooted in the prestigious title of outstanding cook, and she insisted on taking that accomplishment with her.

There is a stark contrast between growing old and growing whole. For those of us who choose the latter, life becomes a series of new beginnings. As we shift gears in response to the here and now, we become more adept at distinguishing between what is meaningful and what is meaningless. We begin in earnest the necessary cleansing process of elimination and prioritization. We remove superficial distractions. We discard many of the trappings of youth such as inflated egos and quests for worldly power and status. We free up precious time and energy to engage life as a spiritual experience that promises a plethora of pleasures. We cannot begin to live freely until we have completed the young-adult and middle-year duties of rearing children and attaining financial security.

With our children grown and independent, we have the pleasure of knowing we served them well and helped position them to leave the nest and engage life on their terms. Having prepared financially for our golden years, we finally have time to consider and explore new possibilities. This is an exciting period in our lives. We have big plans, a lengthy bucket list, and a craving for the freedom to do as much or as little as we desire.

Perhaps for the first time in our lives, we become intimately acquainted with who we really are. We are growing into our own identity, becoming more self-confident, discovering our strengths, and accepting our weaknesses. The desire for a higher level of satisfaction has never been stronger as we give ourselves permission to explore our desires and passions.

Age-related norms are being shattered every day, and new paradigms are emerging. We are finding value in embracing elderhood. We are a commanding force in the world marketplace, and we are demanding seats at the table as discussions about the economic and public policy implications of longevity are underway. Our attitudes and beliefs about possibilities and potentialities are expanding, and we hold tremendous inspirational power.

Conscious aging reflects a deeply personal decision to view the golden years as the single most important stage of life. We are making concerted efforts to harmonize our inner and outer selves and to discover the value of longevity. We are enjoying our role as ambassadors for the aging phenomenon, which offers unexpected pleasures as we explore uncharted territories.

Throughout history decisions have been made by the world's leaders that were clearly ego driven and fear-based rather than spiritually motivated and love-based. This false sense of arrogance that often accompanies power has led us to the present condition of being on the brink of global disaster. Bitterness, climate degradation, environmental pollution, cynicism, endless wars, hatred, health and wealth disparities, pandemics, racial unrest, and disrespect for humanity are symptoms of spiritual depravity that permeates the human experience.

When we accept God as our Creator, the meaning and purpose of life has a distinct reference point that offers viable alternatives to the dire circumstances we face. With age and life experiences, we begin to shift our attitudes and reframe the conversations about our current predicament. We become more adept at envisioning life from a more loving perspective. We start seeing ways we can transform the dream of a better life into reality. Longevity is a gift on so many levels. Most profound is the gift of spiritual wisdom. Over time and through intentional efforts, we can become great examples of what it means to be a child of the holy Trinity.

As we age, the lens through which we see the world expands to make room for inner growth, development, and new levels of awareness. We become less self-centered and more selective in our choices. We replace our large, superficial social circles with smaller, tight-knit groups where authentic and supportive relationships thrive.

Accommodating aging is different from any of our previous challenges. Letting go of who we used to be is a prerequisite to fully embracing who we are now and who we have the potential to become. This is especially challenging for people who enjoyed leadership status and power. They no longer have an army of minions at their beck and call to perform menial tasks. They become the responsible party, and that brings with it a level of humility. God smiles when we begin to strip away the fluff in favor of the authentic.

We are spiritual beings having physical experiences. For reasons we often do not comprehend, this is our destiny, the predetermined pathway to oneness and wholeness with our creative source. Transformation from our physical, egotistical selves to our spiritual, authentic essence is a journey into the depths of our souls. It will take time and a commitment to doing the tough inside work required, but it can move us closer to the spiritual abundance we desire.

Societal Implications of Longevity

Gone is the three-stage model of education, career, and the golden years. The period of retirement is increasing, and we are witnessing firsthand a movement that will redesign our sense of who we are and why we are here. The goals of procreation and accumulation of wealth have been met, our children are independent and busy living their own lives, and we have checked off the realistic items on our bucket list. *Now what? Will we simply continue to exist and just let life happen? Are we destined to become couch potatoes awaiting the grim reaper? What are we to do with all these extra years? What is the spiritual meaning of this added time?*

Interesting ideas and thought-provoking public conversations abound, and many of us are privately asking ourselves these same questions. Life expectancy at the turn of the twentieth century was forty-five, but living into your eighties or nineties is now commonplace. Today's newborns have more than a 50 percent chance of realizing centenarian status. The financial, physical, psychological, social, and spiritual implications of this are huge.

Multiple careers and then retirements are becoming the norm, and our worldview is expanding to envision a lengthy, passionate, and productive lifespan with almost endless possibilities. There are things we know at the more mature stage of our lives that we could not have known earlier. The academic and experiential knowledge and understanding we accumulate over time makes us a formidable force for innovation as society grapples with the reality of an aging population. We have much to contribute to the conversation particularly when we consider that the actual experience of aging is the only firsthand knowledge we have. Aging is not an intellectual exercise; while surveys and research can inform us, many answers must come from lived realities.

Life is a series of stages that have their own assignments, challenges, opportunities, and realizations. During our early years, we are students of academic and experiential knowledge. We then transition to a vocational stage where we implement what we have learned and expand our awareness to include consciousness of the spiritual component of life. Finally, we are released from the workforce with thanks for services rendered and best wishes for a life of leisure. Because this post-employment phase is lasting longer, we now have extra time to meditate on the previous stages and decide how much will be assimilated into our present lifestyle. Some information from our previous stages is relevant to our capacity to age consciously, but much of it is not. The kindest thing we can do with inputs we no longer need is to relegate them to our memory.

The revolution is occurring in the domain of assimilation. As we dig into the significant events of our previous years and analyze and dissect their meaning and sacred purpose, a metamorphosis takes place. We can finally discard everything that inhibits expansion. Armed with the tools we obtained while transforming our worldview from one that was fear-based to one fueled by love, we can breathe deeply and allow ourselves to expand our vision of possibilities and grow spiritually.

Longevity gives us far more than extra years. The human developmental trajectory has sufficiently slowed at every stage to accommodate the phenomenon of life spans stretching into the tenth decade. I recently read a thought-provoking article about delayed maturation and emerging adulthood, which was identified as the phase of life between adolescence and young adulthood. People in this stage are taking longer to assume traditional adult roles and responsibilities. They are choosing to stay home well into their twenties and thirties. A similar experience is occurring at the middle period of life. People in this stage are increasingly displaying a willingness to move back home when their grown-up responsibilities become too hard for them to bear. This phenomenon has created a category of boomerang kids who are redefining adulthood.

These realities are being experienced more frequently by the baby boomers, the parents and grandparents of these children who refuse to leave home or return at the first sign of struggle. Something important is happening from a spiritual perspective that we do not understand yet. Since we are the beneficiaries of this phenomenon, we baby boomers should add our collective wisdom to the conversation. While there are challenges that require our attention, intergenerational households contribute to efforts toward growing whole in creative and interesting ways. Grandparents, parents, and children benefit from the learned experiences and perspectives of each other. *The Twelve Functional Dimensions of Humankind* framework is a catalyst for such a conversation. Opportunities for spiritual growth are inherent in each of the dimensions, and close-knit, intergenerational contact supports lifelong vitality in ways that nothing else can.

Growing Whole is a book about fully embracing the gift of longevity, living well so that we age well, looking forward to and enjoying our golden years, and along the way finding the deep meaning and sacred purpose of life. Once we find the answers we seek, it is our task to become inspirational agents of change. Through the medium of wisdom teaching, we can make a significant contribution to improving the human condition.

Embracing Mindfulness

One of the greatest gifts of longevity is the uncluttered time and space to live in a state of mindfulness. Finally, we can slow down long enough to fully engage in and enjoy the present moment and absorb the beauty and magnificence that surround us. We get the unobstructed opportunity to integrate the lengthy years of accumulated knowledge, understanding, and wisdom and to cultivate and reap the benefits of discovering our true selves.

We live our lives in stages loosely associated with youth, middle age, and senior status. Each of these stages is so distinct that they hardly resemble each other. Think for a moment about who you were during your teenage and early adult years. I expect that most people would not choose to relive many of those experiences. As you transitioned to middle age, you evolved into a more mature and enlightened version of yourself. Your decisions were more thoughtful and contemplative, and your priorities were beginning to line up with your authentic self. Elderhood is even more alien to your years of naive, youthful existence.

At this stage, we are purposely shedding much of what we worked so hard and so long to gather. We are growing by leaps and bounds as we say goodbye to our egotistical, physical selves and move into the spiritual realm, which brings us closer to who we really are. Learning to live in the sacred space of authenticity is a blessing. We are drawn to pursue reconciliation with our creative source, with ourselves, and with others.

Mindfulness is the ability to be fully attentive to the present. It offers a superior quality of awareness far beyond our everyday levels. We are mentally invested in what we are doing and where we are, yet we are sufficiently emotionally distant that we can put our egotistical needs on the back burner, and we lose all judgment. We simply appreciate, experience, and witness. When we practice mindfulness, we create time and space for ourselves to grow in grace and gratitude. The blessings of everyday life reveal themselves more readily, and we can see the miracles of God everywhere.

One of my favorite spots in the world is readily available whenever I need sacred space. It is my backyard patio, which is usually adorned with potted plants that are aesthetically pleasing. There, I am easily transformed and elevated to a space that is beyond my physical self. I am so filled with grace and gratitude that I become one with the divinity and serenity of the universe. During these moments, there are no irregularities between my mortal, physical self and my immortal, spiritual self. I can sit in my chosen spot and enjoy sprawling oak trees, lush flowerbeds whenever the deer allow them to sprout, and other natural wonders. As my eyes scan the landscape, I am in awe of God's creativity and wisdom. I am unable to fully comprehend the depth and breadth of this experience, but I somehow sense that I am touching heaven.

God's nature pervades everyone and everything. When we sit in silence and quiet our minds, the divine principles that organize our lives and give us meaning and sacred purpose are evident. As I pray and meditate, the distractions of life that sometimes creep into my psyche and cause friction and frustration melt away. I can focus on what matters and explore interesting ways of living that support the principles of my personal life code. Coming to terms with what I think and feel and having the courage to synchronize those thoughts and feelings with my actions are necessary for me to reflect emotional integrity. Feeling compelled to be honest and truthful even when others are compromising their ethics, morals, and values is an integral component of mindfulness. This process of cleansing and reconciliation significantly improves my sense of self and brings me closer to Christ-centeredness.

Growing Whole while Celebrating the Gift of Years

Growing whole as it relates to celebrating the gift of years is diverse and multifaceted. It is common for people who were goal oriented and production driven during their years in the workplace to make a conscious decision to settle into a lifestyle and mindset of leisure and relaxation during retirement. They gladly trade in their alarm clocks and meeting schedules for shoreline strolls at sunrise and breathtaking oceanic vistas at sunset. They quickly discard the three-piece suits for T-shirts and Bermuda shorts. *And who could blame them?* To finally be in a position to relax for hours, lose yourself in contemplation and thought, play in the dirt in a flowerbed, or rekindle friendships that took a back seat to other priorities during the earlier years are privileges that should be experienced.

To age consciously, we must grapple with the profound question of what we do with ourselves when the rigorous workdays are behind us. As with any other stage of life, success during this period requires clarity of intent, planning, and preparation. Take the time to think about the happiest and most fulfilling vision for your golden years. Do not transition into a retirement lifestyle by default. Do not allow retirement to be thrust upon you. By aging consciously your retirement years can be the best years of your life. *Do you see yourself spending time with the grandchildren? Hosting dinner parties? Traveling? Volunteering at a mental health clinic? Mentoring?* The pivotal choice is between a life of leisure and a commitment to serve. Conscious aging means objectively evaluating the implications of the decision you make.

While selecting one does not exclude the other, these two options offer different experiences. If you choose a lifestyle of leisure you are certainly not alone. Recreation is one of the fastest growing industries in the world.

Flexibility and freedom from responsibility are great short-term remedies for years of crowded schedules and routines. However, too much free time can start to feel more stressful than pleasant. Feelings of loneliness and unproductiveness can creep in and erode your confidence. If you choose service over leisure, you are also not alone. For many retirees, productivity leads to self-fulfillment and fosters a sense of viability and vitality. By maintaining a modicum of structure and purpose you can enjoy a more relaxed lifestyle and realize the spiritual benefits of serving others. Be mindful that meaningful service must reflect the basic principles that support this righteous goal. Our intentions, thoughts, words, and deeds must be honorable and loving, and our godliness must be evident. We live in perilous times that require a commitment from each of us to offer the best of who we are to God's universe.

Finding rewarding ways to contribute to society while embracing the aging process is challenging. We have earned the right to a less hectic, slower pace, yet we remain accountable from a spiritual perspective to serve the common good. This responsibility never subsides. For the duration of our time on earth, we are required to do our part to ease pain, exemplify high moral and ethical standards, support efforts to help ensure a fair and just society, and use our gifts and talents to glorify God.

The forces that define the quality of a lengthy life are complicated and intertwined; they are at a minimum financial, medical, physical, psychological, sociological, and spiritual. When navigating a long life, the choices we make during our youth and middle years must stand up to the scrutiny of what life brings for decades to come. The longer we live, the longer we are impacted by our early decisions, and even if we choose service over leisure our efforts must be motivated by purity of heart.

Growing whole as it relates to the gift of years requires us to clearly understand that we get from the universe whatever we project into it. If we project ungratefulness and a general lack of appreciation for life, this feeling will manifest itself. Life will offer us mediocre experiences and opportunities that resonate on the energy level of our ungratefulness. If we desire exciting and fulfilling lives, we must raise our energy level. We cannot focus on the negative. Every moment is a godly moment, and when we develop the skill to see God in every experience, our latter years can be our best years. Maintaining a positive attitude and outlook is critical to growing whole while celebrating the gift of years.

Regardless of how bad you perceive your situation to be, there is always someone facing worse circumstances. Every difficulty brings with it an equal or greater benefit. *Have you ever met a person who is grumpy even when surrounded by people exhibiting great joy?* No matter what, you can count on him or her to focus on the negative and bring everybody's spirit down.

Think about a time when you felt happiness and joy. *What were the circumstances? How can you allow that feeling to manifest itself in your life more often?* Start by keeping a mental record of the things for which you are grateful. Regardless of your situation, there is something positive you can concentrate on. Whenever a negative thought enters your mind, do not let it linger there; immediately shift your focus to a positive aspect of the issue you are pondering. As you practice this strategy, you are reengineering your negative internal thought processes through repetition. Write down things for which you are thankful and revisit that list regularly.

This is a great strategy to ease tension between you and your significant other. During moments of anger, focus on what initially attracted you to that person and realize that those characteristics are still there. This will help your feelings of anger subside and give you the opportunity to think logically rather than emotionally about the present circumstance. Work hard to consciously create the outcome you desire, and do not allow yourself to be governed by the natural tendency to focus on the negative. You fell in love with this person for a reason, so go back to that place in your heart and allow the happiness associated with the freshness and newness of that love to flow.

Conscious aging requires effort. We must challenge and stretch our capacities. We cannot allow ourselves to become comfortable and complacent. Most people want to be productive in life. Growing whole while celebrating the gift of years means creating an internal climate for ourselves that sets the tone for accentuating the myriad opportunities for excitement and enjoyment, while fully embracing and participating in the experiences we encounter. Meaning and sacred purpose are the building blocks for the spiritual abundance that we desire. By integrating the dual goals of celebration and growth we realize the perfect balance between a life of leisure and a commitment to serve.

One time when I was in the checkout line at a store, I overheard a conversation between two young women. One said that she had been having a pleasant day but then bumped into someone she did not think highly of. She said, "Everything was great until I ran into Eleanor. She still makes my flesh crawl every time I see her. I expect my day will be downhill from here." I wondered how such a minor event could shift her positive outlook to a negative outlook for the remainder of her day. We often find it easier to focus on and remember negative encounters rather than allow the positivity that surrounds us to saturate our essence. Allowing someone who evokes negative emotions to ruin our day is unfortunate. From the perspective of conscious aging, this example of human interaction presents an opportunity for growth that should not be overlooked.

We do not necessarily control our encounters, but we do have the power to determine how we react to them and whether we grow from them. Perhaps no single aspect of life lends itself more to growth than the spirit of grace does. We will always face problems and challenges; they are an important part of our spiritual journey. Without them, we would not be able to learn the lessons required of us to grow. Cultivating a spirit of grace, which is unmerited favor, is the best defense against our natural proclivity toward the negative rather than the positive aspects of an experience. We often ask God to extend His grace to us. *Why, then are we not willing to extend grace to each other*? If the young woman whose conversation I overheard had been immersed in a sense of benevolence and grace, it is unlikely that seeing someone she did not particularly care for could have shifted her energy frequency from positive to negative so easily.

Be Careful Whom You Listen To

The search for oneness and wholeness requires us to take advantage of every reliable resource available. Awareness comes to us through offerings from the physical environment as well as from the spiritual environment. God gives us the discernment necessary to make wise choices. While the ultimate resource for believers is the Bible, we receive information from other documents and experiences as well. It is incumbent upon each of us to take the time necessary to ensure the credibility and validity of our resources.

I am reminded of a story about a serious conflict between Valerie, a former coworker, and her husband. James was working with a financial advisor who suggested they purchase rental properties to diversify their portfolio and create an additional income tax shelter. This advice came just after the real estate fiasco in 2008 when the bubble burst, and people were losing their homes to foreclosures and short sales.

From the start, Valerie was uncomfortable with the suggestion. While properties were cheap and easy to buy, she was hesitant to trust that the market would recover as quickly as the financial advisor had suggested. After several arguments over a four-month period, James purchased a property without her knowledge. She was livid when she found out. His action fostered a serious relationship breach that for some reason he claimed he had not anticipated. His version of the story was that he wanted to surprise her with this present because he felt he knew what was best for the family. His plan was to repair and flip the property to make a quick profit.

Unfortunately, the market did not rebound quickly, and they were unable to sell the property for years. When they did, they lost money. Valerie felt betrayed and the damage to the marriage was significant. Although they are still a couple, she is not happy. James had decided to listen to their financial advisor rather than honor the concerns of his wife and move forward with caution. One reason she is having a hard time putting this matter behind them is his refusal to take responsibility for violating one of the basic tenets of a relationship—trust.

We receive inputs from a multitude of sources daily, and it can be hard to distinguish fact from fiction as technology continues to churn out data. This makes it even more critical that we assess the origin of the information. *Is it presented from the perspective of the secular or the sacred? Does it comport with biblical teachings? Is the data research based, or does it come from an otherwise credible source? Is it opinion camouflaged as fact?* In Ephesians 4:11–16 (NIV), Paul reminded us of the importance of Christian maturity and our need to grow into it.

> So, Christ himself gave the apostles, the prophets, the
> evangelists, the pastors, and teachers, to equip his people
> for works of service, so that the body of Christ may
> be built up until we all reach unity in the faith and in

the knowledge of the Son of God and become mature, attaining to the whole measure of the fullness of Christ. Then we will no longer be infants, tossed back and forth by the waves, and blown here and there by every wind of teaching and by the cunning and craftiness of people in their deceitful scheming. Instead, speaking the truth in love, we will grow to become in every respect the mature body of him who is the head, that is, Christ. From him the whole body, joined and held together by every supporting ligament, grows, and builds itself up in love, as each part does its work.

This maturation is aided by gifted teachers and leaders who help us to grow in our faith. Paul emphasizes individual and corporate growth. God has given each Christian special gifts and talents for building up the church. As we mature spiritually and better understand what our gifts and talents are it is crucial that we look for opportunities to utilize them to strengthen and encourage the church.

As you do the work required to grow in the fullness of Christ, there are credible sources that offer commentary to further illuminate God's Word and expose our iniquity. It is incumbent upon us to ensure that our sources of information are based on biblical teachings.

Chapter 8 Important Points

- Conscious aging is essential to lifelong vitality and well-being.
- There is an unmistakable connection between aging and spirituality.
- Everyone should have a conscious aging plan. It helps you to prepare for and preserve the lifestyle you choose.
- The body goes through myriad changes as you age, but these challenges pale in comparison to what you gain.
- A lifetime of accumulating knowledge, understanding, and wisdom gives you insight from a vantage point that youth cannot offer.
- People over sixty-five are the fastest growing population group in the world.
- Input from people who possess experiential, intellectual, and intuitive knowledge related to aging is critical to the success of public policy discussions and planning strategies.
- As you age, you expand your worldview to include the redemptive work of the soul.
- Longevity is a privilege reserved for a select few.
- There is a stark contrast between growing whole and growing old.
- Age-related norms are being shattered every day, and new paradigms are emerging. The value and role of elders is becoming readily apparent in Western cultures.
- Multiple careers and associated retirements are becoming the norm, and lengthy, passionate, and productive lifespans usher in new possibilities.
- Longevity offers us so much more than just extra years.
- Mindfulness is the basic human ability to be fully attentive to the present moment.
- One of the greatest gifts of longevity is the uncluttered time and space to live in a state of mindfulness.
- Be selective about whom you listen to.

9

THE SPIRITUAL
SIGNIFICANCE OF TIME

As I sit on the balcony of a beautiful, rustic log cabin in the Blue Ridge Mountains, I am in a particularly nostalgic mood. As I did most mornings, I woke at the crack of dawn, brewed coffee, and made my way outdoors. I enjoy communing with nature in the early hours, which offer unique experiences. The spiritual messages I receive during this time seem to disappear as the day unfolds.

I am overwhelmed by the magical beauty of what my senses reveal. Layers of mountain peaks are before me offering a visual so vibrant that it takes my breath away. The robust waterfall emits soothing sounds as it cascades into the babbling brook below. Brightly colored trees provide a stunning backdrop for the few cabins peeking through. Clusters of pine trees seem so close to the edge of the balcony that I feel I can almost reach out and touch them.

To my left is a family of wild turkeys feeding on the undisturbed droppings from the pine trees towering above them. They are unwittingly contributing to my excitement as I survey the diverse landscape. The falling leaves signal the onset of autumn. The natural aroma of fresh air gives me permission to claim this moment as mine. The dew is so thick that I cannot resist sampling its slightly sweet taste. Off in the distance, I see deer roaming a valley.

My mind drifts to thoughts about life, its sacred purpose, and the meaning of and reason for longevity. Modern medicine and a focus on healthy living and disease prevention have increased life expectancy so much that centenarian status around the world is now common. From a spiritual perspective, there are sacred reasons for this phenomenon that should be explored and explained in ways that uplift the human experience and give meaning to the gift of years.

I am celebrating my seventy-first birthday this weekend, so time is in the forefront of my mind. I am reminded of major events in America's history that impacted me. I was born and raised in the south, so realities such as Jim Crow laws, segregation, and systematic lynching were woven into the fabric of my life. Other noteworthy events included the assassinations of President John Kennedy and Dr. Martin Luther King Jr., the Black Is Beautiful movement, the civil rights movement, the covid pandemic, the election of the first Black president, landing on the moon, massive demonstrations and riots, the passage of the Civil Rights Act, the Persian Gulf war, personal computers and the iPhone, terrorist attacks on September 11, 2001, the Vietnam War, Watergate, widespread police brutality almost singly focused on Black and Brown people, and the women's liberation movement—all parts of my experiential history.

These stories reveal the gamut of the human spirit. We see examples of compassion, creativity, fairness and justice, fear, greed, hatred, hope, inhumanity, pain and loss, progress, rejection, sacrifice, and support. They reveal opportunities and challenges for each of us as we pursue meaning and sacred purpose. They are vivid reminders of our ability to be cruel as well as our capacity to love. These stories refresh our memories about the human relations work that is still undone. Even as we enjoy our well-deserved golden years, we are obligated to use our gifts and talents to glorify God. The mandate to serve is embedded in our Christ-centered lifestyle. It requires us to work diligently to ease pain, calm fears, comfort the brokenhearted, feed the hungry, be positive role models, love and be loved, and share wisdom.

From the perspective of meaning and sacred purpose, time is of the essence. For it to serve our spiritual growth efforts, we need to consider two of its major characteristics. First, time is cyclical; there is a dependable and predictable rhythm to it. We expect certain events to reoccur—day follows night and spring follows winter. Tides come in and go out. Death follows life.

Second, time is linear. Here, we see God actively orchestrating time and events in the direction of His kingdom. Time is moving the universe and everything in it forward to this predetermined destiny. Time is neither friend nor foe; it just is. The cyclical and linear natures of time alert us to its urgency. We have a job to do, and we have only a certain amount of time within which to do it. This truism compels us to find the meaning of life. Then we must passionately pursue what implements our sacred purpose.

The Blessing of Longevity

A seventy-two-year lifespan is 864 months or about 26,280 days. As I pause to consider my lengthy journey and how God has patiently worked with me and supported my growth, I realize how blessed I am. It has taken me a long time to remove the most damaging notions that lodged themselves in my psyche years ago. Some of those limiting beliefs were an innate part of being Black in America. Others were passed on to me from unresolved issues with people in my inner circle. Still others were of my own creation. Over time, I have systematically dismantled many of them; however, vestiges linger.

The spiritual significance of time should not be lost on us. Time does for us what it needs to do. With time, we can right wrongs. With time, we can develop the critical skills of foresight, insight, and hindsight. Time gently nudges us when we are heading down the wrong path and need to change course. With time, we distinguish between the real and the superficial. With time, we become more spiritual, and we look beyond the temporary toward the eternal. With time, we learn to love more, laugh more, and serve more. We become more humble and less haughty. We forgive and let go. Time heals deep wounds. With time, we become efficient at separating the wheat from the chaff. With time, we learn the value of gratitude, compassion, and empathy. With time, we gain sufficient knowledge, understanding, and wisdom to serve as role models and wisdom teachers. Yes, for each of us, time does exactly what it needs to do.

Ahh, the Golden Years!

If you are like me, you have looked forward to the golden years for a while. This is supposed to be your time. With healthier lifestyles and modern medicine, elders often enjoy independence well into their eighties and nineties; that could mean another twenty or thirty years beyond retirement before they begin to experience age-related physical, emotional, or cognitive limitations.

There is something exhilarating about the thought of no more alarm clocks, boring meetings, or insane project completion deadlines. No more office politics or doughnuts in the conference room, no more buying things you do not need to support the latest fundraising effort of your coworker's child, and no more commutes, performance evaluations, and chats with your supervisor.

So where does sacred purpose fit into this picture? The thought of having the freedom to do nothing is intoxicating. No one could blame you if you decided to immerse yourself in a lifestyle of leisure. You have paid your dues. We all must decide what sacred purpose looks like during our golden years. This question must be considered within the context of a larger one: *Why were we gifted with extra years?* Psalm 90:10 (ESV) tells us, "The years of our life are seventy, or even by reason of strength eighty; yet their span is but toil and trouble; they are soon gone, and we fly away."

For those who choose to remain engaged, there are myriad opportunities to contribute to the common good. I grew up during the civil rights movement. I remember my parents expressing concerns about job security on many occasions. While they respected our interest in taking part in certain activities, they worried about backlash. They felt certain that their bosses would fire them if they suspected their children's involvement in protests. Later, as an adult, over the span of my own career, I had ample opportunities to participate in peaceful demonstrations. As I considered them, I could hear my parents' warnings. Many baby boomers like myself wrestled with similar dilemmas. Finally, in our golden years, we have the freedom to make decisions about civic engagement based on our convictions rather than fear of reprisal.

One blessing of longevity is having the unfettered time to envision meaning and sacred purpose in personal and practical ways. Many of the hectic demands of our middle years are no longer present. Our children are grown and independent. Our financial future is reasonably secure. *So what do we do with this extra time?*

Those of us who survived for seven plus decades are quite adept at navigating the stormy waters of change. As enlightened elders, we are natural wisdom teachers and role models. Time has taught us invaluable lessons, and our view of sacred purpose has been refined. The insight, knowledge, understanding, and wisdom we have accumulated have elevated us to a level of spirituality that makes us formidable assets. It makes perfect sense for us to use our gifts and talents to mentor and mold younger generations into leaders who are compassionate and visionary. There are endless opportunities for us to demonstrate how universal implementation of the godly principles of love, joy, peace, patience, kindness, goodness, and faithfulness can alter history.

Time Supports the Process of Growing Whole

From the natural perspective, time began with creation of the universe. From the supernatural perspective, time always was and always will be. Time belongs to God, and His timing is perfect. Each of us has been given a small segment of time on earth. The gift of free will allows us to use a portion of our time to pursue personal goals. As people of faith though, we are here primarily to glorify God and support His kingdom.

We view time as past, present, and future. We cannot change the past, and the future is unpredictable. The limited here and now is where meaning and sacred purpose lies. For this reason, we must use our time wisely. As we go about our days busily moving from one activity to another, it is easy to forget why we are here. Jesus made it clear that we were to "seek first the kingdom of God and his righteousness, and all these things will be added to you" (Matthew 6:33 ESV).

How we spend our time is a clear indicator of what matters to us. The activities of daily living are important, and they rightfully deserve our attention, but our task is to efficiently manage the limited time we have. Growing whole involves setting priorities and staying focused on the eternal as we attend to the temporary. We must balance our time so that we effectively support life while doing kingdom work and glorifying God.

When we implement sacred purpose, we glorify God. When we put our faith in action, we glorify God. When we serve others, we glorify God. When we attend to the needs of our families, we glorify God. When we pray for peace or show compassion to the vulnerable, we glorify God. As we do our best under trying circumstances, we glorify God. This is sacred purpose.

Throughout the lifelong process of growing whole, we continue to refine the skills and sensibilities we have acquired; they allow us to be better servants to those who need us, and we become more effective ambassadors for God. Time gives us the knowledge, understanding, and wisdom to organize our lives in ways that allow us to offer our best.

Time Answers the Deep Questions of Life

To view aging as a sacred, transformational experience, we must first fully comprehend that we are spiritual beings who are witnessing life in temporary physical form. The deep questions of who we are and why we are here can be answered satisfactorily only when we view life as temporary. We are here for a specified period to accomplish specific goals. When sacred purpose is realized, we transition to immortality and return to the fullness of the spiritual beings we always were.

It is natural for us to question the reason for life, death, and the hereafter. These are complex issues, and as we age, our desire for answers becomes more persistent and profound. Our interest in the secular wanes, and we yearn for deeper insight into the spiritual. Our ego-centeredness subsides as we seek the authentic realm of our being, the place in us where divinity thrives.

By the time we reach elderhood, myriad life lessons have molded us into people who closely resemble our originally intended characters. Many of the layers we added in a misguided effort to shield our humanness have been peeled away. The body, soul, and spirit are more closely aligned, and the subjective nature of time reminds us of the inevitable. Time molds and shapes. Time affords us the insight and wisdom to listen to the soft, still voice of God gently nudging us in the direction of understanding and acceptance. While each of us must grapple with the deep questions in our own ways, our faith offers perspective and promise.

We are an integral part of the metanarrative of the kingdom story. As this grand story continues to unfold, our place in it becomes clearer. Time helps us sort through the drama of our lives and find what matters, and then it helps us comprehend why it matters. The spiritual benefits associated with aging are most apparent when we spend time in contemplation answering the why questions. The emotions that accompany growing whole are felt more vividly, and we settle into a mental state of reflection. We become more sympathetic toward others as our hearts expand to make room for deeper expressions of love. Retrospection is a regular visitor, and we spend more time considering and reconsidering the roads not taken. These are spiritual experiences that only the gift of time can offer. Even if we never find answers to the why questions, the self-examination and self-exploration in search of them are sacred and therefore are enough.

Time Clarifies Meaning and Sacred Purpose

The gold standard for a meaningful life and the fulfillment of sacred purpose is the same for all of us. There are untold opportunities to serve the common good and glorify God. Two biblical stories make it abundantly clear why we are here. Both stories reveal that meaning and sacred purpose can be fulfilled only through fellowship and relationship. We are social creatures; we were not meant to exist long term in isolation and solitude.

The first story relates to the great commandment. One day, in hopes of confusing Him, the Pharisees asked Jesus, "Teacher, which command in God's Law is the most important?" Jesus said,

> Love the Lord your God with all your passion and prayer and intelligence. This is the most important, the first on any list. But there is a second to set alongside it: "Love others as well as you love yourself." These two commands are pegs; everything in God's Law and the Prophets hangs from them. (Matthew 22:37–40 TM)

We are required to love God with our entire being. Second, when we learn to love God this completely, loving ourselves and our neighbor flows naturally because we love what He loves.

The second story relates to the Great Commission, when Jesus said to His disciples,

> God authorized and commanded me to commission you: Go out and train everyone you meet, far and near, in this way of life, marking them by baptism in the three-fold name: Father, Son, and Holy Spirit. Then instruct them in the practice of all I have commanded you. I'll be with you as you do this, day after day after day, right up to the end of the age. (Matthew 28:18–20 TM)

Here we see the symbolism inherent in this twofold directive to baptize and instruct. Baptism symbolizes the inside-out cleansing that occurs when we become people of faith. Instruction includes demonstrating how God wants His people to live.

It took me a while to fully grasp that we all have the same sacred purpose. We are to model our love for God, ourselves, and others in every aspect of our lives. By doing this, we glorify God. To accomplish this holy calling, genuine feelings of love must permeate our every intention, thought, word, and deed. To assist, our gifts and talents offer important clues to guide us into specific areas, but ultimately, our task is to glorify God through service. Myriad options to reflect our creative genius as we implement our holy calling are available to us. Through the medium of service, we glorify God, implement sacred purpose, and bring souls into our faith family.

Time Cleanses and Heals Wounds

The cleansing and healing power of time cannot be overstated. As we age, something quite beautiful, natural, and predictable happens. The physical, egotistical self wanes and makes way for the spiritual, authentic self to take center stage. For life to have meaning beyond simply existing and reveling in selfish pursuits, we must constantly strive to become better versions of ourselves. Time sensitizes us to the urgency of this calling.

When we adopt the principle of growing whole, we begin to experience a fundamental transformation. We envision aging not as a period of physical and mental decline but as the ideal time to cultivate our inner selves and resolve any remaining discrepancies. Herein lies the magnificent mystery of spirituality. In our youth, we lack the capacity to appreciate that time does something positive for us in a way nothing else can. Time gives us the space we need to grow in character. Time offers us the insight to recognize the logic behind our seemingly chaotic lives.

Our unique gifts and talents give us distinct clues about how to best serve others, but it takes time and experience to get us ready for the calling. Time shines a light on our transgressions thereby softening our hearts so we can forgive our transgressors. Time helps us to comprehend the principle that everything unfolds as it should by divine design. Time erases the messiness of our younger years. It helps put our disappointment and pain into perspective. As we search our hearts and souls for meaning, we see that the combination of time and spiritual growth is a gift from God.

Sometimes, the nagging guilt of an imperfect life lived among imperfect and wounded people becomes unnecessarily burdensome. When this occurs, the extra weight undermines our sense of self-worth and robs us of our capacity to thrive. Efforts to remedy this condition require reconciliation on three levels. First, our relationship with our Creator must be reconciled. Second, our inner and outer selves must be synchronized. Third, the quality of our relationships with others must be elevated to the levels of love and sacred purpose. Time gives us the space we need to undertake this daunting task. Efforts to realize oneness with God, self, and others require commitment and patience. When we take the time to allow God to do His spiritual work in us, we move closer to the state of wholeness.

Time Enlightens and Gives Perspective

When we were born, whom we were born to, and where we were born give us important clues to the answers we seek. Our gifts, talents, interests, motivations, and worldview collaborate in interesting and rewarding ways to move us closer to enlightenment. From the outset, there is the life we are given and the life we choose to live. While we often see them as the same, they are different, and it is our job to reconcile the discrepancies. Options and decision points permeate our everyday lives. This is the level on which the heart and soul of our personal stories evolves. The central theme, major characters, events and circumstances, antagonists and protagonists, and the intimate details upon which the story is built unveil disappointments, dreams, fantasies, fears, realities, responsibilities, and truisms that make our stories ours.

The role of longevity in all of this is simple but profound and mystical. Obviously, the longer we live, the more opportunities we get to edit and reconcile. I see this as a blessing because we need the extra time to figure out what meaning and sacred purpose look like in our unique stories. Embedded in every great artistic work is authenticity and passion. The popularity of reality shows confirms that truth really is more compelling and more interesting than fiction. Even though many situations are dramatized, there is just enough truth to keep us hanging on for the next episode. What we are subconsciously drawn to are the truisms of life. *What are the things that tug at our hearts? How do we successfully battle our personal demons? How do we express love in ways that support our godly principles? How do we serve as positive role models and teachers? Which path will we take—the sacred or the secular?* Once we can see portraits of ourselves and our real-life struggles in the reality show characters, we are hooked.

My youngest daughter once said that she loved watching the television series *My 600 Pound Life*. She is an insightful person, so I was surprised at that. My biases about what I perceive as extreme gluttony clouded my capacity to understand her interest in this show. Armed with years of educational and professional experience in the mental health field, she searches for deeper meaning in everyday encounters, and once she explained her curiosity about this show, it made perfect sense. She is intrigued by the emotional and mental circumstances that allowed these individuals to get to a weight of six or seven hundred pounds. At the time of our conversation, I had never watched one of the episodes in its entirety. I had made a completely unjustified assumption that these individuals were greedy and undisciplined. But once I watched three or four episodes, I saw my daughter's attraction. The producers do a great job of engaging viewers in the details of each story. The reality of the pain, physical limitations, health consequences, relationship challenges, fears, shame, vulnerability, and the overall quality of their lives help explain their food addiction. Like any other addiction, it begins as a strategy to escape troubling realities in life and evolves into an out-of-control monster.

Whether we realize it or not, each of us has at least one addiction. By paying close attention to the challenges inherent in the lives of the main characters, I felt compelled to be more honest about searching for the addictions innate to my own life. This story represents one of my many humbling moments. I feel convicted for allowing myself to fall into the trap of judging others. Feeling superior to others because I am focused on their addictions rather than mine, I glaringly violated one of the fundamental principles of my life code.

Matthew 7:1–5 (TM) reminds us,

> Don't pick on people, jump on their failures, criticize their faults—unless, of course, you want the same treatment. That critical spirit has a way of boomeranging. It is easy to see a smudge on your neighbor's face and be oblivious to the ugly sneer on your own. Do you have the nerve to say, "Let me wash your face for you," when your own face is distorted by contempt? It is this whole traveling road-show mentality all over again, playing a holier-than-thou part instead of just living your part. Wipe that ugly sneer off your face, and you might be fit to offer a washcloth to your neighbor.

Time Helps Us Accept the Inevitable

I do not recall having any serious thoughts or concerns about aging until that dreaded day when my American Association of Retired Persons (AARP) welcome package arrived in the mail. I felt aggravated at the nerve of the organization, but over time, my feelings softened especially once I educated myself about the senior discounts.

Over the next decade, I thought about aging intermittently, but I purposely avoided allowing myself to get too deeply invested in the impending reality. In my mind, as long as I was actively engaged in the workforce, I could avoid addressing this matter. Aging itself was not the troubling factor; however, concerns about outliving my relevance and vitality and having a reduced quality of life as I lost my independence plagued me.

With twenty years of health care regulatory experience under my belt, I had seen far too many people being warehoused in assisted living facilities and nursing homes. Granted, as a regulator, I was usually exposed to the worst examples of long-term care, and the negative imprint on my psyche was unfair and unjustified. At any rate, I was motivated to avoid these environments at all costs, and somehow in my mind, retirement moved me eerily closer to the institutionalized residential settings I abhorred. So I held onto my job until every ounce of me resisted its conventional rituals.

At some point, rising early, getting dressed, driving to the office, trying to be productive and avoid the mindless chatter that often permeates the workplace, then facing traffic jams on the way home became too much to bear. I understood it was time to go, but something in me was begging to stay. I had a long-standing relationship with the production side of me. I was comfortable with this aspect of my being that for years had helped define my self-worth. The busyness of my middle years allowed me to deny something profound that was happening inside. That AARP card was a stark reminder that I needed to pay attention to the transitory messages I was avoiding.

When I meditated and prayerfully explored the source of my discontent, it became clear that my spiritual house was not in order, so I learned more about the faith I professed. I was pleasantly surprised to experience a more relaxed lifestyle as I grew in knowledge, understanding, and wisdom. Simultaneously, I was employing the newly acquired skills of self-exploration and discovery to address my unresolved emotional issues. My need to control events and people was subsiding, and I witnessed firsthand the joy of allowing life to unfold as it should. I am continuing to grow spiritually, and I remain in awe of the myriad ways blessings flow when we are in sync with meaning and sacred purpose.

Many of the familiar landmarks of my life were disappearing, but I had not yet found the courage to fully embrace the great transformation that was unfolding. I no longer needed credentials and executive jobs to validate my self-worth. My children were grown and independent, so the role of caretaker was evolving into something deeper and far less needy. I was losing my appetite for yet another dress, or shoes, or just the right piece of furniture. Being in charge had lost its luster. Longevity has taught me so many things one of which was that there is a whole new world of discovery that cannot begin until we let go of the facades we created during our middle years. When we embrace the almost unlimited potential of enlightenment and clarity of purpose that await us we set in motion the invigorating excitement of endless possibilities. Once I was able to relieve myself of the superficial trappings of position, power, prestige, and production, I began to stitch together a creative tapestry that more closely resembled my authentic core.

At some point in our lives, we seek answers to the same deep questions: *Who am I? Why am I here?* What we are really asking is, *How does my individual story fit into God's kingdom narrative? In this world of billions of people do I matter?* My serious pursuit of answers came late in life. During my first fifty years, I was so busy dreaming and living and doing that I failed to consider the intrinsic value and true meaning of life and its sacred purpose. I naively thought purpose was connected to my career. What I have since learned is, when purpose is elevated to *sacred* status the opportunity to implement it is everywhere. Whether it is our jobs, families, churches, or communities is not the issue. Wherever we are, as Christians, we are compelled to find meaningful ways to glorify God through service.

Time Helps Us Find God and Strengthens Our Faith

My early church leaders taught me that God hovered above the clouds. They told me He would smile when I abided by my Christian teachings and exact wrath upon me when I erred. Even worse, all my errors were noted in the Book of Life, and before I entered the pearly gates of heaven, I would have to face God and explain each one of those errors. I remember being afraid of God because according to the grown-ups in my life, I often erred, so I expected I would have some explaining to do. I envisioned the Wizard of Oz–style experience Dorothy and her friends had when they stood before this presumed larger-than-life figure who terrified them as they attempted to register their special requests.

I was a young adult the first time I flew in an airplane. I was so excited, and as the plane ascended above the clouds, I halfway expected to see something miraculous, perhaps a glimpse of God. Before you laugh at that, consider that I was the product of a rural upbringing and my worldview was limited then. I do not need to tell you that I did not see God that morning, but for the first time, I came face to face with a profound conflict between a long-standing belief and reality. *Had I misinterpreted something I had been told all my life*? I was compelled by this experience to reconcile the discrepancy. This inspired my serious, intentional examination of the merits and demerits of issues rather than simply accepting what the grown-ups in my inner circle had instilled in me.

It is amazing how we never bother to question much of what we are told. We form opinions of people and things based solely on others' views and pass them on to others who trust our words. It is natural for children to believe what their parents tell them, but as they age, they have a responsibility to examine everything and thoughtfully consider it against the backdrop of their principles. We are here to contribute to the universal good. Anything that crosses our paths that does not help us find meaning and sacred purpose should be quickly disposed of.

I came to accept that my elders had been far more symbolic in their description of God hovering above the clouds than my childish literal interpretation had suggested. I think they were attempting to drive home the point that God's kingdom is heavenly and eternal but is also available to us here and now. They wanted me to understand that how I lived mattered and that my actions had consequences. This explanation works for me; it allows me to retain the nostalgic notion that my elders were gifted with wisdom and were legendary in their understanding of the mysteries of life. Certainty is a rare commodity, but maybe my elders already knew what I would later learn—God is everywhere.

I can see how it must have been difficult for the elders to describe the spiritual principles of my faith-based religion in a manner that a naive child could understand. I was born into a Christian household and thus exposed to the biblical teachings of the Trinity at an early age. The concept of a beautiful kingdom in the sky that would be inhabited only by kind and loving people intrigued me. It had all the makings of a great story, and it had a happy ending to boot. It was sufficiently mysterious and elusive, and in the battle of good versus evil, good prevails.

Jesus used parables to contrast the kingdom and the world and to teach us that we could find God everywhere at any time. Within the boundaries of the profane, the sacred is readily evident. There is always something extraordinary about the ordinary. The benefits of the eternal promises can be found in everyday experiences. Pure joy is available to us in rain and sunshine alike.

As we pursue answers to the deep questions of life, God patiently and quietly nudges us closer to oneness with Him. At the same time, He helps us mend our broken spirits and become whole. This is the journey of our lifetime. With much gratitude and thankfulness, we will discover many ways to strengthen our relationship with Him, and His promises will be revealed to us.

Faith is one of the foundational principles of the Christian religion. Through faith, we place our full confidence in an all-knowing, ever-present, and supreme God we cannot see as the essential provider of all we need. The Trinity represents the three-dimensional view of how we experience God. Our human limitations make it impossible for us to comprehend in its totality this complex, infinite, and ultimate source of spiritual energy. But there are ample everyday and divinely designed clues that bring us closer to the full realization of meaning and sacred purpose.

Time Helps Us Right Wrongs

We cannot begin to understand the gift of longevity without fully embracing meaning and sacred purpose. For us Christians, this state of being far exceeds our personal comforts and pursuits. It even goes beyond the salvation experience. It is all about becoming the best versions of ourselves for a greater good. Time offers us multiple chances to get it right and to position ourselves as the skilled wisdom teachers we are destined to be. The biblical promise of three score and ten and maybe more is a God-ordained blessing that brings with it responsibilities that support this notion of the greater good. We are here to serve others, but thoughtful preparation must take place before we are ready to assume this sacred assignment.

We are inundated with negative stimuli that at first glance suggest we have made such a mess of life and have missed the opportunity to move ourselves closer to peaceful coexistence and spiritual abundance. While all may seem lost sometimes, upon closer examination, we see indicators that despite our imperfections and challenges, we can make positive contributions to the human condition. With God's blessing, we can self-correct, change course, and embrace our sacred purpose. Global societal expansion is an individual-by-individual undertaking. *What if one reason for the gift of extended life is to give us extra time to right some of our wrongs?* Finding the courage to accept our contribution to the messiness of life takes time. Accumulating sufficient foresight, insight, and hindsight to organize the events of our lives into teachable moments takes time. When we grow as individuals, we do our part to elevate humanity.

Time Perfects Memories

I have so many outstanding memories of my children growing up, but one of my favorites is the pure happiness they exhibited whenever I baked a cake. They would sit around the kitchen table, watch me mix the ingredients, all the while displaying their intense excitement. Our conversations were even more special during this ritual. After I blended the ingredients and emptied them into the baking pan, they licked the spoon and bowl. They would then sit back and wait for the oven to work its magic and transform the mixture into a delicious cake. When I reminisce about that, I realize their excitement was not caused by the cake itself but by the simple pleasure of the milestones along the way. All the preparation I put into the process of baking created a special, multisensory experience that appears at the top of their lists of childhood memories. The time we spent together cannot be reclaimed, but it does not need to be. It was special enough then to produce a lifetime memory of enjoyment.

We all get to decide which aspects of our experiences we hold onto and what messages they offer us. Growing whole requires us to always consider the big picture from a vertical rather than a horizontal perspective. When we look back and make the story about us, we miss the spiritual point. But when we view the story from the larger perspective and consider the extenuating circumstances of everyone involved, we just might find the underlying blessing.

Time Reveals Our Authentic Selves

When you look in the mirror, whom do you see? Do you really know the person at whom you are staring? Do you know his or her beliefs, dreams, emotions, fears, and values? Do you know what makes him or her happy or sad? Do you know how he or she views the world? Do you see a lost soul drifting through life in search of meaning or someone aware of his or her sacred purpose? Growing whole requires us to get to know who we are at our core; over time and with determined effort, our true nature is revealed.

I try to live life with vigor and on point. We had no voice in how our lives began and will probably have little to say about how they will end. We do however have a whole lot to say about what happens in the meantime.

To age well, we must live well. To live well, we must be authentic and rooted in the principles of our Christian faith. We must live with integrity so that what we say can be trusted. Our personal life codes should clearly delineate what we stand for. Our private selves should comport with our public personae; there should be no misalignment there. Our Christ-centered lifestyle must be genuine and leave no room for hypocrisy. We should learn to love as God loves—unconditionally. We will falter as we strive for these ideals because the human condition makes it impossible for us to do otherwise, but our efforts should align with the goal of growing whole.

We Christians should focus on finding our authentic, pure, holy spaces and systematically dismantle any vestiges of unholiness that hinder our ability to find meaning and pursue sacred purpose. This is a lifelong endeavor, but it begins with a personal decision to raise the standards by which we live. Authentic living should be our goal. While we live and love in an imperfect world and we ourselves are imperfect, authenticity must become our gold standard.

To serve this present age, we must be genuine. If our intentions, thoughts, words, and deeds do not match, we are revealed as hypocritical. If we are motivated by ego rather than the sincerity of a servant's heart, people will detect the false pretense. Authentic living requires us to align our faith talk with our faith walk. We must decide whether the quality of our relationship with God is authentic or hypocritical. Sacred purpose cannot be realized under the cloak of hypocrisy. We cannot glorify God if we are not in a pure and sincere relationship with Him. Under false pretenses, we can do irreparable harm to someone who is seeking the truth about God.

More than once, I have heard people express disdain for the behavior of certain Christians. As ambassadors for God, we must remain mindful of the awesome responsibility we have assumed. Our light must shine so brightly that it attracts rather than repels. Our habits and practices should be structured in ways that effectively implement our quest for authenticity. Every human has an innate need to grow spiritually. Our task is to manage our lives in ways that this elevation from the secular to the sacred supports God's metanarrative. When we consistently function on this level, we are doing His work and we are allowing Him to shape us in miraculous ways.

One of the greatest benefits of adulthood is having the freedom to examine and explore a vast array of practices and teachings. Our faith requires us to pursue sacred purpose from a Christ-centered perspective, therefore it is incumbent upon each of us to ensure that the principles we adopt and implement in our lives are based on the truisms actually taught by Christ. Sound doctrine originates with God, it is recorded in the Word, it supports our spiritual growth, and it adds value to our efforts to establish a Christ-centered lifestyle. Otherwise we are disingenuous and inauthentic.

Hiding our true feelings is a common yet misguided relationship practice. We often do this to avoid confrontation, but in doing so, we undermine the authenticity of our connection to others. As we look forward to our golden years, we must be sure that the present versions of ourselves provide the building blocks for the future versions we envision. Along the way, the decision to grow whole will reveal certain things about us that we may not be proud of. As our life stories unfold and we continue along the journey to wholeness, buried feelings will rise to the surface and disturb our inner peace until we face them. This is normal, and when these feelings arise, we must be sufficiently courageous to allow God to do His work in us.

Several years ago, Edith, a coworker, confided in me some ill feelings she harbored toward Mindy, her best friend. Guilt haunted her, and she decided it was time to confront these emotions. She told me this.

Since third grade, Mindy and I were inseparable. During our teenage and early adult years, our lifestyle was less than stellar. Mindy and I regularly engaged in activities that brought shame to us and our families. I do not know why, but we went wild and rebelled against our home training.

By our late twenties though, we had settled into a more respectable pattern. We had good jobs with benefits. Believe it or not, she and I found our true loves and married only seven months apart. This is when I first started to notice some feelings I must have long ago buried. As they surfaced, I felt ashamed. It was hard for me to accept that I was jealous of my best friend!

Mindy's husband worked in the construction industry. He was skilled in his craft and made good money. In four years, they had a nice home and two children and were happily moving forward realizing their dreams. My husband and I were not as lucky. Our relationship was questionable from the beginning, and by the end of year two, we called it quits. We had no children, so the divorce was easily attained.

I struggled financially for years. At times, I had to rely on my parents to help me make ends meet. Gradually though, after three promotions, I became independent and was taking care of myself. I thought I was happy for Mindy despite how things turned out for me. She and her husband are still doing well, and whenever I sense any ill feelings toward her situation as compared to mine, I quickly bury them and move forward.

I bought my first home after fifteen years of struggling. Although my home is not as spacious or as beautiful as Mindy's, I love it, and I feel a great sense of accomplishment. I did this all by myself! I am happy most of the time, but lately, these feelings of jealousy toward her success are showing up more often. Mindy and I did things during our youth we should not have, and I am being punished and she is not. I love her, yet I struggle to understand why life is treating her so much better than it is treating me.

I commended Edith for having the courage to be honest about her emotions. As we continued to explore her feelings and their causes, she went deeper into the minefield of their relationship, which was far more complicated than she had first presented to me.

Over a period of six weeks, we met and continued the self-examination she had started. The more she talked about the related circumstances, the better she seemed to feel. Edith finally decided to my surprise to confess everything to Mindy.

Several months after our last session, Edith called me to say that she and Mindy had gotten together to engage in what she called "real talk." Armed with ample bottles of their favorite wine, they explored Edith's feelings of jealousy and other unresolved issues they had ignored for years. It seemed neither had wanted to hurt the other, so they had done what we often do—they buried their concerns in that place deep inside where we stow our messes. At some point, their out of sight–out of mind strategy stopped working, so they faced their truths. They cried, laughed, prayed, and reminisced for hours, and their relationship ended up stronger. They had gotten raw and real, and they benefitted from this display of courage and love. Their willingness to be vulnerable and reveal the ugliness of their feelings brought them closer to authenticity and elevated the level of their love for each other to that sacred space deep within.

When we are honest, life has meaning and proper perspective. We are more fulfilled and more joyful. Sacred purpose tells us that yes, we have a legitimate reason to be here and our contributions matter. Holy intention says we have declared our strong desire to be active participants in elevating society to a more compassionate and loving level. When meaning, sacred purpose, and holy intention intersect, all is well with our souls.

We are spiritual beings having a human experience that is divinely designed to move us away from the egotistical, physical version of ourselves and toward our pure, authentic essence. This process takes longer for some than it does for others, so we must stay the course no matter how many entanglements we encounter. Patience really is a virtue, and the ability to forgive ourselves when we falter is critical. Our task is to accept and embrace the lives we have been given and see them from a vertical rather than a horizontal perspective. When we comprehend that our stories are tiny parts of the kingdom story, we gain the fortitude and insight required for spiritual growth, and we lose our selfish appetite for making everything about us.

God's power to fully transform us is a living force that is accessible once we accept by faith this divine truth. Everything that happens to us and everyone we encounter are perfectly designed to support our transformation from the physical to the spiritual. There are distinct lessons we need to learn to realize our full potential and be of good service. Nothing in life is accidental or arbitrary; it is all on purpose and for a purpose. Our unique biological and environmental circumstances were predetermined to support the roles we play in the fulfillment of the greatest story ever told.

Deciding to discover our authentic selves is a pivotal decision. To be relevant, we must be authentic. To serve God and create the Christ-centered lifestyle we desire, we must be authentic. Today's youth are desperately seeking authentic connections. In this age of technology, they are finding it harder to establish mature, meaningful relationships. Having grown up during the time when people routinely interacted with each other face to face, we might have something of value to share with young people. I remember my dad drilling into our brains the requirement to look others in the eye when we talked to them. This way, he said, we could discern the sincerity of their intention. If we truly intend to serve this present age, we must be authentic. We cannot help someone else develop character traits that we ourselves have not mastered.

Chapter 9 Important Points

- The spiritual significance of time should not be lost on you in your daily activities.
- Time does for you exactly what it needs to do.
- Time supports the process of growing whole. It

  a. answers the deep questions,
  b. cleanses and heals,
  c. enlightens and gives perspective,
  d. helps you accept the inevitable,
  e. helps you find God and strengthens your faith,
  f. helps you right wrongs,
  g. perfects memories, and
  h. reveals your authenticity.

- Time gives you the knowledge, understanding, and wisdom to contribute to the common good.
- From the natural perspective, time began with the creation of the universe. From the supernatural perspective, time always was and always will be.
- You are an important part of the metanarrative of the kingdom story.
- The fundamental principles of Christianity are embedded in the great commandment to love and the Great Commission to evangelize.
- You had no voice in how your life began. You will have little to say about how it will end. You do however have a whole lot to say about what happens in the meantime.
- Every Christian should be singly focused on finding authenticity and holiness.
- As an ambassador for God, you must remain mindful of the awesome responsibility you have assumed.

- One of the greatest benefits of adulthood is having the freedom to examine and explore a vast array of practices and teachings. Your faith requires you to pursue sacred purpose from a Christ-centered perspective, therefore, you must ensure that the principles you adopt and implement in your life are based on the truisms actually taught by Christ.
- Sound doctrine originates with God, it is recorded in the Word, it supports your spiritual growth, and it adds value to your efforts to establish a Christ-centered lifestyle.

10

SPIRITUAL ABUNDANCE AND THE PROMISED-LAND LIFESTYLE

> May the God of hope fill you with all joy and peace in believing, so that by the power of the Holy Spirit you may abound in hope. (Romans 15:13 ESV)

Imagine the pure joy of having ready access to the deepest, most authentic part of yourself, the part where love flows freely and fuels your soul. Imagine how wonderous life would be if you had already done the inside-out work required to address the unresolved issues that cause you unnecessary pain and sabotage your dreams. Imagine if your personal goals and God's sacred purpose for your life were aligned. Imagine how rich life would be if this state of euphoria was a routine part of your Christ-centered lifestyle. Imagine what loving God, self, and others would look like in such a heightened state of awareness. Imagine if you could hear the voice of God so vividly that His words and their meaning are unmistakably clear. Imagine if you could feel His spiritual presence so strongly that you knew beyond a doubt you were in the company of divinity. This state of spiritual abundance is available to us when we sow the seeds of "love, joy, peace, patience, kindness, goodness, faithfulness, gentleness, and self-control." (Galatians 5:22–23 ESV)

Fruit of the Spirit

The journey toward wholeness has its share of ups and downs, victories, and defeats. Many times, our hearts will be broken, disappointments will bring us to our knees, and the agony of loss will temporarily cripple us. But we persevere and stay the course because we are clear about the promises of God. As we continue our spiritual growth trajectory and move closer to oneness and wholeness, we raise the level of our energy and our worldview is elevated from world-centeredness and ego-centeredness to Christ-centeredness. At that point, we have moved into the territory of promised-land living.

While we will never experience perfection on earth, when we invite God's holiness into our lives, His power and presence give us joy and peace that defy human understanding. We were born with a yearning for spiritual abundance. This is one of the basic building blocks of God's reconciliation plan. He gives us the gifts and talents we need to realize this strong desire and He also gives us the free will to make conscious choices about who and what we will rely on to satisfy this yearning. *Will you rely on money, possessions, power, or prestige, or will you put your complete faith in Him?* God offers us the same opportunity to choose that He offered Adam and Eve. *There is secular fruit and there is spiritual fruit. Which will you choose?* Choices have consequences.

Soon after His baptism, Jesus had a remarkable wilderness encounter with Satan. During this interchange, the devil urged Jesus to provoke God. Jesus had prepared for His ministry by fasting and praying for forty days and forty nights. As a result, He was probably exhausted and hungry. Satan thought he saw an opportunity to persuade Jesus to rebel against God, but he was mistaken. Jesus passed each of His tests, and Satan eventually accepted defeat and left him alone.

Similarly, as newly anointed members of the Christian faith, we are set apart from the world yet we are still in it physically, emotionally, and spiritually. To experience promised-land living in the earthly realm, we must figure out how to be true to our faith within the parameters of this reality. We are challenged to reconcile any unresolved issues that hinder realization of sacred purpose while living with the same temptations we faced before our salvation experience. As He did with Adam and Eve, God leaves the temptations right there in full view. We must choose this day and everyday whom we will serve.

Joy

The joy and peace of promised-land living is available to us in the here and now. When we can see the all-knowing, all-powerful, and ever-present God of the universe, no matter the circumstances, spiritual abundance is ours to enjoy and revel in. Functioning on this higher level of Christ-centeredness requires leaving all the remnants of world-consciousness and ego-consciousness behind despite our continued exposure to the secular pleasures they offer. While the enticing fruit might be delicious, it might also be poison.

The concept of joy holds deep spiritual significance in the Christian faith. As one of the fruits of the spirit, it is the pure delight of being alive regardless of the difficulties of the present moment. It is unshakable faith in the God of the universe. It is the peace of knowing who we are and whose we are.

The book of Matthew breaks a four-hundred-year period of silence between the book of Malachi and the birth of Jesus Christ. During this period of silence God did not speak to the Jewish people. Matthew, who was one of Jesus' twelve disciples, tells us that Jesus began His ministry by calling His first disciples and giving what is now widely known as the Sermon on the Mount. The preamble to the sermon, the Beatitudes, describes the lifestyle that God requires of His people and it establishes a code of conduct for them. It contrasts kingdom values with worldly values. It distinguishes between superficial faith and Christian faith, and it clarifies how the Old Testament expectations will be fulfilled in the new kingdom. The preamble focuses on specific ways to receive God's blessings, which are experienced by us as a state of internal joyfulness that does not depend on external circumstances and situations.

Joy is more than an emotion. It is far deeper than feelings of happiness. It is a gift from God—it is an essential spiritual practice. Our worldly possessions and our accomplishments are blessings that make us happy, but they are external and situational. We are taught to consider everything that happens to us from a spiritual perspective—even when we falter. We are to trust that our life will unfold as it should and we will learn what we need to learn from every experience. During our valley moments we must find the strength to endure and be patient. God is preparing us for sacred purpose. The source of all joy is the Lord. As a result, joy is an innate part of our Christian faith. It is our leaning post when we are weak. It deepens our relationship with God, Jesus Christ, and the Holy Spirit. As one of the fruits of the spirit, it is foundational to realizing the benefits of sanctification and growing whole. Joy supernaturally comforts us and sustains us during our periods of pain and sorrow. Joy is calm and easy; it does not require drama or fastidiousness. It is not complicated, and we can find it in the simplest expressions of life.

As we shift our worldview from ego to spirit, transformation occurs in myriad ways. Fear and insecurity no longer control us. The chains of selfishness no longer bind us. When the lens through which we see the world is based on love and sacred purpose, we learn to relax and enjoy life as it unfolds. We understand and accept that some degree of pain and suffering is a natural part of life. This allows us to relinquish the physical urge to control matters in favor of humble submission to God's divine design for our lives.

Every life has meaning and purpose. Salvation and sanctification give purpose its sacred status because God anointed it. Once we are adopted into His family, everything changes. We no longer serve temporary, worldly idols; we now serve our eternal God and His kingdom. As we continue our efforts to grow whole, revelation and clarification of this salient point occur over time. As our spiritual senses awaken and we become more comfortable functioning on this higher level of consciousness, the intensity of fear-based emotions wanes and love-based emotions permeate our personal life codes. We internalize the spiritual truth that while our physical selves can be harmed, our eternal selves are never in danger.

> Do not be anxious about anything, but in every situation,
> by prayer and petition, with thanksgiving, present your
> requests to God. And the peace of God, which transcends
> all understanding, will guard your hearts and your minds
> in Christ Jesus. (Philippians 4:6–7 NIV)

While happiness is often situational, joy is our ever-present companion whether or not things are going well. Life offers many disappointments and tragedies. As a result, it is tempting to settle into a woe is me mindset and lower our expectations to support the belief that we are victims of circumstances. If we are not careful, we can become addicted to our miseries and settle for mediocre lives that sabotage our divine destiny and limit our capacity to witness God's miracles.

Worldly treasures such as money, position, power, and prestige can be taken away by people with more money, higher positions, and greater power and prestige. A single stock market crash can reduce your bank account in seconds. Enactment of a law or a business realignment can eliminate your prestigious job and strip you of its accompanying power without any consideration for your welfare. The fleeting, egotistical nature of prestige is tenuous at best while God's promise of spiritual abundance is secure and eternal. Situational whims do not add to or detract from the joy and peace of promised-land living.

Growing up on a family farm offered me many wonderful experiences. One of my fondest memories is of the fruit trees that adorned our property. Readily available were varieties of kumquats, oranges, pears, scuppernongs, and tangerines. Vegetables were plentiful as well, but I was more interested in the fruit.

During growing season, the scuppernongs were so abundant that my siblings and I entered into a business partnership with our grandmother; we would pick and package the grapes, and she would haul them to the local farmers' market to sell. It was a lucrative arrangement all around. This delicious fruit nourished us, earned us some pocket money, and grandmother was rewarded with her fair share of the proceeds. Just as the abundant natural fruit of my childhood was pleasant, plentiful, and beneficial to the quality of my life, the fruit of the spirit is also pleasant, plentiful, and beneficial to the quality of my life.

Joy is an important by-product of growing whole. The key to realizing and sustaining this coveted euphoric state is learning the art of authentic contentment regardless of our situations. When circumstances make it hard to tap into that space deep within us where peace and authentic contentment reside, we must keep the faith and rest in the certainty that all things good and bad will ultimately lead us to a place where spiritual transformation is realized.

Reflections on Abundance and Scarcity

Advances in technology make it possible for us to communicate within seconds with anyone in the world. Despite such incomprehensible access, depression, distress, and loneliness abound. We are disconnected emotionally even in the company of thousands. There is a sadness that is hard to explain. Something significant is missing in our lives, and we cannot find it by searching outside ourselves. The disconnection is not external; it is in our souls. Internal harmony and unity are critical components of our efforts toward wholeness, and the contentment we innately seek is beyond our grasp until we learn to experience life through the lens of abundance rather than scarcity.

Deep within each of us lies a wellspring of abundance. The human story is one of creation and recreation. The circle of life gives us dates and times to enter and exit it. During this period, with a little effort on our part, the miracle of discovery makes our journey sufficiently exciting to keep us engaged and passionate about the gift of life. Spiritual laws and universal principles tell us that everything we need to successfully navigate life is in us and is accessible at will.

> His divine power has given us everything we need for a godly life through our knowledge of him who called us by his own glory and goodness. Through these he has given us his very great and precious promises, so that through them you may participate in the divine nature, having escaped the corruption in the world caused by evil desires. For this very reason, make every effort to add to your faith goodness; and to goodness, knowledge; and to knowledge, self-control; and to self-control, perseverance; and to perseverance, godliness; and to godliness, mutual affection; and to mutual affection, love. For if you possess these qualities in increasing measure, they will keep you from being ineffective and unproductive in your knowledge of our LORD Jesus Christ. (2 Peter 1:3–8 NIV)

Motivational speakers offer us inspiring messages about abundance and prosperity, which is often associated with power, prestige, and wealth. As the atmosphere is shifting and leading us toward a heart-centered way of being, we are learning that abundance is far more expansive than worldly possessions.

Unfair and unjust distribution of these resources set up the dichotomy of abundance versus scarcity and create ill will among humankind. The powerful decision makers who drive policy and stir the passions of greed have created a system that encourages needless competition. We live in an abundant universe with plentiful resources. When life is viewed from the lens of us versus them, the mindset that someone else's gain is at our expense becomes the cultural norm. Fear-based emotions flourish in such an environment. We become comfortable with the level of disrespect and hatred that supports manipulating others for our selfish gains.

From a human perspective, secular abundance is a complicated phrase with myriad components. When we peel back its layers, we see that it is influenced by internal and external factors. It is at once egotistical, emotional, materialistic, physical, and psychological. It is subjective rather than objective. What feels like abundance to you might not rise to that level for someone else. The point where abundance ends and greed begins is a slippery slope. Ours is one of the richest nations in the world. Most Americans live well above the poverty level with ready access to life's necessities and some of the desires of their hearts. *So the question is, when is enough enough?* In our efforts to grow whole, this dilemma requires our ongoing attention.

By comparison, spiritual abundance is simple and straightforward. When we position ourselves to hear the voice of God, we make room for creativity, expansion, and positivity to flourish. Our steps are ordered in ways that authentic moments of joy and inner peace thrive, and we allow compassion and love to transform us. Spiritual abundance is a decision of the heart. We choose to live in the sacred space of contentment. We learn to be grateful for the present moment, and we block out the stressful complexities of our frantic and frazzled secular world. Through prayer and meditation, we connect with our life source and live in this state of heightened awareness. Life has meaning, and we have clarity of purpose. We are not concerned with worldly trappings, and the principles that guard and guide our lives are rooted in our Christ-centered lifestyle.

Spirituality and Lifelong Learning

Learning to implement the principles of spiritual abundance in our everyday lives is an important catalyst for wholeness. When we decide to grow beyond an emotional and theoretical discussion of godliness, we elevate our mundane, ordinary experiences to transcendent status. We tap into a reservoir of divine intervention that elevates us from the secular to the sacred.

Embedded in every intention, thought, word, and deed are seeds of holiness. When the miracle of waking up each morning is greeted with gratitude and thanksgiving and when we forgive our perceived offenders, the principle of spiritual abundance is present. When we show kindness and love, when we serve the less fortunate, or when we end our day with prayer, the principle of spiritual abundance is present. When we live in this joyous space, we move ever so close to oneness with God and wholeness with self and others.

Growing whole requires a lifelong commitment to learning. Every experience is a teachable moment. No matter our current status, we are created on purpose for purpose. New learning and fresh insight are invigorating and allow us to develop the skills required for holy expansion and growth. When we know better, we usually do better. To remain relevant, we must be awake and informed. According to the Four Stages of Learning theory, learning takes place in the basic categories of unconscious incompetence, conscious incompetence, conscious competence, and unconscious competence. While the origin of this theory is uncertain, Gordon Training International played a major role in promoting its use during the 1970s. I have adapted the four learning stages for use as a model for spiritual growth.

- At the unconscious incompetence stage, we are ignorant of the need to change or learn a new skill. We do not accept our deficiency; in fact, we are unaware there is one, and we function on this low level of achievement and productivity. Deep within us are seeds that yearn to be fertilized and nurtured, and even at this fat, dumb, and pseudo-happy stage, dissatisfaction festers and shows up in myriad ways. We unleash our fear-based emotions and bad attitudes on the world all the while lacking the capacity to recognize the cesspool we have created. We settle for a lifetime of ill health and the numbness of a hopeless existence. We lack vision and are devoid of the energy and gusto that accompanies meaning and sacred purpose.

If we are lucky, the events of life will disturb the false realities we have created to support this mediocre existence, and the previously dormant seeds of growth will be aroused. If this happens, we will begin to ask probing questions and examine our worldview. In doing so, glimpses of possibility will show up. If we choose to ignore the opportunity for expansion that accompanies the disturbance, we in effect choose a lifetime of low self-esteem and low productivity. On this level, we are incapable of maintaining healthy relationships and the ever-present sting of missed opportunities is the central theme of our life story. On the other hand, if we find the courage to step out on faith and explore possibilities, we sow and reap bountifully. The potential for transformation is ever present. It is up to us to discover its blessing.

- At the conscious incompetence stage, we are acutely aware of our deficiency, and we feel compelled to change. We realize that by dealing with unresolved internal conflict, life can be more fulfilling and the joyful existence we innately desire is achievable. We step out of our "less-than" reality and envision a life saturated with meaning and sacred purpose. We ask probing questions, and we seek enlightenment. We accept responsibility for our present condition, and we kindle the powerful flames of desire and passion to propel us to a higher level of existence. We release the bad habits of self-sabotage that chain us to guilt and shame, we forgive ourselves and others, and we create new habits that lead to fulfillment and productivity.
- At the conscious competence stage, we have acquired new life skills and we are performing on a higher, more productive level. We are slowly becoming more comfortable with our new normal. The fruits of our labor are paying big dividends, and we are committed to a lifestyle of expansion and growth. Self-awareness, vigilance,

and early detection of the triggers that threaten our progress are critical assets. Success at this stage requires practice, practice, and more practice until the positive changes become habitual.

- At the fourth and final stage, we are functioning on the unconscious competence level. This means we can consistently and reliably perform our newly acquired skills, and the behavioral and cognitive adjustments we made no longer require extra attention and effort. They are embedded in us, and life as we know it begins undergoing a miraculous metamorphosis. Having experienced a spiritual transformation, we now serve as role models and wisdom teachers for those in our circles of influence. We offer them a real-life example of what is possible when we make a conscious decision to be guided by a holy calling that far exceeds what our human limitations could envision.

My husband and I live in an area of our city with an abundance of deer. After much trial and error, we ceded the back yard to them. They have proven time and again that we will not have the lush flowerbeds of my dreams. In an apparent act of compromise, they do allow me though to inundate my patio with potted plants.

The patio is my laboratory. This sacred space has offered me untold hours of enjoyment as I commune with nature in general and my plants in particular. Their beauty, aroma, and vibrant colors and the hybrids I have inadvertently created always offer me a spiritual experience. Sometimes, I get busy and ignore my plants but many of them survive and thrive despite my neglect.

Jessica, a dear friend, once asked me to recommend a plant for her screened porch that was guaranteed to survive. I suggested four that were likely to do well, but just as with everything in life, there are no guarantees. This interchange sparked a delightful conversation that reminded us about the Parable of the Growing Seed. This is a story about a man who scatters seed on the ground and then allows nature to take its course. Even though he went about his business and ignored the seed it sprouted, then it produced a stalk and leaves, then a new head of grain appeared. Finally, fully developed kernels emerged. The moral of this story is all this new growth happened without the man's assistance.

And he said, "The kingdom of God is as if a man should scatter seed on the ground. He sleeps and rises night and day, and the seed sprouts and grows; he knows not how. The earth produces by itself, first the blade, then the ear, then the full grain in the ear. But when the grain is ripe, at once he puts in the sickle, because the harvest has come." (Mark 4:26–29 ESV)

Jesus often used parables to describe the new life being offered by God. Parables are simple stories about ordinary, everyday events that illustrate moral principles or spiritual lessons. The metaphoric style of Jesus' stories made them difficult to understand without the assistance of the Holy Spirit. One of my favorite parables is the Parable of the Sower. In this story the man scatters seed on four different types of ground; hard ground, stony ground, thorny ground, and good ground. The hard ground prevents the seed from sprouting and it becomes nothing more than bird food. The stony ground provides enough soil for the seeds to germinate and begin to grow, but because the ground is shallow the plants do not take root and soon die. The thorny ground allows the seed to grow, but the competing thorns choke the life out of the plants. The good ground receives the seed and produces bountiful fruit. The seed represents God's Word. The types of ground represent the condition of our hearts. The hard ground symbolizes someone who hears God's Word but does not understand it. The stony ground symbolizes someone who professes their love for God's Word, but their heart is not changed and when trouble arises their weak faith quickly disappears. The thorny ground symbolizes someone who receives the Word but their love for worldly treasures is stronger than their love for God's Word. The good ground symbolizes someone who hears, understands, receives, and allows God's purposes to be accomplished in their life. We believe and receive God's Word through our heart and by faith. The moral of this story is the condition of our heart determines whether God's Word will take root in our lives and exemplify the good soil.

Spiritual abundance and promised-land living are natural experiences when God's seeds are planted in our hearts and we patiently allow them to grow and produce good fruit. God's power and presence will abound, and the quality of our lives will improve exponentially. Meaning and sacred purpose will permeate our being, and we will thrive in the joy of salvation and sanctification. When we get busy and allow the events of lives to distract us, God will gently nudge us back to what really matters—glorifying Him. Through an intimate, personal relationship, we will continue to enjoy God's grace and mercy, despite our missteps. Oneness and wholeness will become our new normal, and worldly temptations will no longer find fertile ground in us. The fruit of the spirit will become the guiding principles for our lives and meaning and sacred purpose will undergird our efforts toward growing whole.

God promises us that His harvest will be magnificent and prolific—the best fruit ever grown. "And God is able to bless you abundantly, so that all things at all times, having all that you need, you will abound in every good work" (2 Corinthians 9:8 NIV).

Chapter 10 Important Points

- The state of spiritual abundance is available to you when you commit to the lifelong process of growing whole.
- When you sow the seeds of "love, joy, peace, patience, kindness, goodness, faithfulness, gentleness, and self-control" (Galatians 4:22–23 ESV), you reap a bountiful harvest.
- You were born with a yearning for spiritual abundance. This is one of the basic building blocks of God's reconciliation plan.
- The joy and peace of promised-land living are available to you here and now.
- When you shift your worldview from ego to spirit, transformation occurs in ways that move you closer to the Christ-centered lifestyle you desire.
- Every life has meaning and purpose. Salvation and sanctification give purpose its sacred status because God anointed it.
- While happiness is often situational, joy is your ever-present companion no matter the circumstances.
- There is a distinct difference between secular abundance and spiritual abundance.
- Unfair and unjust distribution of worldly resources sets up a dichotomy of abundance versus scarcity and creates ill will among humankind.
- Learning to implement the principles of spiritual abundance in your everyday life is an important catalyst for wholeness.
- Growing whole requires a lifelong commitment to learning. Every experience is a teachable moment.
- New learning and fresh insight are invigorating, and they allow you to develop the skills required for holy expansion and growth.
- To remain relevant, you must be awake and informed.
- Learning takes place in four basic stages—unconscious incompetence, conscious incompetence, conscious competence, and unconscious competence.

- Learning to implement the principles of spiritual abundance in your everyday life is an important catalyst for wholeness.
- Spiritual abundance and promised-land living are natural experiences when God's seeds are planted in your heart and you patiently allow them to grow and produce good fruit.

EPILOGUE

Let thy hands be as the hands of a good watch, through every golden moment marking the worthy progress of the inner life. (James Lendall Basford[20])

Growing whole is a lifelong process of being molded into the character and image of God. This process begins with a decision to do the work necessary to transition from a worldly, ego-centered existence to a Christ-centered lifestyle.

We are unable to find meaning and sacred purpose on our own. Even under the best of circumstances, we fall short as our diligent efforts are consistently thwarted by the reality of human imperfection. Without God's guidance, we lack vision, so we cannot see the big picture. We do not comprehend that our individual lives connect to the metanarrative of the kingdom story. As a result, we go about our days in pursuit of self-gratification. We behave in ways that hinder rather than help the common good because we fail to comprehend the interconnectedness of God's world. We do not understand that our actions and reactions to the events of life matter not only to us but also to the universal human condition.

For those who choose to accept the biblical account of human existence, the gold standard for how one individual should interact with another is clear. God's Word explains the meaning of life and the sacredness of its purpose. Without this account of why life matters, we have no point of beginning. We are subject to being "tossed to and fro by the waves and carried about by every wind of doctrine, by human cunning, by craftiness in deceitful schemes" (Ephesians 4:14 ESV).

---

[20] https://quotegarden/james_basford/self.html

God promises a kingdom of redeemed people who will participate with Him in an eternal, blissful spiritual state. In the meantime, He calls us to fulfill earthly assignments to serve humankind. For most of us, sacred purpose will not rise to the level of our favorite Bible characters, but our assignments matter, nonetheless. Maybe we are here to help end world hunger or urge governments to lay down their weapons of mass destruction in favor of peaceful coexistence. Maybe we are here to find a cure for a chronic disease that plagues humanity. Maybe we have the gifts and talents to improve environmental protection laws and regulations. Maybe our contribution lies in research, or the arts, or teaching, or sharing God's Word in ways that people can comprehend and apply to their daily lives.

God gives us clues about where our meaning and sacred purpose lie. *What are your special gifts and talents? What are you passionate about? What propels you out of bed each morning? What makes you lose track of time? What makes your soul smile?* Our job is to find the reason for being here and then committing wholeheartedly to implement the calling.

The process of growing whole requires a personal decision that our best years are yet to come. There is something so exhilarating about such a declaration. If we believe life will continue to get better, our attitude toward it will remain positive and we will exude confidence that is contagious. Longevity is a blessing only if we believe it is. Otherwise, we miss opportunities that are unique to our golden years. We have so much to look forward to. Having the freedom to live life more on our terms while continuing to serve energizes and invigorates us. Believing our quality of life can always improve strengthens our resolve and undergirds our genuine efforts to grow. Lifelong relevance and vitality are key to appreciating the gift of years.

From a spiritual perspective, as children of God, we assume the awesome, ever-present responsibility for glorifying Him in all our efforts. We abandon worldly ego-centeredness in favor of Christ-centeredness. We serve others rather than indulge ourselves. We abandon fear in favor of faith. We exemplify love, joy, peace, patience, kindness, goodness, faithfulness, gentleness, and self-control. Our relationship with the world is forever changed, and we begin to put the broken pieces of our souls together in ways that serve the common good.

We live in a divided world, and we are required to do our part to facilitate reconciliation. Everything we intend, think, say, and do matters. *Will we reflect God's righteousness, or will we promote self-righteousness? Will we use our gifts and talents to support the kingdom, or will we become stumbling blocks? Will we treat others with the respect they deserve, or will we allow our biases and prejudices to make us act in unholy ways?* The gift of free will offers us that choice.

We heal the world by healing ourselves. We change the world by changing ourselves. During the 1960s, a mathematician and meteorologist named Edward Lorenz earned the title of Father of Chaos Theory when he made a remarkable discovery that he called the butterfly effect. According to Lorenz, small differences in a dynamic system such as the atmosphere could trigger vast and often unsuspected effects.

> Even the slightest change can cause entirely different results. The wing movements of a butterfly in Peru may later, through an extremely complex series of unpredictably-linked events, magnify air movements and ultimately cause a hurricane in Texas.[21]

The principle that the smallest change triggers a chain reaction of unexpected and epic proportions is now routinely applied to other dynamic systems, not just the weather. (See *The Vibrational Universe*, Kenneth J. MacLean). Lorenz was simply trying to explain why it was so hard to make good weather forecasts, but he wound up unleashing a scientific revolution called chaos theory.

This same principle can be applied to growing whole, finding meaning, and sacred purpose. One small harmonious act of kindness can have a revolutionary, universal effect. One smile might be the difference in a despondent person following through with plans to commit suicide or deciding there is a reason to live. This same individual whose life was spared by a smile may one day conduct research that supports early detection and prevention of epidemics and pandemics.

We were not born simply to immerse ourselves in worldly pleasures and treasures. We are here to serve humanity, and we cannot accomplish this without an intimate, one-on-one relationship with God. As our relationship

---

[21] K. J. Maclean, *The Vibrational Universe* (2005).

with Him strengthens, we learn more about His requirements for our lives. We gain knowledge, understanding, and wisdom. We become comfortable relying on Him and seeking His guidance. As we learn to love others as God loves us, to forgive others as God forgives us, and to serve others as God serves us, like the flutter of a butterfly's wings, we can cause a chain reaction of epic proportions.

Growing whole includes acknowledging the interconnected nature of all that is. God created the universe and everything in it. From the human soul to the vast dimensions of the cosmos, it all belongs to Him and is subject to His spiritual truths. These truths clarify that He is orderly, precise, and predictable in His response to us. When we are faithful and obedient, life is easier, more meaningful, and more fulfilling. When we transgress, we bring unnecessary pain and suffering to ourselves and others. Everything matters. We either help or hinder the kingdom story.

When we ignore our interconnectedness, it is easier to demonize and distrust others because we see them as separate and different from us. On the other hand, when we fully embrace the reality of interdependence, the seeds of compassion and empathy are planted and nurtured. All pathways to oneness and wholeness require reconciliation, which is made possible only through fellowship and relationship. We are to love God and our neighbor as ourselves, and everyone is our neighbor.

Growing whole requires clarity of sacred purpose. Without this, we do not appreciate our relevance to the kingdom story. We struggle with the evils that accompany low self-esteem, and we become disillusioned. We lose ourselves in worldly pursuits and settle for self-serving existences. We tolerate less than peak performance, and we engage in activities that demean and disrespect ourselves and others. Our intentions, thoughts, words, and deeds are misaligned, and disharmony prevails.

Growing whole requires deep, objective self-examination and self-exploration. It relies heavily on a strong sense of self-awareness. We must find the courage to get raw and real with ourselves and analyze our unresolved issues. This vital spiritual cleansing expands our hearts to make room for inside-out reconciliation. We strip away layers of disappointment and hurt. We recognize and rectify indiscretions. We make amends and seek forgiveness. These peacemaking initiatives establish the critical framework for opportunities to expand and grow. Socrates's famous saying

"The unexamined life is not worth living" is a profound recognition of the value of self-exploration and reconciliation.

When we are clear about who we are and what really matters to us, we demonstrate a level of emotional integrity that supports expansion and growth. Our inner and outer selves align, and when we falter, we take ownership of our missteps. Self-awareness empowers us to manage our lives in ways that model our spiritual essence. As we engage in daily living, we continuously send and receive messages. As God's earthly ambassadors, the messages we send should exude the principles of compassion, faithful service, and love. When we know who we are and whose we are, our lives are living testimonies of godliness.

We all have gifts and talents that were bestowed by God to serve His purposes. The five-sensory, multisensory, and multidimensional combinations that make up our individual character is uniquely ours. There is a divinely inspired reason for this phenomenon. We have the free will to use these gifts and talents to pursue meaning and sacred purpose in creative ways. Our contributions to the kingdom story are unique to us. This makes life challenging, exciting, and interesting.

When we move into the spiritual space where meaning and sacred purpose feel personal yet interconnected to the metanarrative of all that is, we experience spiritual abundance. Our commitment to growing whole is reaping its harvest, and our hearts expand. The struggle to find this spiritual space is the story of our lives. The accomplishments and setbacks, the happiness and sadness, the harvest and heartache, the jubilation and pain, the moments of compassion and seasons of anger, the stepping-stones and stumbling blocks come together to support our transformation from the physical to the spiritual. Through our unique expressions of love for God, self, and others, we contribute to the greatest story ever told.

The decision to invite God into our lives is a critical prerequisite for growing whole. Without His divine guidance, we are lost souls muddling through life pursuing one selfish desire after another. The gift of salvation connects us to God, and the lifelong, hard work of sanctification cleanses and purifies our souls. When we invite God in, we make room for systematic transformation to a higher level of consciousness that elevates us beyond our human limitations. Through the work of the Holy Spirit, we spend the remainder of our lives growing into the being that God intended when He created original man. Our desires and habits change, and we shift our focus from temporary, worldly pursuits to our eternal, sacred purpose.

Growing whole begins with a simple yet profound conscious choice and a willingness to commit. Once you choose and commit, God sets the forces in motion to support your profound transformation. Your level of spiritual energy is raised. Your world-centered and ego-centered desires wane as you undertake the journey of a lifetime. Almost immediately, you begin to attract events, conditions, circumstances, and people who are pivotal to your spiritual expansion and growth.

Just as the acorn gives rise to the oak tree, each of us was born as a diamond in the rough with the imperative to transition into a precious jewel. Through our myriad experiences in growing whole, we learn the lessons predetermined for us by God. We find meaning and pursue sacred purpose as He intended. The story of creation is a story of holy intention, and the role we play in the metanarrative of the kingdom story is important. For this reason, we are here.

As we endure the struggles of life and marvel in its blessings, we can trust that God knows exactly what He is doing. By divine design, He is molding and shaping us into His character and image. Finding meaning and sacred purpose in the parameters we are given leads to oneness with God and wholeness with self and others.

> Blessed are those who trust in the Lord. They are like trees planted along a riverbank, with roots that reach deep into the water. Such trees are not bothered by the heat or worried by long months of drought. Their leaves stay green, and they go right on producing delicious fruit. (Jeremiah 17:7–8 NLT)

GLOSSARY

Term	Definition
Christ-centered Lifestyle	A life that is committed to Jesus Christ, the Son of God, as Lord and savior. You focus your attention, energy, and time on spiritual growth, internalizing His teachings, and applying your knowledge, understanding, and wisdom in ways that demonstrate love for God, self, and others. You put your Christian faith into action by serving the common good and actively pursuing your sacred purpose.
Cocreate	The lifelong sanctification work we undertake in partnership with the Holy Spirit.
Conscious aging	A decision to be proactive about preserving your chosen lifestyle by 1) remaining engaged in meaningful and productive activities while successfully coping with life's age-related challenges, 2) understanding and appreciating the unique benefits that accompany longevity, and 3) entering elderhood with a positive attitude and a sense of eagerness in anticipation of a future filled with exciting options.
Ego-centered	An unhealthy focus on yourself and what matters to you rather than being concerned about the welfare of others.
Five-sensory	The natural, physical ability to hear, see, smell, taste, and touch.

Growing whole	A willful decision to live a Christ-centered lifestyle by focusing on spiritual growth and the ongoing purification of your soul. To integrate the principles of the *Twelve Functional Dimensions of Humankind* model to support sustained spiritual growth. To actively pursue internal and external harmony by engaging in activities that promote alignment, balance, and reconciliation. To fully immerse yourself in the Godly principles of love and sacred purpose. To view spiritual growth from a whole-person perspective.
Horizontal perspective	A selfish focus on how circumstances and events affect you. Having little regard for how others are impacted.
Metanarrative	The grand story of God, through Jesus Christ, building a kingdom of redeemed people for their eternal enjoyment and for His glorification. The overall message of the Bible story of creation (the way things were), the fall (the way things are), redemption (the way things could be), and restoration (the way things will be). This story begins in the Garden of Eden, with the creation of all things and ends in a City of God, the New Jerusalem, with the renewal of all things. In between, it offers a vision of the meaning and sacred purpose of life and how we fit into God's grand story.

Multidimensional	An explanation of the spiritual interconnectedness of the physical and nonphysical aspects of human existence. A comprehensive description of how the body, soul, and spirit interact with each other and how they impact the dimensions within which they function. When the tripartite nature of humankind and the functional dimensions of the body, soul, spirit are aligned and integrated, life is experienced and interpreted from a whole-person perspective.
Multisensory	When salvation occurs God takes up permanent residence in the body of the newly anointed believer in Jesus Christ. The believer no longer relies solely on his or her natural, physical abilities to navigate life. With the indwelling of the Third person of the Trinity, the Holy Spirit, the individual's five-sensory capacities are elevated to holy status.
Sacred purpose	Your God-ordained reason for living and the basis for understanding how you fit into the kingdom-building metanarrative.
Spiritual transformation	The lifelong process of inside-out cleansing and renewing of the heart and mind (soul) so they no longer conform to the ways of the world, but are now committed to pleasing God. This process requires the conscious discarding of negative ideologies and replacing them with positive ones that honor God and are in accordance with His Word.

Vertical perspective	A focus on how circumstances and events fit into the metanarrative of biblical teachings by compassionately considering the impact on everyone involved.
World-centeredness	Seeking happiness by focusing on temporary, secular pleasures and treasures rather than God's promises of eternal joy and spiritual abundance.
Worldview	The lens through which we see the universe and everyone and everything in it. The essence of who we are as human beings-our attitudes, beliefs, deeds, desires, dreams, emotions, sense of right and wrong, and value system.

ABOUT THE AUTHOR

Gloria Crawford Henderson is a life coach whose specialty areas include personal growth and development, relationship dynamics, spirituality, wellness, and women's empowerment. For more than forty-five years, she was a government manager and public policy administrator with the State of Florida. The array of her executive and legislative branch subject matter expertise spans corrections and criminal justice, public finance, health care administration and regulation, and substance abuse and mental health crisis services. She has a bachelor's degree in political science and a master's degree in public administration. According to Gloria,

> The common denominator of my professional portfolio is the ongoing revelation that people hurt themselves and others in myriad ways when they lack meaning and sacred purpose. One of the strongest human desires is the need to expand and grow. When we are not in active pursuit of the highest and best version of ourselves, the agony of mediocrity is relentless. We are built for greatness, and when we, for whatever reasons, fall short of that universal urge, the insidious nature of "less than" attacks us at our core. Then, it shows up in the form of anger, bitterness, disease, and dysfunction. We act out in ways that disrespect our humanity, and we forfeit our God-given right to flourish. Greatness resides within each of us, and we must never stop growing!

Following a serious medical scare Gloria made a pivotal quality of life decision to make health and wellness and spiritual growth a priority. She set out on a journey of discovery that yielded amazing results. Life is far more enjoyable, and opportunities to encourage and motivate others abound. She now spends her time coaching, speaking, and training. She says,

> Simple, whole-person lifestyle changes can alter the trajectory of our lives in ways we are just beginning to understand. People are living longer, and it is incumbent upon each of us to make the latter years better than the former. Life really does get better when we commit to the process of growing whole rather than simply growing old. We do this by actively pursuing life and all of its accompanying miracles through the lens of love and by treating spiritual transformation as the priority it should be. To grow whole, we must be authentic, awake, and aware. As we learn to live in accordance with our God-ordained plan, the true meaning of life and its sacred purpose are revealed in ways that elevate our energetic frequencies and offer riveting glimpses of heaven on earth.

With their years of experiential knowledge and understanding, elders are perfectly positioned for their important roles as wisdom teachers. As we do the inside-out work required to reconcile unresolved issues and heal our wounds, we model behaviors that serve the common good. We feel better, live happier and healthier lives, and offer the universe fruitful examples of lifelong wellbeing. Gloria's mantra is,

> With the blessing of a growth mindset and a positive attitude, I am poised to continue discovering and enjoying life to its fullest. This gift is so precious, and when we express our appreciation through the lens of grace and gratitude, meaning and sacred purpose thrive.

References

Chapter 1

Priscilla Shirer Quotes. Goodreads.com. Retrieved June 22, 2021, from
https://www.goodreads.com/quotes/priscilla_shirer_15514706.

Carl Jung Quotes. (n.d.). BrainyQuote.com. Retrieved March 30, 2021,
from https://www.brainyquote.com/quotes/carl_jung_717969.

Frankl, V. E. *Man's Search for Meaning.* Boston: Beacon Press, 2006.

Chapter 2

Joyce Meyer Quotes. BrainyQuote.com. Retrieved July 16, 2021, from
https://www.brainyquote.com/quotes/joyce_meyer_565164.

Pew Research Center (https://www.pewforum.org/?attachment_id=32199).

Pew Research Center (https://pewforum.org/2021/02/16/faith-among-black-
americans/pf_02-16-21_black-religion-00-0/).

Warren, Rick. *The Purpose Driven Life: What on Earth am I here for?* Grand
Rapids: Zondervan Press, 2002.

Chapter 3

Bryan Stevenson Quotes. Goodreads.com. Retrieved August 14, 2021,
from https://www.goodreads.com/bryan_stevenson_4396806.

Chapter 5

Funk, Mary Margaret. *Humility Matters for Practicing the Spiritual Life.* Continuum Press, 2005.

Alder, Shannon. Quotes by Shannon Alder.

Chapter 6

Emmanuel Teney Quotes. BrainyQuote.com. Retrieved June 30, 2021, from https://www.brainyquote.com/quotes/emmanuel_teney_105084.

Gary Rudz Quotes. TopFamousQuotes.com. Retrieved July 5, 2021, from https://www.topfamousquotes.com/quotes/gary_rudz_179331.

Ellis Havelock Quotes. Goodreads.com. Retrieved August 22, 2021, from https://www.goodreads.com/quotes/ellis_havelock_98081.

Mandela, Nelson R. From *Nelson Mandela By Himself: The Authorized Book of Quotations.*

Henri Nouwen Quotes. Goodreads.com. Retrieved September 16, 2021, from https://www.goodreads.com/quotes/henri_nouwen_303173.

Mahatma Gandhi Quotes.BrainyQuote.com. Retrieved August 14, 2021, from https://www.brainyquote.com/quotes/mahatma_gandhi_107039.

Pope John Paul II and His Message of Forgiveness. Loyola Press.

Finley, Deborah. *What Your Future Holds and What you can do to Change it* (2007).

John Templeton Quotes. AZquotes.com. Retrieved September 28, 2021, from https://www.azquotes.com/quotes/john_templeton_14517.

Epilogue

James Lendall Basford Quotes. Quote Garden. Retrieved May 12, 2021, from https://www.quotegarden.com/quotes/james_lendall_basford/self.html.

Maclean, Kenneth J. *The Vibrational Universe.* 2005.

Printed in the United States
by Baker & Taylor Publisher Services